COOK
HEALTHY
& QUICK

Contents

Introduction

Eating healthily is easiest when it's convenient. So in *Cook Healthy and Quick* we have collected together recipes that are speedy to prepare and that will help you make good choices. We have grouped them around mealtimes – a protein-filled breakfast, say, or a plant-based main meal. Then we have done a detailed nutritional analysis for you: not just the calories per serving, but also the amount of carbohydrates, fats, salt, and fibre that you will be consuming.

We hope that this will help you to make healthy choices throughout your day, and keep within recommended daily intakes. For an adult consuming 2000 calories, these are as follows: no more than 90g sugars; 70g fats, with only 20g saturated fats; and about 1 teaspoon (6g) salt. You should also try to eat 18g fibre per day. Alongside this analysis we have added colour bands so that you can identify the key benefits of a recipe at a glance.

Remember, none of this is complicated – or restrictive. Eating well does not have to mean dialling down on your enjoyment. Some days, what you want is a brownie. So go ahead, have one. Just make it yourself, with our recipe that uses fruit to reduce the sugar content.

True, reducing the sugar does not mean that a brownie can be for every day. Nor can cheesecake or ice cream. But whether you want a snack or you're planning dinner for friends, here are recipes that are full of flavour and mindful of healthy principles. Take a look at the nutritional analysis, and make your choice.

If you have specific dietary needs, there are also recipes here that do not use dairy products or that avoid gluten. And many more can easily be adapted to be dairy-free and gluten-free. The colour bands will help you to identify these quickly.

Additionally, we offer easy Variations – simple ideas for you to create new dishes just by substituting just one or two ingredients. We also highlight on each recipe the time it will take, first to prepare and then to cook. Many recipes need no cooking and can be both prepared and cooked within 30 minutes. Only the time required for marinating, say, or freezing is excluded from our calculations.

So when your time is short, flip through these pages. With more than 300 recipes to choose from, you won't find it hard to *Cook Healthy and Quick*.

Cheap and healthy

It's easy to assume that eating healthily is a costly business. These recipes prove that anyone with a well-stocked store cupboard can eat well on a budget.

20 minutes

1 Pad Thai page 162
PREP 5 MINS **COOK** 15 MINS

2 Mint frittata page 24
PREP 5 MINS **COOK** 10–15 MINS

25 minutes

3 Prawn and garlic courgetti
page 208
PREP 20 MINS   **COOK** 5 MINS

4 Chicken liver with Marsala
page 168
PREP 15 MINS, PLUS SOAKING   **COOK** 10 MINS

5 Spicy raw vegetable spaghetti
page 176
PREP 20 MINS   **COOK** 5 MINS

30 minutes

6 Sweet potato cakes   page 174
PREP 10 MINS   **COOK** 20 MINS

7 Quinoa salmon cakes   page 260
PREP 10 MINS, PLUS CHILLING
COOK 20 MINS

8 15-minute soup   page 66
PREP 5 MINS   **COOK** 25 MINS

9 Quinoa and polenta muffins
with eggs, bacon, and avocado
page 44
PREP 10 MINS   **COOK** 20 MINS

35 minutes

10 Spinach and coconut prawn
curry   page 248
PREP 15 MINS   **COOK** 15–20 MINS

11 Baked tomatoes stuffed with
couscous, black olives, and feta
page 192
PREP 20 MINS   **COOK** 15 MINS, PLUS RESTING

Low-fat but filling

Sometimes a low-fat meal can be unsatisfying. These recipes are all low in saturated fat, but they're full of flavour and they won't leave you hungry.

15-20 minutes

25 minutes

30-35 minutes

Fish in a flash

Fish and seafood are low in fat and a good source of protein, so they are a healthy choice at any time of day. They can be quick to prepare too: these dishes are ready within 20 minutes.

5-10 minutes

1 Nori maki page 257
PREP 5 MINS

2 Prawn, sweet chilli, and Greek yogurt wraps page 120
PREP 10 MINS

3 Pilpil prawns page 244
PREP 5 MINS **COOK** 1–2 MINS

15-20 minutes

4 Crayfish panini with herbed mayonnaise page 123
PREP 15 MINS

5 Crispy polenta fish fingers with easy tartare sauce page 317
PREP 10 MINS, PLUS CHILLING **COOK** 5 MINS

6 Baked fish with a herby crust page 221
PREP 5 MINS **COOK** 10 MINS

7 Blackened salmon page 236
PREP 5 MINS, PLUS RESTING **COOK** 10 MINS

8 Prawn kebabs page 318
PREP 10 MINS, PLUS MARINATING
COOK 6 MINS

9 Cajun-spiced salmon page 238
PREP 10 MINS **COOK** 10 MINS

10 Red mullet in raki sauce
page 218
PREP 5 MINS **COOK** 12 MINS

11 Pan-fried prawns in garlic butter page 247
PREP 5 MINS **COOK** 10 MINS

Spice up the salad

A salad can be so much more than lettuce. Make it from whatever you like – seeds, nuts, grains or fruits. Take inspiration from these recipes, which are all ready in 35 minutes or less.

20–30 minutes

35 minutes

Easy vegetarian

A vegetarian meal is often naturally high in fibre, which is good for digestion, keeps your heart healthy, and keeps you feeling full for longer.

15-20 minutes

1 Gazpacho page 80
PREP 15 MINS, PLUS CHILLING

2 Black-eyed bean, spinach, and tomato curry page 183
PREP 5 MINS COOK 15 MINS

3 Spaghetti with garlic, oil, and red chilli page 198
PREP 10 MINS COOK 10 MINS

4 Broad bean tortilla page 30
PREP 5 MINS COOK 10–15 MINS

20-35 minutes

5 Veggie burgers page 310
PREP 15 MINS, PLUS CHILLING
COOK 12–15 MINS

6 Roasted asparagus with aïoli sauce page 288
PREP 10 MINS COOK 20 MINS

7 Mexican quinoa salad page 90
PREP 10–15 MINS, PLUS COOLING
COOK 20 MINS

35+ minutes

8 Millet cashew stir-fry with chilli and lime sauce page 272
PREP 20 MINS COOK 20 MINS

9 American-style soaked buckwheat pancakes with cherry almond sauce
page 52
PREP 10 MINS, PLUS SOAKING COOK 30 MINS

10 Avocado and lime cheesecake
page 384
PREP 30 MINS, PLUS CHILLING COOK 20 MINS

Fabulous with five

Eating well can often mean eating simply. There are ideas here for breakfasts, main meals, snacks and desserts and none contain more than five ingredients.

5 minutes

1 Kiwi and pear juice   page 338
PREP 5 MINS

2 Almond and apricot energy balls   page 302
PREP 5 MINS

3 Strawberry and macadamia smoothie   page 349
PREP 5 MINS

10 minutes

15-20 minutes

25-35 minutes

Quick and easy desserts

You might have to factor in time for chilling or freezing, but none of these recipes will take more than 30 minutes to prepare.

5-10 minutes

1 Quick banana ice cream page 376
PREP 5 MINS, PLUS FREEZING

2 Summer fruit fool page 366
PREP 10 MINS, PLUS CHILLING

3 Espresso granita page 380
PREP 5 MINS, PLUS COOLING AND FREEZING
COOK 5 MINS

4 Mango, orange, and passion
fruit fool page 373
PREP 10 MINS, PLUS CHILLING

15 minutes

5 Strawberry mousse
page 371
PRFP 20 MINS, PLUS CHILLING

6 Moroccan orange salad
page 356
PREP 15 MINS

20-30 minutes

7 Vanilla pudding with raspberries
page 368
PREP 10 MINS **COOK** 10 MINS, PLUS CHILLING

8 Warm fruit compote page 362
PREP 10 MINS **COOK** 10 MINS

9 Banana and cranberry ice cream
page 378
PREP 10 MINS, PLUS FREEZING **COOK** 10 MINS

10 Sweet spiced freekeh with fresh
figs page 358
PREP 5 MINS **COOK** 25 MINS

BREAKFASTS

Protein-packed

Feelgood fillers

PROTEIN-PACKED

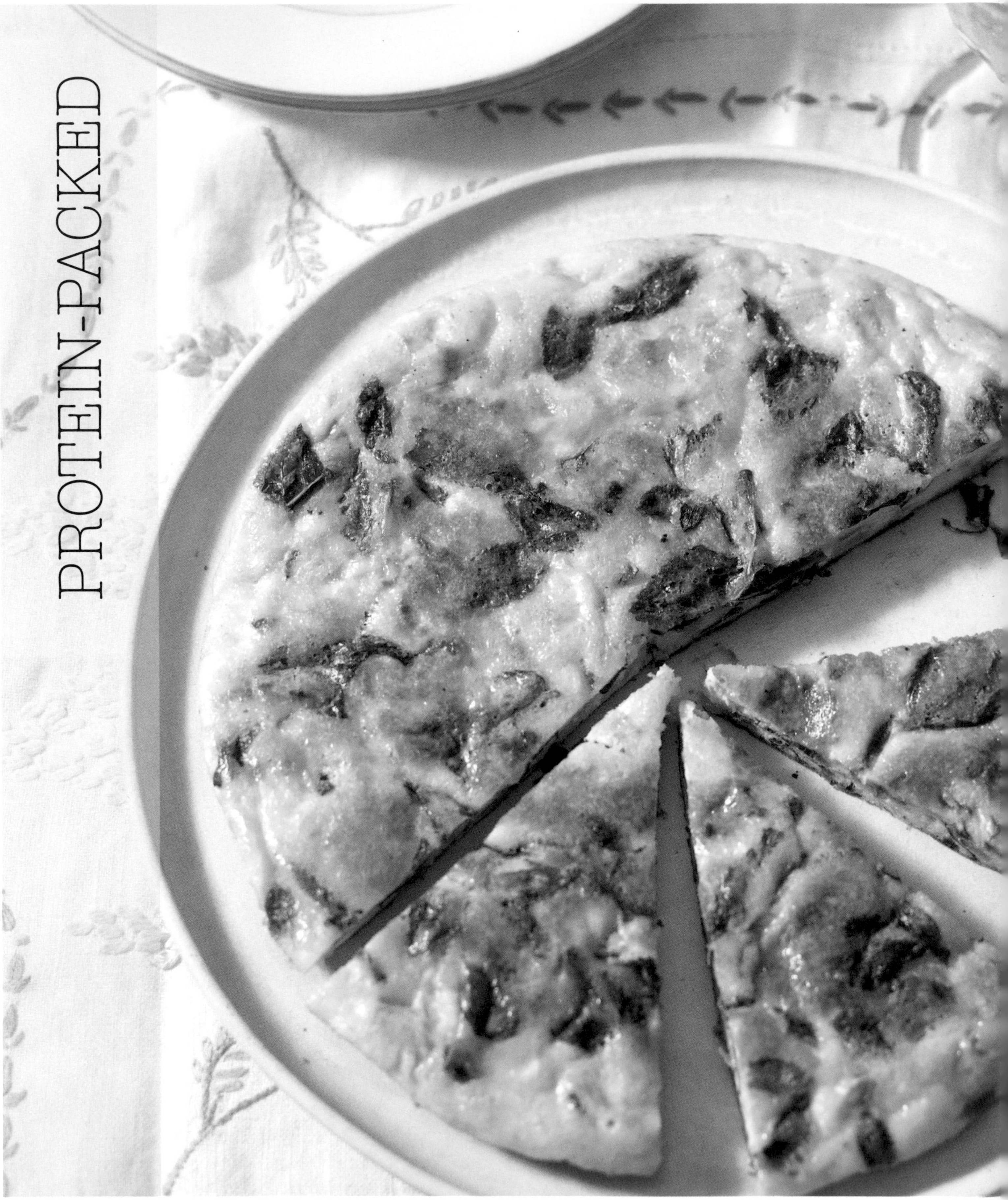

Mint frittata

Mint is a popular herb in southern Italy where the Middle Eastern influence is strong. It flavours this Italian version of the Spanish tortilla beautifully.

Low carb

Gluten free

Low salt

SERVES 8
PREP 5 MINS
COOK 10–15 MINS

8 large eggs

3 tbsp grated pecorino or Parmesan cheese

salt and freshly ground black pepper

3–4 tbsp olive oil

1 small onion, finely chopped

generous handful of mint leaves, roughly torn

1 Beat the eggs with the cheese and season. Set aside.

2 Heat 2 tablespoons of the oil in a frying pan. Add the onion, salt lightly to get the juices running, and fry gently until just soft – do not let it brown. Stir in the mint and cook for another minute.

3 Remove the pan from the heat and allow the mixture to cool. In a bowl, mix the onion and mint with the eggs.

4 Reheat the pan with the remaining oil. As soon as the oil is lightly smoking, pour in the egg mixture.

5 As soon as the first layer sets, pull the edges to the middle, then leave to cook gently, running a palette knife round the rim to loosen the edge. Shake the pan to keep the base from burning.

6 As soon as the top begins to look set, remove the pan from the heat. Slide the tortilla onto a plate, place a second plate on top, and invert so that the cooked side is on top. Slide the tortilla back into the pan and cook for a further 1–2 minutes.

NUTRITION PER SERVING	
Energy	156kcals/653kJ
Carbohydrate	0.75g
of which sugar	0.5g
Fat	12g
of which saturates	3.5g
Salt	0.35g
Fibre	0.2g

try this....
Pea, salmon, and mint frittata

Add 150g (5½oz) cooked **peas** and 150g (5½oz) flaked, poached **salmon** at the end of step 3.

Turkish eggs

There are many interpretations of *shakshouka*, but it is primarily a pepper and tomato dish with eggs. It is a popular street food in Turkey.

Low carb

Low saturated fat

Dairy free

Gluten free

Low salt

SERVES 4
PREP 10 MINS
COOK 15 MINS

2 tbsp olive oil

1 onion, halved and finely sliced

2 red or green bell peppers, finely sliced

2 garlic cloves, finely chopped

1 red chilli, deseeded and finely chopped

1 tsp sugar

400g can chopped tomatoes

salt and freshly ground black pepper

4 large eggs

small bunch of flat-leaf parsley, finely chopped

1 Heat the oil in a heavy-based frying pan and fry the onion and peppers for 2–3 minutes, until soft. Toss in the garlic and chilli, and fry until the vegetables begin to colour.

2 Add the sugar and tomatoes, and cook over a medium heat for 3–4 minutes, until the mixture is slightly pulpy. Season well.

3 Using a wooden spoon, make four indentations in the tomato mixture and crack an egg into each one. Reduce the heat, cover the pan, and cook until the whites are set. Scatter over the parsley and serve.

NUTRITION PER SERVING	
Energy	203kcals/848kJ
Carbohydrate	11g
of which sugar	10g
Fat	14g
of which saturates	3g
Salt	0.4g
Fibre	3g

Poached eggs in garlic yogurt

This Turkish classic is accompanied by garlic-flavoured yogurt. Serve with a salad to enjoy later in the day.

Low carb

Gluten free

Low salt

SERVES 4
PREP 5 MINS
COOK 10 MINS

500g (1lb 2oz) thick, creamy yogurt

2 garlic cloves, finely chopped

salt and freshly ground black pepper

2–3 tbsp white wine vinegar

4 large eggs

1–2 tbsp butter

1 tsp pimentón (Spanish paprika) or dried red chillies, finely chopped

a few dried sage leaves, crumbled

1 In a bowl, beat the yogurt with the garlic. Season to taste. Spoon the yogurt into a serving dish or individual plates, spreading it flat to create a thick base for the eggs.

2 Fill a pan with 900ml (1½ pints) water, add the vinegar, and bring to a rolling boil. Stir the water with a spoon to create a mini whirlpool in the centre. Crack one egg into a small bowl and gently slip it into the water. As the egg spins and the white sets around the yolk, stir the water again for the next one. Poach each egg for 2–3 minutes, so that the yolks are still soft. Drain the eggs using a slotted spoon and place on top of the yogurt base.

3 Quickly melt the butter in a small pan. Stir in the paprika and sage leaves, then spoon over the eggs and sprinkle a little salt over the top. Serve immediately.

NUTRITION PER SERVING

Energy	288kcals/1205kJ
Carbohydrate	6g
of which sugar	5g
Fat	22g
of which saturates	12g
Salt	0.5g
Fibre	0.1g

Broad bean tortilla

This tortilla is made with broad beans instead of potatoes and is flavoured with marjoram, a herb that works well with all members of the bean family.

Low carb

Low saturated fat

Dairy free

Gluten free

Low salt

SERVES 6
PREP 5 MINS
COOK 10–15 MINS

500g (1lb 2oz) broad beans, shelled

4 tbsp olive oil

2 tbsp white wine or dry sherry

4 large eggs

salt and freshly ground black pepper

1 tsp fresh marjoram leaves

1 Slip the beans out of their skins, unless they are very tiny and the skins are unwrinkled and tender. Heat 1 tablespoon of the oil in a small frying pan and stir in the beans, and turn them. Add the wine, allow the alcohol to evaporate, then cover the pan and leave to simmer gently for 5–6 minutes, until the beans are just soft and the liquid has almost evaporated. Leave to cool.

2 In a bowl, beat the eggs with seasoning and the marjoram leaves, then add the beans and stir.

3 Reheat the pan with the remaining oil. Tip in the egg-bean mixture and cook gently as a thick pancake, neatening the edges with a spatula and lifting up the edges to let the uncooked egg run underneath.

4 Cook until the top is beginning to set and the base is golden brown. Then slide the tortilla onto a plate, remove the pan from the heat, place a second plate on top, and invert so that the cooked side is on top. Slide back into the pan and cook for 2–3 minutes more on a low heat, until the tortilla is firm but still juicy in the middle. Serve warm or cool.

NUTRITION PER SERVING	
Energy	194kcals/812kJ
Carbohydrate	6g
of which sugar	1g
Fat	12g
of which saturates	2g
Salt	0.2g
Fibre	6g

Classic omelette

The ultimate fast food, omelettes are extremely quick to make and very tasty too – perfect for a nutritious and satisfying breakfast or brunch.

Low carb

Dairy free

Gluten free

Low salt

MAKES 1
PREP 2–3 MINS
COOK 5 MINS

2 large eggs

salt and freshly ground
black pepper

1 tsp butter

1 Beat the eggs in a bowl and season to taste. Melt the butter in a frying pan over a moderate heat and pour in the egg mixture.

2 Tilt the pan to spread the egg mixture evenly. Stir the eggs with a fork, stopping as soon as they are set. Fold the side of the omelette closest to the handle halfway over itself.

3 Sharply tap the handle so the bottom side of the omelette curls over. Slide the omelette to the edge of the pan. Transfer to a serving plate, and serve with a fresh green salad on the side.

NUTRITION PER SERVING	
Energy	221kcals/925kJ
Carbohydrate	0g
of which sugar	0g
Fat	17g
of which saturates	6g
Salt	0.6g
Fibre	0g

Greek tomato omelette

A breakfast and supper dish in the Peloponnese, this is flavoured with dill and melted cubes of salty *kefalotiri*, a cheese made with ewe's or goat's milk.

Low carb

Gluten free

Low salt

SERVES 4–5
PREP 15 MINS
COOK 15 MINS

4 tbsp olive oil

2 large ripe, firm tomatoes, thickly sliced

1 garlic clove, chopped

100g (3½oz) *kefalotiri*, mozzarella, or taleggio cheese, diced

6 large eggs

1 tbsp chopped dill

salt and freshly ground black pepper

1 Heat the oil in a small frying pan. Spread the tomato slices in an even layer over the surface, sprinkle with garlic, and cook gently until the tomato is soft and slightly dry. Top with the cheese but do not stir.

2 Meanwhile, beat the eggs with dill and a little seasoning. As soon as the cheese has melted a little, pour over the egg, turn up the heat, cover loosely, and cook until the top begins to look set. Flip the cake over and cook the other side. You can also slip the pan under the grill.

NUTRITION PER SERVING	
Energy	312kcals/1305kJ
Carbohydrate	2g
of which sugar	1.8g
Fat	26g
of which saturates	8g
Salt	0.7g
Fibre	0.7g

Scrambled eggs with smoked salmon

This is the ultimate feel-good brunch recipe. Smoked salmon is rich in omega-3 fats and a source of iron – but do remember, it is high in salt.

SERVES 4
PREP 10 MINS
COOK 10 MINS

6 eggs

2 tbsp milk

salt and freshly ground
  black pepper

15g (½oz) unsalted butter

160g (5¾oz) smoked salmon,
  cut into thin strips, or hot
  smoked salmon, flaked

2 tbsp snipped chives

4 wholemeal muffins, split
  and toasted, to serve

1 Beat the eggs with the milk, and season to taste with salt and pepper.

2 Melt the butter in a medium non-stick saucepan and, when foaming, pour in the eggs. Stir with a wooden spoon over medium heat until almost set, then stir in the smoked salmon.

3 Cook until the eggs have just set, sprinkle with chives, season with pepper, and serve at once on toasted muffin halves.

NUTRITION PER SERVING	
Energy	392kcals/1640kJ
Carbohydrate	30g
of which sugar	2g
Fat	17g
of which saturates	5.5g
Salt	2.5g
Fibre	2g

Poached eggs with chargrilled asparagus

For a grown-up breakfast, dip the asparagus in the egg yolk as if it were a toast soldier.

Low carb

Dairy free

Gluten free

Low salt

SERVES 4
PREP 5 MINS
COOK 10 MINS

1 bunch of asparagus, woody ends removed

1 tbsp olive oil

salt and freshly ground black pepper

4 eggs

1 Heat a griddle pan and rub the asparagus spears with the oil. Cook on the pan over a medium heat for 5–7 minutes (depending on thickness), turning occasionally, until they are tender and charred in places. Sprinkle them with salt and pepper.

2 When the asparagus is nearly ready, bring a large pan of salted water to the boil. Crack an egg into a teacup and gently slide into the bubbling water. Repeat for all the eggs (using a teacup helps them maintain their shape). Poach the eggs in very gently simmering water for about 3 minutes until the white is set but the yolk is still runny. (The trick to perfect poached eggs is that they must be very fresh; this helps the white to stay together in a neat shape.)

3 Transfer the asparagus to warmed plates, place an egg on top of each pile, and sprinkle with black pepper.

NUTRITION PER SERVING	
Energy	128kcals/530kJ
Carbohydrate	1g
of which sugar	1g
Fat	10g
of which saturates	2g
Salt	0.2g
Fibre	1.5g

Fried eggs with garlic

Egg dishes are very popular in the Middle East, where they are served for breakfast, as street snacks in busy markets, or as a late-night snack at home. Garlic is a rich source of vitamin B_6 and manganese, which contributes to bone health.

Low salt

SERVES 4
PREP 5 MINS
COOK 6–8 MINS

2 tbsp olive oil

knob of butter

2–3 garlic cloves, crushed

1–2 tsp sumac

8 eggs

1 tsp dried mint

salt

1 In a heavy-based frying pan, heat the oil and the butter. Add the garlic and sumac, and cook for 1–2 minutes, until it begins to colour. Crack the eggs into a bowl and pour into the pan.

2 Sprinkle the mint over the eggs and cover the pan with a lid. Reduce the heat and cook until the whites are just set.

3 Sprinkle a little salt over the eggs, divide into four portions, and serve with toasted flat or leavened bread.

NUTRITION PER SERVING	
Energy	243kcals/1007kJ
Carbohydrate	0g
of which sugar	0g
Fat	21g
of which saturates	5.5g
Salt	0.7g
Fibre	0g

Cuban-style rice

Cuban rice, named for the fried bananas served on the side, is loved in Spain as much for its pretty colours as for the sweet-salty flavours. Leftover paella makes a particularly good version.

Low saturated fat

Dairy free

Gluten free

Low salt

SERVES 4
PREP 10 MINS
COOK 10 MINS

about 300g (10oz) ready-cooked rice

3–4 tbsp olive oil

4–8 eggs

4 small bananas, skinned and halved lengthways

500g (1lb 2oz) fresh or canned tomatoes

1 thick slice of onion, chopped

1 garlic clove, chopped

1 fresh red chilli, deseeded and chopped (optional)

1 Heat the rice through in a low oven or microwave and transfer to a warm serving dish.

2 Heat the oil in a large frying pan. Crack the eggs in and fry sunny-side up. Remove with a slotted spoon, arrange on top of the rice, and keep warm.

3 In the same pan, fry the bananas just enough to caramelize them a little. Remove and arrange them with the eggs.

4 Meanwhile, liquidize the tomatoes, onion, and garlic with the chilli, if using. Pour the tomato mix into the same frying pan and bubble up for 1–2 minutes to concentrate the juices and develop the flavours. Serve the rice with its toppings, and the tomato sauce on the side.

NUTRITION PER SERVING	
Energy	393kcals/1644kJ
Carbohydrate	48g
of which sugar	22g
Fat	15g
of which saturates	3g
Salt	0.5g
Fibre	3g

Mexican eggs

A cheap, filling breakfast. Add chilli for more heat. If you don't have any passata, simply blend a can of tomatoes in a food processor, then strain.

Low saturated fat

Dairy free

SERVES 4
PREP 5 MINS
COOK 25 MINS

1 tbsp olive oil

2 garlic cloves, crushed

400ml (14fl oz) tomato passata

1 tsp smoked paprika

salt and freshly ground black pepper

1 tbsp chopped coriander leaves

4 eggs

4 thick slices of wholemeal or Granary bread

1 Heat the oil in a 25cm (10in) heavy-based, ovenproof frying pan over a medium heat and fry the garlic for 1 minute until it begins to colour. Add the passata and smoked paprika and season well. Bring to the boil, reduce to a gentle simmer, and cook for 20 minutes until thickened and reduced.

2 Five minutes before it is ready, preheat the grill on its highest setting. Stir most of the coriander into the tomato mixture.

3 When the sauce is ready, take it off the heat. Make four holes in the sauce with the back of a spoon. Crack an egg into each hole and put the pan under the hot grill for 2 3 minutes, until the eggs have just set. Meanwhile, grill or toast the slices of bread.

4 Scoop a little of the tomato sauce over the top of each piece of toast, then top it with an egg and sprinkle over the reserved coriander to serve.

NUTRITION PER SERVING	
Energy	228kcals/958kJ
Carbohydrate	22g
of which sugar	4g
Fat	10g
of which saturates	2.5g
Salt	1.2g
Fibre	2g

Potato, pancetta, and red onion hash

A hash is perfect if you fancy something more substantial in the morning. Try serving each portion topped with a fried egg – keep the yolks runny, if you like, as they will form a "sauce" for the hash.

Gluten free

High fibre

SERVES 2
PREP 10 MINS
COOK 20 MINS

salt and freshly ground black pepper

500g (1lb 2oz) floury potatoes, such as King Edward or Maris Piper, peeled and cut into bite-sized chunks

2 tsp olive oil

1 red onion, finely chopped

½ red pepper, diced

50g (1¾oz) pancetta lardons

1 tbsp finely chopped chives

50g (1¾oz) grated mature Cheddar cheese, to serve

1 Bring a pan of salted water to the boil, add the potatoes, and cook for 10 minutes. Drain.

2 Meanwhile, heat the oil in a large, non-stick frying pan over a medium heat and cook the onion and red pepper for 5 minutes. Add the pancetta, season well, and cook for a further 5 minutes, stirring occasionally.

3 Add the boiled potatoes to the frying pan and cook over a high heat for about 10 minutes, stirring frequently.

4 Divide the hash between warmed plates, and sprinkle with the chives. Serve with a grating of Cheddar cheese or, if you prefer, baked beans and tomato ketchup.

NUTRITION PER SERVING	
Energy	347kcals/1452kJ
Carbohydrate	52g
of which sugar	7g
Fat	17g
of which saturates	7.5g
Salt	1.3g
Fibre	9g

Grilled mushrooms with scrambled eggs on toast

A lovely way to serve eggs, this makes an unusual and luxurious breakfast. One Portobello mushroom has only 19 calories.

SERVES 4
PREP 10 MINS
COOK 20 MINS

2 tbsp olive oil

2 tbsp chopped parsley leaves

salt and freshly ground black pepper

4 large flat mushrooms, such as Portobello, stems discarded

4 large eggs

4 tbsp semi-skimmed milk

1 heaped tbsp finely chopped chives

1 tbsp butter

4 thick slices of wholemeal bread

1 Preheat the oven to 200°C (400°F/Gas 6). In a bowl, mix the oil and parsley and season. Brush the mixture all over the mushrooms, place on a baking tray, and bake for 20 minutes until tender.

2 Just before the mushrooms are ready, whisk together the eggs, milk, and chives, and season well.

3 Heat a large, heavy-based saucepan and melt the butter. Scramble the eggs in the pan over a low heat for 3–4 minutes, using a wooden spoon and a slow, scraping motion to move them around so all the egg comes in contact with the heat. Be sure to get into every area of the base and the corners of the pan, so the egg cooks evenly.

4 Meanwhile, grill or toast the bread. When the toast is ready, spoon over the juices from the mushrooms and top each piece with a mushroom, gill-side up.

5 While the egg is still a little soft or liquid (it will continue to cook off the heat), place one-quarter of it into each mushroom to serve.

NUTRITION PER SERVING	
Energy	306kcals/1280kJ
Carbohydrate	21g
of which sugar	2g
Fat	16g
of which saturates	5g
Salt	0.9g
Fibre	4g

French toast with blueberries

Blueberries are low in calories and high in antioxidants – more so than any other fruit. Many studies have shown that they help reduce blood pressure.

SERVES 2
PREP 10 MINS
COOK 10 MINS

4 eggs

240ml (8fl oz) skimmed milk

¼ tsp ground cinnamon

4 slices thick wholemeal bread, cut into triangles

1 tbsp sunflower oil

250g (9oz) blueberries

maple syrup, to serve

1 Crack the eggs into a mixing bowl. Add the milk and cinnamon and whisk together.

2 Pour the mixture into a shallow dish. Soak the bread in the mixture for about 30 seconds.

3 Heat half a tablespoon of the oil in a frying pan on a low heat. Carefully place two triangles in the pan.

4 Fry the triangles on both sides until they turn golden. Repeat steps 3 and 4 for the remaining bread triangles.

5 Serve the eggy bread warm, with blueberries and maple syrup or try it with butter and jam.

NUTRITION PER SERVING	
Energy	243kcals/1017kJ
Carbohydrate	26g
of which sugar	10g
Fat	9g
of which saturates	2g
Salt	0.7g
Fibre	2g

Quinoa and polenta muffins with eggs, bacon, and avocado

Rich in wholegrains, these savoury muffins make a perfect start to your day. Serve with eggs, bacon, and avocado for a hearty breakfast.

SERVES 8
PREP 10 MINS
COOK 20 MINS

1 tbsp light olive oil

4 large eggs

8 bacon rashers

large knob of butter, to serve

2 avocados, pitted and cut into thin slices, to serve

FOR THE BATTER

125g (4½oz) polenta

60g (2oz) wholemeal flour

150g (5½oz) prepared quinoa

1 tbsp baking powder

½ tsp baking soda

¾ tsp sea salt

250ml (9fl oz) milk

3½ tbsp light olive oil

1 tbsp honey

3 large eggs

1 Preheat the oven to 200°C (400°F/Gas 6). Grease and line an 8-hole muffin tin with paper cases. For the batter, place the polenta, flour, quinoa, baking powder, baking soda, and salt in a large bowl and mix to combine.

2 In a separate bowl, whisk together the milk, oil, honey, and the eggs until well combined. Then gently fold the liquid mixture into the dry ingredients and mix until just combined.

3 Divide the batter equally between the eight muffin cases and transfer the tin to the oven. Bake for about 20 minutes or until a toothpick inserted into the centre comes out clean.

4 Meanwhile, heat the oil in a frying pan over a medium heat and fry the eggs. Then add the bacon rashers and fry until crisp. Split the muffins, top with some butter, and serve with the fried eggs, bacon, and avocado.

NUTRITION PER SERVING	
Energy	499kcals/1871kJ
Carbohydrate	30g
of which sugar	5g
Fat	28g
of which saturates	7g
Salt	2.3g
Fibre	3.1g

Traditional American buttermilk biscuits

In America, "biscuits" (similar to British scones) are often served at breakfast with bacon, sausage, or scrambled egg.

MAKES 6
PREP 10 MINS
COOK 10–12 MINS

300g (10oz) self-raising flour, sifted, plus extra for dusting

2 tsp baking powder

½ tsp fine salt

100g (3½oz) butter, chilled and cut into cubes

200ml (7fl oz) buttermilk

1 egg, lightly beaten

1 Preheat the oven to 230°C (450°F/Gas 8). In a large bowl, or the bowl of a food processor, mix together the flour, baking powder, and salt. Add the butter and rub it in, or pulse-blend, until the mixture resembles fine breadcrumbs.

2 Make a well in the centre of the flour mixture and stir in the buttermilk. You will need to use your hands to bring the dough together. Gently knead the mixture on a floured work surface to form a soft dough.

3 Gently roll the dough out to a thickness of 2.5cm (1in). Cut rounds out of the dough with a 7cm (2¾in) biscuit cutter. Gently bring the dough back together and re-roll it to cut out as many as possible.

4 Brush each biscuit with a little of the egg. Bake in the top of the oven for 10–12 minutes, until they have risen and are golden brown.

NUTRITION PER SERVING	
Energy	318kcals/1336kJ
Carbohydrate	37g
of which sugar	2g
Fat	16g
of which saturates	9g
Salt	1.5g
Fibre	2g

Savoury cheese and bacon muffins

The perfect breakfast on the go or handy snack, bacon adds a delicious twist to these cheesy mini-cakes that will keep you full all morning.

SERVES 4

PREP 10 MINS

COOK 25 MINS

4 lean back bacon rashers

150g (5½oz) Cheddar cheese, cut into small pieces

125g (4½oz) fresh wholemeal breadcrumbs

small bunch of spring onions, finely chopped

3 eggs

100ml (3½fl oz) semi-skimmed milk

handful of fresh chives, chopped

salt and freshly ground black pepper

butter, for greasing

1 Preheat the oven to 190°C (375°F/Gas 5). Heat a frying pan over a medium–high heat and add the bacon rashers. Fry until cooked, but not too crispy, then cut into bite-sized pieces and set aside.

2 In a large bowl, mix together the cheese, breadcrumbs, spring onions, eggs, and milk. Stir through the bacon and chives, and season well.

3 Grease four 150ml (5fl oz) metal pudding moulds or ramekins with the butter and divide the batter equally between them. Bake in the oven for about 25 minutes, or until the muffins are well risen and golden and a skewer inserted into the middle comes out clean. Transfer to a wire rack and leave to cool slightly. Serve warm.

NUTRITION PER SERVING	
Energy	221kcals/925kJ
Carbohydrate	6g
of which sugar	2g
Fat	21g
of which saturates	5g
Salt	1.5g
Fibre	1g

Banana and oatmeal muffins

These muffins are a healthy choice for a leisurely brunch; delicious eaten when they're still warm. One muffin offers a good amount of fibre.

MAKES 12
PREP 20 MINS
COOK 20 MINS

160g (5¾oz) plain flour

1 tsp bicarbonate of soda

1 tsp baking powder

1 tsp ground cinnamon

100g (3½oz) oatmeal

50g (1¾oz) chopped walnuts (optional)

110g (3¾oz) butter, softened

100g (3½oz) demerara sugar

2 eggs, lightly beaten

3 ripe bananas, mashed

120ml (4fl oz) skimmed milk

1 Preheat the oven to 190°C (375°F/Gas 5). Place 12 paper muffin cases in a 12-hole muffin tin, or simply place the cases on a baking tray.

2 Sift the flour, bicarbonate of soda, baking powder, cinnamon, and oatmeal into a large bowl. Tip in any bran left in the sieve. Add the walnuts (if using). Stir well.

3 Place the butter and demerara sugar in a separate mixing bowl and cream together, using an electric hand-held whisk, until very light and fluffy. (This could take as much as 5 minutes, so be patient!) Add the eggs and mix well. Stir in the bananas and milk.

4 Pour the wet mixture into the dry and stir to combine. Do not over-mix or the muffins will be heavy. Divide the mixture between the paper cases.

5 Bake for 20 minutes (start checking after 15), or until a cocktail stick inserted into a muffin comes out clean. Transfer to a wire rack to cool.

NUTRITION PER SERVING	
Energy	254kcals/1063kJ
Carbohydrate	30g
of which sugar	13g
Fat	12g
of which saturates	5.5g
Salt	0.5g
Fibre	2g

Banana and yogurt pancake stack

Try stacking pancakes for a luxurious breakfast treat. Younger children especially love their sweet fluffiness.

Low salt

SERVES 6
PREP 10 MINS
COOK 15–20 MINS

200g (7oz) self-raising flour, sifted

1 tsp baking powder

40g (1¼oz) caster sugar

250ml (8fl oz) whole milk

2 large eggs, lightly beaten

½ tsp vanilla extract

30g (1oz) unsalted butter, melted and cooled, plus extra for frying

2–3 bananas

200g (7oz) Greek yogurt

runny honey, to serve

1 Sift the flour and baking powder into a large bowl and add the sugar. In a jug, whisk together the milk, eggs, and vanilla extract. Make a well in the centre of the flour mixture and whisk in the milk mixture, a little at a time, bringing in the flour as you go. Finally, whisk in the cooled, melted butter until the mixture is smooth.

2 Melt a knob of butter in a large, non-stick frying pan. Pour tablespoons of the batter into the pan, leaving space between them for the batter to spread. Each pancake should become about 8–10cm (3¼–4in) in diameter, but don't worry too much.

3 Cook over a medium heat, reducing the heat if they seem to be cooking too fast. Turn the pancakes when small bubbles appear on the surface and pop. Cook for another 1–2 minutes until golden brown and cooked through.

4 Slice the bananas on the diagonal to produce 5cm- (2in-) long strips. Place a warm pancake on a plate and top with a spoonful of yogurt and slices of banana. Top with another pancake, more yogurt, banana, and honey. Finish the stack with a third pancake, topped with a spoonful of yogurt and drizzled generously with honey.

NUTRITION PER SERVING	
Energy	317kcals/1336kJ
Carbohydrate	40g
of which sugar	17g
Fat	13g
of which saturates	7g
Salt	0.8g
Fibre	2g

Potato pancakes with smoked salmon

Cook extra mashed potato in the week and you'll have the basis of this fabulous brunch dish. Dill helps in digestion and also has antibacterial properties.

SERVES 4
PREP 10 MINS
COOK 10–15 MINS

450g (1lb) cooked, cold mashed potato

1 egg, beaten

25g (scant 1oz) plain flour, plus extra for dusting

salt and freshly ground black pepper

2 tbsp olive oil

100g (3½oz) smoked salmon, thinly sliced

4 tbsp soured cream

2 tbsp chopped dill

lemon wedges, to serve

1 Place the potato, egg, and flour in a mixing bowl. Season well and stir to combine. Divide into eight equal portions and, with flour-dusted hands, shape into rounds about 7cm (2¾in) in diameter.

2 Heat the oil in a large, non-stick frying pan over a medium heat. Carefully add the pancakes to the pan. Cook for 10–15 minutes, occasionally turning the pancakes carefully with a fish slice, until they are browned and hot right through.

3 Transfer the pancakes to warmed plates. Top each with smoked salmon, soured cream, and dill. Season well with black pepper and serve with lemon wedges.

try this....
Green potato pancakes

Rinse 200g (7oz) **kale** and steam for 6–8 minutes. Squeeze the excess water from the kale, then roughly chop the leaves and stir into the mashed potato. Alternatively, replace white potatoes with **sweet potatoes**.

NUTRITION PER SERVING	
Energy	288kcals/1199kJ
Carbohydrate	21g
of which sugar	2g
Fat	18g
of which saturates	7g
Salt	0.9g
Fibre	2g

American-style soaked buckwheat pancakes with cherry almond sauce

Buckwheat makes an incredible gluten-free flour and is even kinder on your digestion when soaked overnight. A good source of B vitamins, it is also rich in magnesium, copper, and easily digestible protein.

SERVES 8
PREP 10 MINS,
PLUS SOAKING
COOK 30 MINS

FOR THE BATTER

150g (5½oz) buckwheat flour

65ml (2¼fl oz) plain yogurt

200ml (7fl oz) milk

2 eggs

¾ tsp baking soda

¼ tsp baking powder

½ tsp vanilla extract

⅛ tsp salt

1–2 tbsp coconut oil, plus extra if needed

Greek yogurt, to serve

FOR THE SAUCE

350g (12oz) cherries, stoned

3 tbsp sugar

1 tsp almond extract

FOR A GLUTEN-FREE OPTION

use gluten-free baking powder

1 For the batter, place the flour, yogurt, and milk in a large bowl. Mix to combine, cover with a kitchen towel, and leave at room temperature for 8 hours or up to 24 hours.

2 Place the eggs, baking soda, baking powder, vanilla, and salt in a large bowl. Whisk lightly until well blended. Then gradually pour the egg mixture into the flour mixture and whisk until well combined.

3 Heat a large non-stick frying pan over a medium–high heat and add the oil once the pan is hot. Pour tablespoons of the batter into the pan, leaving space between them for the pancakes to spread. Each pancake should spread to about 15cm (6in) in diameter.

4 Cook the pancakes until small bubbles appear on the surface and the underside is firm. Then turn them over and cook for a further 1–2 minutes, or until cooked through. Transfer the cooked pancakes to a warm oven. Continue cooking until all the batter is used up, adding more oil to the pan as needed.

5 For the sauce, place the cherries in a large, lidded saucepan and cover with 100ml (3½fl oz) water. Add the sugar and place the pan over a medium-high heat. Cover and simmer until the cherries have broken down. Then uncover and cook until the liquid becomes syrupy. Remove from the heat and stir in the almond extract. Serve the cherry almond sauce with the pancakes and Greek yogurt.

NUTRITION PER SERVING	
Energy	181kcals/758kJ
Carbohydrate	27g
of which sugar	12g
Fat	6g
of which saturates	4g
Salt	0.6g
Fibre	1g

Pumpkin and cinnamon waffles

Adding canned pumpkin and spices to these waffles gives them a wonderfully autumnal taste. Particularly low in calories, pumpkin is also rich in fibre, minerals, and vitamins.

SERVES 6
PREP 20 MINS
COOK 5 MINS

200g (7oz) self-raising flour, sifted

40g (1½oz) soft light brown sugar

1 tsp baking powder

2 tsp ground cinnamon

2 eggs, separated

300ml (10fl oz) skimmed milk

1 tsp vanilla extract

40g (1½oz) butter, melted and cooled

150g (5½oz) canned pumpkin purée

vegetable oil, for greasing (optional)

maple syrup, apple wedges, or sliced bananas, to serve

1 In a bowl, use a balloon whisk to mix the flour, brown sugar, baking powder, and cinnamon.

2 Whisk together the egg yolks, milk, vanilla extract, melted butter, and pumpkin purée. Using a clean whisk, whisk the egg whites to firm peaks. Stir the pumpkin mixture into the flour mixture until evenly combined.

3 Preheat the waffle maker or waffle iron, and oil it if that is suitable for the model you own. Gently fold the egg whites into the batter until they are well combined. Spoon a ladleful of the batter onto the hot waffle iron (or the amount that is recommended by the manufacturer) and spread it almost to the edge. Close the lid and bake until golden.

4 Serve immediately with maple syrup, apple wedges, or sliced bananas.

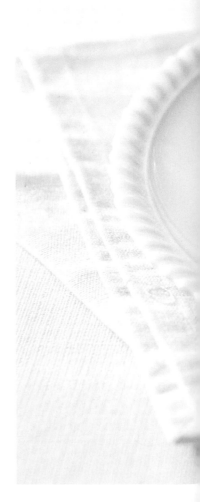

NUTRITION PER SERVING	
Energy	256kcals/1071kJ
Carbohydrate	35g
of which sugar	9g
Fat	9g
of which saturates	5g
Salt	0.7g
Fibre	2g

Overnight oats

Prepare these no-cook oats the night before, then enjoy a delicious instant breakfast the next morning. Oats are rich in beta-glucan, a fibre that lowers cholesterol.

Gluten free

Low salt

SERVES 2
PREP 10 MINS,
PLUS SOAKING

50g (1¾oz) porridge oats

150ml (5fl oz) coconut milk

1 tbsp honey

fresh cherries

toasted walnuts

1 Combine the oats and coconut milk. Transfer the mixture into a sealed jar and leave to soak in the fridge overnight.

2 In the morning, top up with a little more milk, if necessary. Drizzle over the honey, add the cherries, and top with the walnuts. Serve at once.

try this....
Banana and cinnamon overnight oats

Mash 1 **banana** with 2 tablespoons **cocoa powder**, 1 tablespoon **brown sugar**, and 1 teaspoon **cinnamon**. Spoon over the oats, then sprinkle with 1 tablespoon **chia seeds** and some toasted **coconut flakes**.
Serve at once.

NUTRITION PER SERVING	
Energy	653kcals/2372kJ
Carbohydrate	52g
of which sugar	22g
Fat	43g
of which saturates	26g
Salt	0g
Fibre	5.5g

LUNCHES

Broccoli soup with cheesy croutons

Broccoli has an impressive nutritional profile. Low in calories and high in fibre, it is also rich in calcium and potassium, and a good source of vitamin C.

Low saturated fat

High fibre

SERVES 4
PREP 10 MINS
COOK 15–20 MINS

1 large head broccoli, about 500g (1lb 2oz)

1 tbsp olive oil

1 large onion, finely chopped

2 garlic cloves, crushed or finely chopped

900ml (1½ pints) vegetable or chicken stock

5 tbsp half-fat crème fraîche

FOR THE CROUTONS

3 thick slices slightly stale Granary or wholemeal bread, crusts removed

2 tbsp olive oil, plus extra for greasing

50g (1¾oz) Parmesan cheese, grated

1 To make the croutons, preheat the oven to 220°C (425°F/Gas 7). Cut the bread into small cubes and place in a bowl, drizzle over the oil and Parmesan, and mix well. Transfer the croutons to a greased ovenproof dish and cook for 7–10 minutes, or until golden and crispy. Remove and cool.

2 Divide the broccoli into florets, then slice and roughly chop the stalks.

3 Heat the oil in a large pan, add the onion and sauté for 1–2 minutes. Then add the broccoli and garlic, and cook for a further 1–2 minutes.

4 Add the stock, bring to the boil, then reduce the heat, and simmer for 10 minutes, or until the broccoli is soft. Pulse the mixture in a food processor or process using a hand-held blender to form a purée.

5 Return the soup to the pan and gently reheat, stir in the crème fraîche. Divide between four bowls, then scatter over the croutons, and serve.

NUTRITION PER SERVING	
Energy	235kcals/1320kJ
Carbohydrate	20g
of which sugar	7g
Fat	16g
of which saturates	6g
Salt	0.9g
Fibre	8g

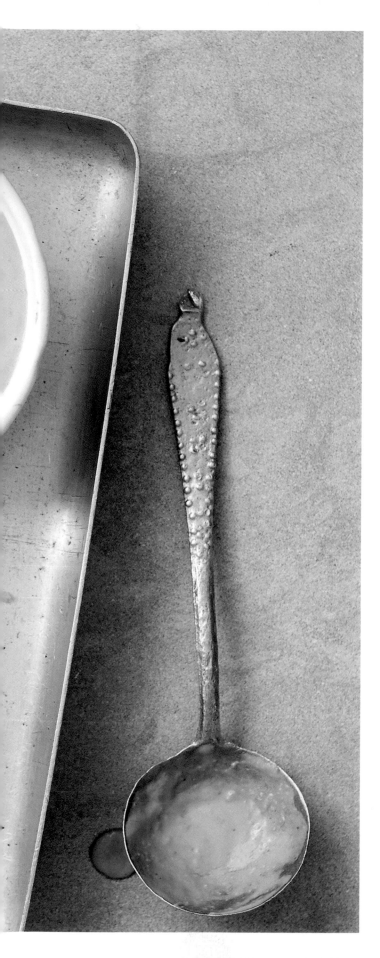

Pea, mint, and avocado soup with quinoa

This light and creamy chilled soup is enhanced by the addition of the nutty flavoured and protein-packed quinoa. Easy to prepare, it makes the perfect summer lunch.

SERVES 4
PREP 10 MINS
COOK 20–25 MINS

50g (1¾oz) uncooked quinoa

2 avocados, pitted

500g (1lb 2oz) frozen peas

20g (¾oz) chopped mint, plus extra to garnish

1 litre (1¾ pints) unsweetened almond milk

1 Rinse the quinoa under running water, drain, and place in a lidded saucepan. Cover with 250ml (9fl oz) of water and bring to the boil.

2 Reduce the heat to a simmer, cover, and cook for 15–20 minutes, or until almost all the liquid has been absorbed and the quinoa is fluffy. Remove from the heat, drain any remaining water, and set aside to cool.

3 Scoop out the flesh from the avocados and place in a food processor. Add the peas, mint, and half the milk and pulse until smooth. Then add the remaining milk and pulse until fully blended.

4 Divide the soup equally between four soup bowls. Top with equal quantities of the cooled quinoa. Garnish with some mint and serve immediately.

NUTRITION PER SERVING

Energy	420kcals/1757kJ
Carbohydrate	28g
of which sugar	10g
Fat	22g
of which saturates	4.5g
Salt	0g
Fibre	11g

15-minute soup

This simple soup is prepared with a ready-made broth in Spain – leftovers from one of the bean soups popular at midday, flavoured with diced Serrano ham and parsley, and fortified with hard-boiled egg.

Low carb

Low saturated fat

Dairy free

SERVES 4
PREP 5 MINS
COOK 25 MINS

1 litre (1¾ pints) hot chicken
  or beef broth

2 tbsp rice

4 tbsp diced Serrano ham

2 eggs, hard-boiled and chopped

1 tbsp finely chopped flat-leaf parsley

1 tbsp finely chopped mint (optional)

FOR A GLUTEN-FREE OPTION
use gluten-free stock

1 In a large pan, bring the broth, rice, and ham to the boil. Reduce the heat and simmer for 15 minutes, or until the rice is nearly tender.

2 Add the eggs and simmer for a further 1 minute. Remove from the heat, then stir in the parsley and mint, if using. Serve piping hot.

NUTRITION PER SERVING

Energy	126kcals/532kJ
Carbohydrate	6g
of which sugar	0g
Fat	6g
of which saturates	1.5g
Salt	2.8g
Fibre	0g

Butternut squash soup

Make this rich, velvety soup more sophisticated with a garnish of sage leaves, quickly fried in light oil. Butternut squash contains antioxidants that are known to promote good eyesight.

SERVES 4–6
PREP 5 MINS
COOK 20 MINS

3 tbsp olive oil

1 onion, chopped

1 leek, white part only, chopped

1 celery stick, chopped

500g (1lb 2oz) butternut squash, cut into 3cm (1in) cubes

750ml (1¼ pints) vegetable or chicken stock

½ tbsp chopped sage leaves

salt and freshly ground black pepper

FOR A GLUTEN-FREE OPTION
use gluten-free stock

1 Heat the oil in a large, heavy-based saucepan with a lid. Add the onion, leek, and celery and cook for 5 minutes until they soften, but do not brown.

2 Add the squash, stock, and chopped sage, and season generously with salt and pepper.

3 Bring to the boil, then reduce the heat to a gentle simmer, cover, and cook for 15 minutes until the squash is tender.

4 Blend the soup, either in a blender or using a hand-held blender, until completely smooth. Check the seasoning and serve.

NUTRITION PER SERVING	
Energy	208kcals/870kJ
Carbohydrate	19g
of which sugar	11g
Fat	10g
of which saturates	6g
Salt	2g
Fibre	5g

Lettuce soup with peas

For the best flavour choose very fresh, crisp lettuces for this refreshing chilled soup. Peas are a good source of vitamin C and other antioxidants.

Low carb

Low saturated fat

Gluten free

Low salt

SERVES 4
PREP 20 MINS,
PLUS CHILLING

125g (4½oz) peas (shelled weight)

1 small garlic clove

sea salt and freshly ground black pepper

2 round lettuce leaves, torn into pieces and solid cores discarded

250ml (9fl oz) plain yogurt

2cm (¾in) piece fresh root ginger, peeled and finely grated

handful of mint leaves

juice of ½ lemon

1 Bring a small amount of water to the boil in a pan, add the peas, and cook for 1 minute. Drain (reserving the cooking water), cool under cold running water, and chill in the fridge.

2 Halve the garlic clove and crush the halves with a pinch of coarse salt. Combine the garlic with all the other ingredients (except the peas) in a blender or food processor, adding just enough of the reserved cooking water to get the blades moving or until the desired consistency is achieved – it is best if you can get it fairly smooth, with a bit of texture.

3 Transfer the soup to a large bowl and chill for 30 minutes. When ready to serve, stir through the cooked peas, leaving a few to garnish.

NUTRITION PER SERVING

Energy	88kcals/368kJ
Carbohydrate	9g
of which sugar	6g
Fat	2.5g
of which saturates	1.5g
Salt	0.1g
Fibre	2.5g

Italian meatball soup

A strong stock enriched with meatballs is traditionally served at the start of a southern Italian Christmas feast. Fresh stock is a good source of calcium.

SERVES 6
PREP 20–30 MINS
COOK 10 MINS

400g (14oz) lean minced meat

175g (6oz) fresh breadcrumbs

1 garlic clove, finely chopped

2 tbsp finely chopped flat-leaf parsley, plus extra to garnish

2 large eggs, beaten

a little milk

salt and freshly ground black pepper

2–3 heaped tbsp plain flour

1.5 litres (2¾ pints) hot strong chicken or beef stock

1 Work the minced meat with the breadcrumbs, garlic, parsley, and eggs to a soft paste – you may need a little milk or more breadcrumbs. Season.

2 Spread the flour on a plate. With damp hands, pinch off little pieces of the paste and form into balls no bigger than a marble. Season the flour and roll the balls through it to coat and reserve.

3 Bring the stock gently to the boil and slip in the meatballs. Reduce the heat to a steady simmer and poach the meatballs until firm, for about 10 minutes. Garnish with parsley.

NUTRITION PER SERVING

Energy	301kcals/1259kJ
Carbohydrate	26g
of which sugar	2g
Fat	11g
of which saturates	4.5g
Salt	2g
Fibre	0.2g

Moroccan fish soup

In the Middle East, fish is generally grilled, fried, or baked. It appears in only a few classic stews and soups, such as this North African recipe, popular in the coastal regions of Morocco, Tunisia, Libya, and Egypt.

Low carb

Low saturated fat

Dairy free

SERVES 6
PREP 10 MINS
COOK 20 MINS

2–3 tbsp olive oil

1 onion, finely chopped

2–3 garlic cloves, finely chopped

2–3 tsp harissa paste

small bunch of flat-leaf parsley, finely chopped

1.2 litres (2 pints) hot fish stock

150ml (5fl oz) white wine (optional)

400g can chopped tomatoes, drained

1kg (2¼lb) fresh firm-fleshed fish fillets, such as cod, haddock, ling, grouper, sea bass, or snapper, cut into bite-sized chunks

salt and freshly ground black pepper

small bunch of coriander, coarsely chopped, to garnish

FOR A GLUTEN-FREE OPTION
use gluten-free stock

1 Heat the oil in a large, deep, heavy-based pan and stir in the onion and garlic, until they begin to colour. Add the harissa and parsley, and pour in the fish stock. Bring to the boil, reduce the heat, and simmer, uncovered, for 10 minutes to let the flavours mingle.

2 Add the wine, if using, and the tomatoes. Gently stir in the fish chunks and bring to the boil again. Reduce the heat, season to taste, and simmer uncovered for about 5 minutes to make sure the fish is cooked through. Scatter the chopped coriander over the top and serve immediately.

NUTRITION PER SERVING	
Energy	218kcals/912kJ
Carbohydrate	4g
of which sugar	4g
Fat	5g
of which saturates	0.8g
Salt	2g
Fibre	0.9g

Sweet potato soup

Rich and velvety, this is a substantial dish. The croutons add
a satisfying crunch. Sweet potatoes are a good source not
just of fibre but also of vitamins A and C.

SERVES 6
PREP 10 MINS
COOK 20 MINS

5 tbsp olive oil

1 onion, chopped

1 leek, white part only, chopped

1 celery stick, chopped

500g (1lb 2oz) sweet potatoes, peeled
and cut into 2.5cm (1in) cubes

½ tbsp chopped sage leaves

750ml (1¼ pints) vegetable or chicken
stock

salt and freshly ground black pepper

30g (1oz) unsalted butter

4 slices of day-old wholemeal or Granary
bread, crusts removed and cut into
1cm (½in) dice

1 Heat 3 tablespoons of oil in a large, heavy-based saucepan.
Add the onion, leek, and celery and cook for 5 minutes, or until
the vegetables are softened but not browned.

2 Add the sweet potatoes, sage, and stock to the pan. Season
to taste and bring to the boil.

3 Reduce the heat to a gentle simmer and cover the saucepan
with the lid. Cook for 10 minutes, or until the sweet potatoes
are tender.

4 While the soup is simmering, in a large frying pan, heat the
remaining oil and butter until hot. Add the bread pieces, then
fry, stirring constantly for 10 minutes, or until golden.

5 Using a slotted spoon, remove the croutons from the frying
pan and drain off the excess oil on a kitchen paper.

6 Using an electric hand-held blender, process the soup until
smooth. Season again, if needed.

7 Ladle the soup into serving bowls, garnish with the croutons,
and serve warm.

NUTRITION PER SERVING	
Energy	309kcals/1293kJ
Carbohydrate	35g
of which sugar	7.5g
Fat	14.5g
of which saturates	4g
Salt	1.4g
Fibre	5g

Salmorejo

A fresh soup from southern Spain, similar to Gazpacho.
Tomatoes helps regulate blood sugar.

Low saturated fat

Dairy free

Low salt

SERVES 4
PREP 15 MINS, PLUS
SOAKING AND CHILLING

115g (4oz) stale white bread,
   crusts removed, torn into
   bite-sized pieces

3 tbsp olive oil, plus extra
   to garnish

2 tbsp red wine vinegar

1 onion, roughly chopped

3 garlic cloves

1 red pepper, deseeded and
   chopped

5 tomatoes, skinned and
   deseeded

1 cucumber, peeled,
   deseeded, and chopped

salt and freshly ground black
   pepper

2 hard-boiled eggs, chopped

2 slices serrano ham, cut
   into strips

1 Place the bread into a bowl. Add the oil and vinegar,
mix well, and set aside to soak for 10 minutes.

2 Place the onion, garlic, red pepper, tomatoes, and most
of the cucumber in a blender or food processor with 90ml
(3fl oz) water, and blend to a purée. Add the bread mixture,
blend again, then season to taste with salt and pepper.

3 Chill for at least 30 minutes, pour into serving bowls, and
top with hard-boiled eggs, strips of ham, and the remaining
cucumber. Serve, drizzled with a little olive oil.

NUTRITION PER SERVING	
Energy	280kcals/1172kJ
Carbohydrate	22g
of which sugar	9.5g
Fat	16g
of which saturates	2.5g
Salt	0.7g
Fibre	4.5g

Watercress soup

Serve this velvety smooth soup hot, topped with Parmesan cheese. Watercress is a powerhouse of nutrients.

SERVES 4
PREP 10 MINS
COOK 15 MINS

1¾ tbsp oil

1 onion, peeled and finely chopped

175g (6oz) watercress

3 ripe pears, cored and roughly chopped

1.3 litres (2 pints) vegetable stock

salt and freshly ground black pepper

100ml (3½fl oz) half-fat crème fraîche

juice of ½ lemon

Parmesan cheese, grated, to serve

olive oil, to drizzle

FOR A GLUTEN-FREE OPTION
use gluten-free stock

1 Heat the oil in a saucepan and cook the onion for 10 minutes, or until soft, stirring occasionally to prevent burning.

2 Meanwhile, trim the watercress and pick off the leaves. Add the watercress stalks to the onion with the pears and stock, and season with salt and pepper.

3 Bring to the boil, cover and simmer gently for 15 minutes. Remove from the heat and pour into a blender along with the watercress leaves. Process until the soup is a very smooth texture.

4 Stir in the crème fraîche and lemon juice, adjust the seasoning and serve sprinkled with Parmesan shavings and drizzled with a little olive oil.

NUTRITION PER SERVING	
Energy	277kcals/1159kJ
Carbohydrate	16g
of which sugar	15g
Fat	12g
of which saturates	5g
Salt	2g
Fibre	4g

Gazpacho

This chilled, no-cook Spanish soup is lovely on a hot day. Use the freshest tomatoes you can find – and celebrate their ripe flavour.

| Low carb |
| Low saturated fat |
| Dairy free |
| Gluten free |
| Low salt |

SERVES 4
PREP 15 MINS, PLUS CHILLING

1kg (2¼lb) tomatoes, plus extra
　　to serve

1 small cucumber, peeled and finely
　　chopped, plus extra to serve

1 small red pepper, deseeded
　　and chopped, plus extra to serve

2 garlic cloves, crushed

4 tbsp sherry vinegar

salt and freshly ground black pepper

120ml (4fl oz) extra virgin olive oil,
　　plus extra to serve

1 hard-boiled egg, white and yolk
　　separated and chopped, to serve

1 Bring a kettle of water to the boil. Place the tomatoes in a heatproof bowl, pour over enough boiling water to cover, and leave for 20 seconds, or until the skins split. Drain and cool under cold running water. Gently peel off the skins, cut the tomatoes in half, deseed, and chop the flesh.

2 Place the tomato flesh, cucumber, red pepper, garlic, and vinegar in a food processor or blender. Season to taste and process until smooth. Pour in the oil and process again. Dilute with a little cold water, or a few ice cubes if too thick. Transfer the soup to a serving bowl, cover with cling film, and chill.

3 When ready to serve, finely chop the extra cucumber and red pepper. Place the cucumber, pepper, and egg yolk and white in individual bowls and arrange on the table, along with a bottle of olive oil. Ladle the soup into bowls and serve, letting each diner add their own garnish. If the soup hasn't had enough time to chill properly, add an ice cube or two to each bowl.

try this....
Green gazpacho

Place 100g (3½oz) **baby spinach**, 2 **garlic cloves**, 1 large **cucumber**, large handful of fresh **basil leaves**, flesh from 1 ripe **avocado**, 4 **spring onions**, 200g (7oz) **plain yogurt**, and 2 tablespoons **sherry vinegar** in a blender and process until smooth. To serve, divide between four bowls, add a couple of ice cubes and garnish with diced **avocado** and **peashoots**.

NUTRITION PER SERVING

Energy	279kcals/1167kJ
Carbohydrate	9.5g
of which sugar	9.5g
Fat	24g
of which saturates	3.5g
Salt	0.1g
Fibre	4g

Mango and curry leaf soup

Alfonso mangoes, renowned for their fragrant flesh and creamy texture, have a short season from early April until the end of May. Other varieties work well too.

SERVES 4
PREP 15 MINS
COOK 20 MINS

FOR THE GARNISH
small handful of curry leaves
vegetable oil, for deep frying

FOR THE SOUP
4 ripe mangoes, Alfonso, if in season
2 tbsp vegetable oil
1 tsp black mustard seeds
handful of fresh curry leaves
1 red chilli, deseeded and finely chopped
2 tsp date palm sugar or dark muscovado sugar
½ tsp turmeric
2 tsp rice flour
300–400ml (10–14fl oz) vegetable stock
300ml (10fl oz) half-fat coconut milk
juice of 1 lime, to taste
salt and freshly ground black pepper
2 tbsp chopped fresh coriander leaves

FOR A GLUTEN-FREE OPTION
use gluten-free stock

1 First make the garnish: deep-fry the curry leaves in hot oil until crisp – it only takes a few seconds. Drain on kitchen paper and set aside.

2 Roughly chop the flesh of three mangoes into small pieces and finely dice the fourth. Set aside. Heat the oil in a medium pan and, when hot, fry the mustard seeds for a few seconds before adding the curry leaves and chilli. Continue frying for 30 seconds, until the leaves stop spluttering.

3 Add the three roughly chopped mangoes to the pan, reserving the diced mango. Turn the heat down low and simmer the fruit until softened. Stir in the sugar and cook until the mango begins to caramelize. Sprinkle over the turmeric and rice flour and fry for 30 seconds, stirring all the time. Pour over 300ml (10fl oz) of the stock and simmer for 10 minutes.

4 Add the coconut milk and simmer for 2–3 minutes. Sharpen with lime juice, season with salt and pepper, and stir in the coriander leaves and diced mango. If the soup is too thick, add a little hot vegetable stock. Divide the soup between the bowls and sprinkle with a few crisp-fried curry leaves.

NUTRITION PER SERVING	
Energy	226kcals/946kJ
Carbohydrate	26g
of which sugar	23g
Fat	11g
of which saturates	5.5g
Salt	0.6g
Fibre	5g

Chilled melon and ginger soup

This is a soup to make in a hurry. All that's needed to bring out its fruity flavour is a seriously good chill – and a perfectly ripe melon.

Low saturated fat

Gluten free

Low salt

SERVES 4
PREP 15 MINS,
PLUS CHILLING

1 ripe Galia melon, peeled and deseeded

2.5cm (1in) piece of fresh root ginger, peeled

1 tsp fennel seeds

200g (7oz) white seedless grapes

grated zest and juice of 1 lime

1 tsp dried mint

4 tbsp Greek yogurt, beaten

salt and freshly ground black pepper

FOR THE GARNISH

2 tbsp mint leaves

pinch of sugar

25g (scant 1oz) crystallized ginger, finely chopped

1 Roughly chop three-quarters of the melon flesh into bite-sized chunks. Finely chop the remainder and set aside. Grate the root ginger and squeeze any juice over the melon chunks. Discard the leftover ginger.

2 Heat a heavy-based frying pan or griddle over a gentle heat and lightly toast the fennel seeds for about 30 seconds, until you smell an aniseed-like aroma. Grind the seeds to a coarse powder using a mortar and pestle.

3 Put the ground fennel seeds into a blender or food processor with the roughly chopped melon and ginger juice. Add the grapes, lime juice and zest, and dried mint. Blitz until smooth and push through a sieve to remove the skins.

4 Stir in the yogurt, season, and chill thoroughly – it's best to half-freeze this soup, then give it a good whisk just before serving. Spoon into bowls, adding a small pile of the reserved melon to each one. Shred the fresh mint, mix with the sugar and crystallized ginger, and scatter over the soup. Serve immediately.

NUTRITION PER SERVING	
Energy	106kcals/444kJ
Carbohydrate	19g
of which sugar	19g
Fat	2g
of which saturates	1g
Salt	0.1g
Fibre	1.4g

Mango and red snapper broth

This is a complete meal in a bowl. Raw mangoes, available from South Asian stores, add bite to a citrussy broth flecked with fiery red chillies.

Low saturated fat

Dairy free

High fibre

SERVES 4
PREP 15 MINS, PLUS MARINATING
COOK 15 MINS

500g (1lb) red snapper fillets, skinless, cut into 2.5cm (1in) cubes

2 stalks lemongrass, finely chopped

2 tbsp vegetable oil

4 birds eye red chillies, finely sliced

4 spring onions, finely sliced

5cm (2in) fresh root ginger, finely shredded

4 garlic cloves, roughly chopped

4 small raw green mangoes, or under-ripe mangoes, peeled and finely chopped

2 tsp date palm sugar or dark muscovado sugar

2 tbsp rice wine vinegar

1.2 litre (2 pints) fish stock

8 lime leaves, torn in half

1 tbsp fish sauce

100g (3½oz) medium egg noodles

100g (3½oz) fine green beans, halved

salt, to season

juice of 1 lime, to taste

2 tbsp chopped fresh coriander leaves

1 tbsp shredded fresh mint leaves

FOR THE MARINADE
1 tbsp light soy sauce

2 tsp fish sauce

1 tbsp toasted sesame oil

1 tbsp mirin

1 tsp sugar

juice of 1 lime

1 Combine the soy and fish sauce, sesame oil, mirin, sugar, and lime juice, and spoon over the fish. Refrigerate for 20 minutes. Pound the lemongrass to a paste with a dash of water, using a mortar and pestle. Set aside.

2 Heat the oil in a wok or large pan and fry the chillies, spring onions, ginger, and garlic for 30 seconds over a high heat. Add the mangoes and fry for 1 minute. Stir in the sugar until it begins to caramelize. Add the vinegar, lemongrass, stock, lime leaves, and fish sauce. Bring to the boil.

3 Stir in the noodles, beans, and fish pieces (not the marinating liquid). Simmer for 3–5 minutes, until the noodles are cooked and the fish flakes easily. Season with salt, sharpen with lime juice, and add the herbs.

NUTRITION PER SERVING	
Energy	402kcals/1682kJ
Carbohydrate	35g
of which sugar	12g
Fat	11g
of which saturates	2g
Salt	3.2g
Fibre	6g

Mussel soup

Mussels, cultivated since ancient times in the Bay of Taranto in the south of Italy, are an excellent source of fatty acids, vitamins, and minerals. They are the most nutrient-dense seafood.

Low carb

Low saturated fat

Dairy free

SERVES 4–6
PREP 10 MINS
COOK 10–20 MINS

1.35kg (3lb) large mussels in shells

150ml (5fl oz) dry white wine

2–3 tbsp olive oil

1 onion, finely chopped

1 garlic clove, finely chopped

1 litre (1¾ pints) hot fish stock

500g (1lb 2oz) ripe tomatoes, skinned and diced

1–2 bay leaves

1 tbsp crumbled fresh or dried oregano

1 tsp capers, drained

salt

bunch of basil, shredded, to serve

FOR A GLUTEN-FREE OPTION
use gluten-free stock

1 Scrub the mussels and trim off the beards. They will close themselves tightly – but if they do not, they are dead and should not be used.

2 In a large soup pan, bring the wine to the boil and pack in the mussels. Cover and steam for 2–3 minutes, giving the pan a shake to move the shellfish around, until all the shells are open. Reject any that remains shut and reserve the ones in their shells. Strain the broth through a fine sieve to remove the grit and set aside.

3 In the same pan, heat the oil and fry the onion and garlic until soft but not browned. Add the stock and the reserved broth, tomatoes, bay leaves, and oregano, and bring to the boil. Simmer for 5 minutes, then tip in the mussels and capers. Reheat and season with salt.

4 Sprinkle with the basil and serve in deep soup bowls.

NUTRITION PER SERVING	
Energy	222–148kcals/ 936–624kJ
Carbohydrate	6–4g
of which sugar	5.5–4g
Fat	8.5–6g
of which saturates	1.3–0.8g
Salt	2.8–1.8g
Fibre	2–1.4g

SALADS

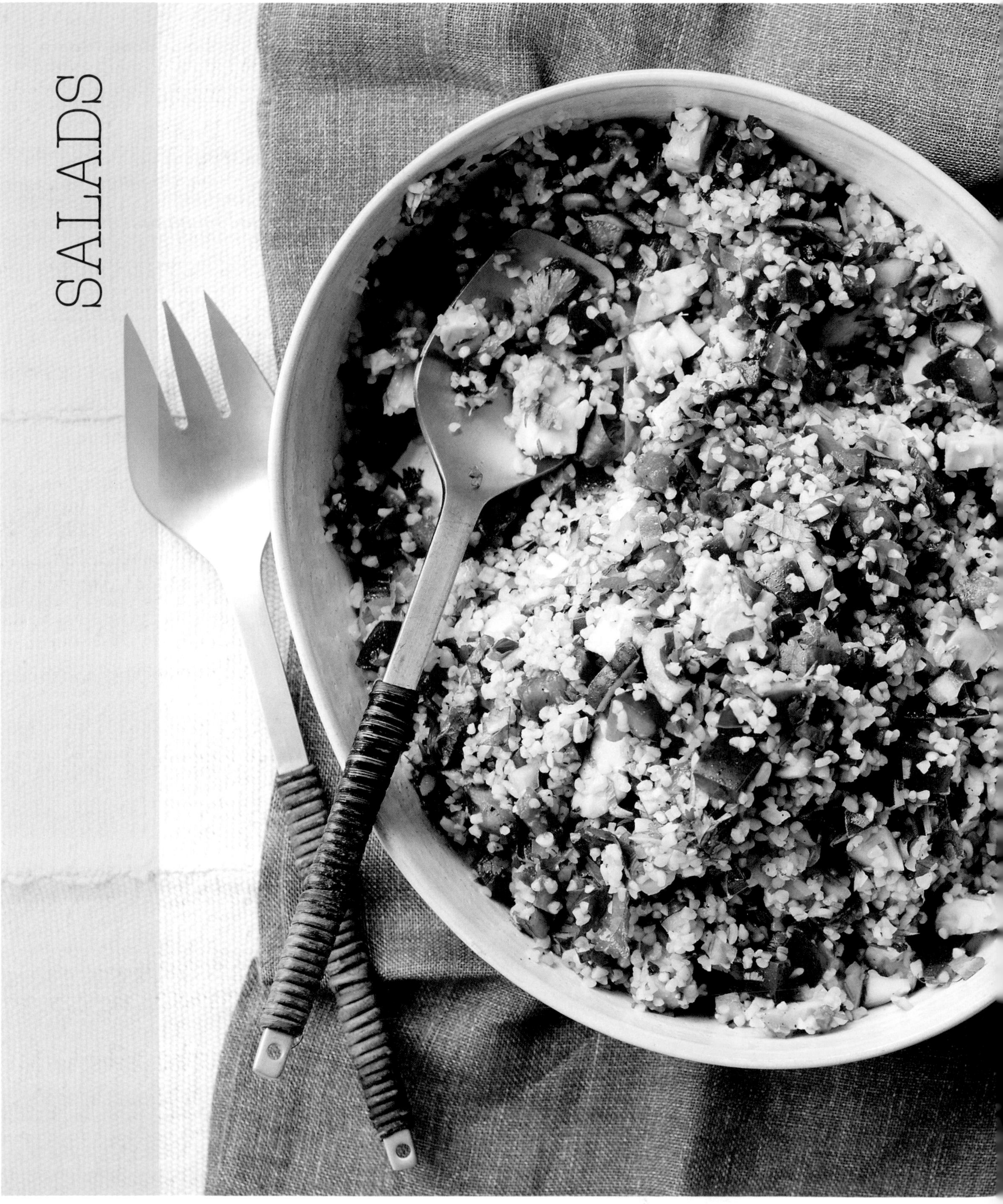

Avocado, coriander, and lime tabbouleh

Tabbouleh is a traditional part of a mezze in the Middle East, but it also makes an excellent salad. The lime and avocado in this version give it a fresh dimension.

Low saturated fat

Dairy free

SERVES 4
PREP 15 MINS, PLUS
SOAKING AND CHILLING

175g (6oz) bulgur wheat

1½ tsp rock salt

2 tomatoes, diced

1 avocado, peeled, pitted, and diced

1 small red pepper, deseeded and diced

60g (2oz) red onion, diced

handful of coriander leaves, roughly chopped

125ml (4¼fl oz) lime juice

2 tbsp extra virgin olive oil

salt and freshly ground black pepper

1 Place 350ml (12fl oz) of water in a large saucepan and bring to the boil. Place the bulgur wheat and rock salt in a large bowl. Pour over the boiling water, cover, and leave to soak for about 30 minutes.

2 Drain any excess water from the bulgur wheat and place it in a large bowl. Then add the tomatoes, avocado, red peppers, onions, and coriander. Mix well to combine. Transfer the mixture to a large serving bowl.

3 Drizzle the lime juice and oil over the mixture. Toss well to coat. Season to taste with salt and black pepper, if needed. Mix well and chill the tabbouleh in the fridge for about 20 minutes before serving.

try this....
Prawn and avocado salad with freekeh

Replace the bulgur wheat with 2 x 250g packs **ready-to-eat freekeh** and 200g (7oz) cooked, peeled **prawns**.

NUTRITION PER SERVING	
Energy	306kcals/1275kJ
Carbohydrate	38g
of which sugar	5g
Fat	14g
of which saturates	2.5g
Salt	1.9g
Fibre	2.4g

Jewelled couscous in a jiffy

A salad that needs no cooking at all. Make the evening before, then pack in a lunchbox for a healthy weekday lunch.

Low saturated fat

Dairy free

Low salt

SERVES 4–6
PREP 12 MINS,
PLUS COOLING

300g (10oz) couscous

1½ tbsp olive oil

1 tbsp powdered vegetable stock or 525ml (17fl oz) hot vegetable stock

50g (1¾oz) pine nuts

100g (3½oz) dried apricots, finely chopped

large handful of coriander leaves, finely chopped

4½ tbsp extra virgin olive oil

juice of 1 large lemon

salt and freshly ground black pepper

2 or 3 tbsp pomegranate seeds, to serve

1 Boil a kettle. Put the couscous into a bowl and drizzle over the olive oil. Rub it into the couscous, scatter over the powdered vegetable stock (if using), and mix it in.

2 Pour over 525ml (17fl oz) of boiling water (if using powdered stock) or hot vegetable stock, and stir briefly. The liquid should just cover the couscous. Immediately seal with cling film.

3 Leave for 5 minutes, then test the grains, which should be nearly soft, and all the water soaked in. Fork over the couscous and leave it to cool, forking it occasionally to separate the grains.

4 Meanwhile dry-fry the pine nuts in a non-stick frying pan over a medium heat, stirring, until they colour. Be careful, as they can burn quickly. Set aside to cool.

5 Toss together the cooled couscous, pine nuts, apricots, and coriander. Mix in the extra virgin olive oil and lemon juice and season to taste. Scatter over the pomegranate seeds to serve.

NUTRITION PER SERVING

Energy	396kcals/1657kJ
Carbohydrate	46g
of which sugar	9g
Fat	18g
of which saturates	2g
Salt	0.7g
Fibre	4g

Chorizo, chickpea, and mango salad

A hearty, main meal salad with great variety of flavour. Chorizo is an excellent source of selenium.

SERVES 2
PREP 15 MINS
COOK 15 MINS

1 tbsp olive oil

150g (5½oz) chorizo, roughly chopped

400g can of chickpeas, drained and rinsed

3 cloves of garlic, finely chopped

handful of flat-leaf parsley, finely chopped

1 tbsp dry sherry

2 ripe mangos, stoned and flesh diced

small handful of fresh basil, roughly chopped

small handful of fresh mint leaves, roughly chopped

small handful of fresh coriander leaves, roughly chopped

250g (9oz) baby spinach leaves

1 Heat the olive oil in a frying pan, add the chorizo and chickpeas, and cook over a low heat for 1 minute, then add the garlic and parsley, and cook for a further minute. Add the sherry and cook for 10 minutes, stirring occasionally.

2 Put the mango and remaining herbs in a bowl and toss together, then add the chickpea mixture and combine well. Spoon onto a bed of spinach to serve.

NUTRITION PER SERVING	
Energy	504kcals/2106kJ
Carbohydrate	31g
of which sugar	5.5g
Fat	24g
of which saturates	8g
Salt	1.5g
Fibre	2.5g

try this....
Spicy chicken, chickpea, and mango salad

Replace chorizo with 350g (12oz) **ready-prepared piri piri chicken**, roughly chopped into bite-sized pieces.

Mexican quinoa salad

Crunchy tortilla chips and spicy chillies create a salad that packs a real punch in flavour and texture, and which everyone can enjoy.

Low saturated fat

Dairy free

Low salt

High fibre

SERVES 2
PREP 10–15 MINS,
PLUS COOLING
COOK 20 MINS

50g (1¾oz) uncooked quinoa

400g can red kidney beans, drained

50g can sweetcorn

½ red onion, finely chopped

1 red pepper, deseeded and finely chopped

4–6 slices pickled jalapeño chillies, finely chopped

1 avocado, pitted and cut into cubes

1 head of romaine lettuce

50g (1¾oz) plain corn tortilla chips, crumbled, plus extra to serve

1 lemon or lime, halved, to serve

FOR A GLUTEN-FREE OPTION
use gluten-free tortillas

1 Rinse the quinoa under running water, drain, and place in a lidded saucepan. Cover with 250ml (9fl oz) of water and bring to the boil.

2 Reduce the heat to a simmer, cover, and cook for 15–20 minutes or until almost all the liquid has been absorbed and the quinoa is fluffy. Remove from the heat, drain any remaining water, and set aside to cool.

3 Place the quinoa, kidney beans, sweetcorn, onions, peppers, and jalapeños in a large bowl. Mix until well combined. Then add the avocado and mix lightly to combine.

4 Roughly shred the lettuce and add to the bowl. Sprinkle the tortillas over the mixture and toss lightly. Transfer the salad to a serving platter or plate. Serve immediately with tortilla chips and lemons or limes to squeeze over.

NUTRITION PER SERVING	
Energy	555kcals/2322kJ
Carbohydrate	57g
of which sugar	10g
Fat	24g
of which saturates	4g
Salt	0.5g
Fibre	20g

Couscous with pine nuts and almonds

A tasty alternative to rice; serve either hot or cold.
Couscous makes a good source of low-fat protein
for vegetarians.

Low saturated fat

Dairy free

Low salt

High fibre

SERVES 4
PREP 15 MINS,
PLUS STANDING

175g (6oz) couscous

boiling water, to cover

1 red pepper, deseeded
and chopped

100g (3½oz) raisins

100g (3½oz) dried apricots,
chopped

½ cucumber, deseeded
and diced

12 black olives, pitted

60g (2oz) blanched
almonds, lightly toasted

60g (2oz) pine nuts, lightly
toasted

4 tbsp light olive oil

juice of ½ lemon

1 tbsp chopped mint

salt and freshly ground
black pepper

1 Put the couscous in a bowl and pour
over enough boiling water to cover it by
about 2.5cm (1in). Set aside for 15 minutes,
or until the couscous has absorbed all the
water, then fluff the grains up lightly with
a fork.

2 Stir in the pepper, raisins, apricots,
cucumber, olives, almonds, and pine nuts.

3 Whisk together the olive oil, lemon juice,
and mint. Season to taste with salt and
pepper and stir into the couscous. Serve
at once while warm, or leave to cool.

NUTRITION PER SERVING

Energy	619kcals/2590kJ
Carbohydrate	63g
of which sugar	31g
Fat	33g
of which saturates	3g
Salt	0.3g
Fibre	7g

Quinoa salad with mango, lime, and toasted coconut

A healthy salad full of big, tropical flavours and bright colours. Try to get Alphonso mangoes, if possible, which are famed for their sweetness.

Dairy free

Gluten free

High fibre

SERVES 4
PREP 15 MINS
COOK 10 MINS

50g (1¾oz) desiccated or flaked coconut

300g (10oz) quinoa

400g can butter beans, drained and rinsed

½ red onion, finely chopped

1 large mango, peeled, stoned, and cut into bite-sized pieces

1 lime, peeled, segmented, and segments halved

handful of mint, finely chopped

handful of flat-leaf parsley, finely chopped

FOR THE DRESSING

3 tbsp olive oil

1 tbsp white wine vinegar

pinch of sugar

salt and freshly ground black pepper

1 Toast the coconut by dry-frying it in a pan over a medium heat for 2–3 minutes until golden, stirring so that it doesn't burn. Remove from the heat and allow to cool.

2 To make the dressing, place all the ingredients in a small bowl or jug and whisk. Taste and adjust the seasoning as needed.

3 Cook the quinoa according to pack instructions. Drain well and tip into a large serving bowl. While the quinoa is still warm, stir through the butter beans, onion, mango, lime, mint, and parsley, and season.

4 Pour over the dressing and stir well. Sprinkle the toasted coconut on top and serve immediately.

try this....
Spicy chicken and quinoa salad with mango and lime

Omit the coconut and butter beans. Cook 200g (7oz) **French beans** in a pan of boiling water for 3–4 minutes. Plunge into cold water to cool, then drain well and slice in half. Continue as above from step 2, adding the beans and 350g (12oz) diced **ready-to-eat chicken tikka**.

NUTRITION PER SERVING

Energy	460kcals/1935kJ
Carbohydrate	54g
of which sugar	12.5g
Fat	20g
of which saturates	8g
Salt	0.8g
Fibre	7.5g

Quinoa and fennel salad

The peppery and aniseed notes of fennel contrast well with the nutty quinoa and the sweet pomegranate seeds.

| Low saturated fat |
| Dairy free |
| Low salt |
| High fibre |

SERVES 4
PREP 10 MINS,
PLUS STANDING
COOK 15 MINS

175g (6oz) uncooked quinoa

350ml (12fl oz) vegetable stock

1 tsp ground cumin

1 whole fennel bulb

3 tbsp olive oil

1 tbsp lemon juice

salt and freshly ground black pepper

4 spring onions, trimmed and thinly sliced

3 tbsp chopped coriander leaves

2 tbsp chopped mint leaves

100g (3½oz) pomegranate seeds

FOR A GLUTEN-FREE OPTION
use gluten-free stock

1 Rinse the quinoa under cold running water. Drain and place in a large saucepan. Add the stock and cumin and bring to the boil, stirring frequently. Then cover and cook over a medium heat for about 10 minutes. Remove from the heat and drain. Return the quinoa to the pan and leave for about 10 minutes, covered, to fluff up.

2 To prepare the fennel, trim the stalks, root end, and any tough outer pieces from the bulb and reserve the fronds. Cut the bulb in half lengthways. Then set each half on a chopping board, flat-side down, and cut into thin slices lengthways.

3 Heat 2 tablespoons of the oil in a large frying pan over a medium heat. Add the fennel slices and cook for about 5 minutes, turning over once, until golden. Remove from the heat and transfer to a bowl. Add the lemon juice and remaining oil, season to taste, and mix well to combine.

4 Add the onions, coriander, mint, and reserved fennel fronds to the bowl. Then add the quinoa and half the pomegranate seeds. Stir to mix, taste, and adjust the seasoning if needed. Divide the salad between four plates and sprinkle over the remaining pomegranate seeds. Serve at room temperature or cold.

NUTRITION PER SERVING

Energy	525kcals/2197kJ
Carbohydrate	28g
of which sugar	7.5g
Fat	11g
of which saturates	1.5g
Salt	0.8g
Fibre	7g

Herbed mackerel salad

Throw together this fragrant salad for a light meal packed with flavour – and then mop up the dressing with a crispy baguette. Smoked mackerel is great to have in the fridge, as it's quick, inexpensive, and high in protein.

Low saturated fat

Dairy free

SERVES 4
PREP 10–15 MINS
COOK 15–20 MINS

salt and freshly ground black pepper

550g (1¼lb) new potatoes, well scrubbed and chopped into bite-sized chunks

200g (7oz) hot-smoked mackerel fillets, skinned

60g (2oz) baby salad leaves

2 tbsp chopped dill

2 tbsp chopped chives

200g (7oz) cooked beetroot (not in vinegar), roughly chopped

baguette, to serve

FOR THE DRESSING

4 tbsp extra virgin olive oil

juice of 1 lemon

1 tsp wholegrain mustard

1 tsp clear honey

1 garlic clove, finely chopped

1 Bring a large pan of salted water to the boil, add the potato chunks, and cook for 10–15 minutes, or until tender. Drain and set aside.

2 Meanwhile, break the mackerel into bite-sized pieces, removing any bones you find as you go, and place in a large serving bowl. Add the salad leaves and herbs, and gently toss together.

3 Place the dressing ingredients in a small jug, season, and whisk together with a fork.

4 Add the warm potatoes to the serving bowl, pour over the dressing, and stir gently. Add the beetroot and serve straight away with the baguette.

NUTRITION PER SERVING

Energy	279kcals/1167kJ
Carbohydrate	26g
of which sugar	6g
Fat	12g
of which saturates	2.5g
Salt	1.1g
Fibre	4g

Panzanella

Good-quality bread is a joy, and even when it is past its best it can be used in this delectable Italian salad. The oil and vinegar moisten the bread and stop it tasting stale.

Low saturated fat

Dairy free

SERVES 4–6
PREP 15 MINS,
PLUS STANDING

350g (12oz) unsliced stale dense-textured bread, such as ciabatta or sourdough, roughly torn into bite-sized pieces

600g (1lb 5oz) mixed tomatoes, at room temperature, such as red, yellow, green, purple baby plum, cherry, or beefsteak, all roughly chopped into bite-sized chunks

1 red onion, finely chopped

2 garlic cloves, finely chopped

2 tbsp capers in brine, drained

salt and freshly ground black pepper

leaves from 1 bunch of basil, roughly torn

FOR THE DRESSING

6 tbsp extra virgin olive oil

3 tbsp red wine vinegar

½ tsp mustard powder

½ tsp caster sugar

1 Place the bread, tomatoes, onion, garlic, and capers in a large serving bowl. Season well and stir to combine.

2 Place the dressing ingredients in a small jug, season, and stir well. Pour over the bread and tomato mixture and stir to coat.

3 Set aside for at least 10 minutes and up to 2 hours, at room temperature, to allow the flavours to mingle. Stir the basil leaves into the salad just before serving.

NUTRITION PER SERVING	
Energy	396kcals/1664kJ
Carbohydrate	47g
of which sugar	8.5g
Fat	19g
of which saturates	3g
Salt	1.7g
Fibre	4.5g

Fattoush

You can vary the ingredients in this tangy toasted bread salad, but sumac, pomegranate syrup, and toasted flatbread are essential components of this traditional dish.

| Low saturated fat |
| Dairy free |
| Low salt |

SERVES 6
PREP 15 MINS

handful of fresh lettuce leaves

2–3 tomatoes, skinned and sliced

1 red or green pepper, deseeded and chopped

4–5 spring onions, trimmed and sliced

small bunch of flat-leaf parsley, coarsely chopped

2 thin flatbreads, such as pitta breads

2–3 tbsp olive oil

juice of 1 lemon

1–2 garlic cloves, crushed

1 tsp cumin seeds, crushed

salt and freshly ground black pepper

1–2 tbsp pomegranate syrup

2 tsp sumac

1 Arrange the lettuce leaves, tomatoes, peppers, and spring onions in a wide, shallow bowl and sprinkle the parsley over the top. Lightly toast the flatbreads, break them into bite-sized pieces, and scatter them over the salad.

2 In a small bowl, combine the oil and lemon juice with the garlic and cumin seeds. Season well and pour over the salad. Drizzle the pomegranate syrup over the top and sprinkle with sumac. Toss the salad gently just before serving.

NUTRITION PER SERVING	
Energy	120kcals/502kJ
Carbohydrate	17g
of which sugar	5g
Fat	4g
of which saturates	0.6g
Salt	0.2g
Fibre	2g

Chicken salad with radicchio and asparagus

This French "salade tiède", or warm salad, is easy to assemble and makes for a healthy supper you can knock together in minutes.

| Low carb |
| Low saturated fat |
| Dairy free |
| Gluten free |
| Low salt |

SERVES 4
PREP 5–10 MINS
COOK 10–15 MINS

4 tbsp extra virgin olive oil

4 chicken breasts, about 150g (5½oz) each, cut into thin strips

1 garlic clove, finely chopped

60g (2oz) roasted red peppers, thinly sliced

salt and freshly ground black pepper

1 small head of radicchio, torn into small pieces

250g (9oz) asparagus spears, each trimmed and cut into 3 pieces

2 tbsp raspberry vinegar

½ tsp sugar

1 Heat 2 tablespoons of the oil in a large non-stick frying pan over a medium–high heat. Add the chicken and garlic and fry, stirring, for 5–7 minutes, or until the chicken is tender and cooked through. Stir in the roasted red peppers, and season to taste with salt and pepper.

2 Meanwhile, put the radicchio leaves in a large serving bowl. Remove the chicken from the pan, using a slotted spoon, and place in the bowl with the radicchio.

3 Add the asparagus to the fat remaining in the pan and fry, stirring constantly, for 1–2 minutes, or until just tender. Transfer to the bowl with the chicken.

4 Whisk together the remaining 2 tablespoons of the oil, the vinegar and sugar, then pour into the pan and stir over a high heat until well combined. Pour this dressing over the salad and toss quickly so that all the ingredients are well mixed and coated with the dressing. Serve straight away.

try this....
Chicken salad with lentils and asparagus

Heat 1 tablespoon **oil** in a pan, add 2 finely sliced sticks of **celery**, 1 finely chopped **red onion**, and 1 diced **red pepper**, then sauté over a medium heat for 5 minutes, or until the onion is starting to soften. Add another 1 tablespoon oil and the chicken, asparagus, and garlic, and cook for a further 5–7 minutes, or until the chicken is cooked through. Allow the chicken mixture to cool, then mix with 1 can **green lentils**. Make the dressing as directed in step 4, pour over the chicken and lentils, and serve.

NUTRITION PER SERVING	
Energy	284kcals/1190kJ
Carbohydrate	3g
of which sugar	3g
Fat	13g
of which saturates	2g
Salt	0.2g
Fibre	2g

Chicken Caesar salad with polenta croutons

Using baked polenta to make the crunchy croutons for this perennially popular salad gives it a twist by providing extra texture to complement the succulence of the chicken and the freshness of the lettuce.

Gluten free

SERVES 4
PREP 20 MINS
COOK 10 MINS

2 tbsp light olive oil

225g (8oz) prepared polenta, cut into 2.5cm (1in) cubes

rock salt and freshly ground black pepper

1 large or 2 small heads romaine lettuce, washed, dried, and torn into bite-sized pieces

225g (8oz) cooked chicken, cut into bite-sized pieces

85g (3oz) freshly grated Romano cheese

FOR THE DRESSING

100ml (3½fl oz) extra virgin olive oil

1 tbsp Dijon mustard

3 tbsp good-quality mayonnaise

4 anchovy fillets, chopped

½ tsp Worcestershire sauce

1 garlic clove, crushed

2 tbsp finely grated Parmesan cheese, plus extra to serve

pinch of caster sugar

1 Heat the oil in a large frying pan over a medium heat. Add the polenta and season with ½ teaspoon of rock salt and ¼ teaspoon of pepper. Cook for 10 minutes, turning over the polenta cubes occasionally, until lightly browned and crisp. Remove from the heat and set aside.

2 For the dressing, place all the ingredients in the small bowl of a food processor and pulse until emulsified into a thick and creamy dressing. Alternatively, place the ingredients in a large bowl and blend well with a hand-held blender. Season with pepper, mix well to combine, and set aside.

3 Place the lettuce, chicken, and cheese in a large bowl and toss lightly to combine. Drizzle over the dressing, a little at a time, and toss until well coated. Arrange the salad on a serving dish and scatter over the polenta croutons. Sprinkle over some Parmesan and serve immediately.

NUTRITION PER SERVING	
Energy	521kcals/2180kJ
Carbohydrate	1.5g
of which sugar	1.5g
Fat	44g
of which saturates	10g
Salt	1.5g
Fibre	0.8g

Spicy Asian chicken salad

This colourful salad requires very little cooking. Toss with the dressing at the last minute to prevent wilting.

SERVES 4–6
PREP 10 MINS
COOK 7–10 MINS

400g (14oz) skinless, boneless chicken breasts

salt

4 tbsp lime juice (about 2 limes)

4 tsp Thai fish sauce

1 tbsp caster sugar

pinch of chilli flakes (optional)

1 small lettuce, shredded

100g (3½oz) beansprouts

1 large carrot, shaved using a vegetable peeler

15cm (6in) piece of cucumber, deseeded and finely sliced

½ red pepper, finely sliced

½ yellow pepper, finely sliced

about 15 cherry tomatoes, halved

handful of mint leaves, chopped

handful of coriander leaves, chopped

50g (1¾oz) salted peanuts, chopped (optional)

1 Poach the chicken in a large saucepan in plenty of simmering salted water for 7–10 minutes, depending on the thickness, until cooked through. Let cool, then thinly slice.

2 Whisk the lime juice, fish sauce, sugar, a pinch of salt, and the chilli flakes, if using, together, until the sugar dissolves.

3 Mix together the salad vegetables, most of the herbs, and the chicken. Mix in the dressing and scatter with the remaining herbs and the peanuts, if using, to serve.

try this....
Asian chicken salad with a peanut dressing

Make the salad as directed above. To make the peanut dressing, place 100g (3½oz) **crunchy peanut butter**, 1 tablespoon **toasted sesame oil**, 1 tablespoon **soy sauce**, 1 tablespoon **rice wine vinegar**, 1 teaspoon **honey**, 1 crushed **garlic clove**, and 100ml (3½fl oz) leftover poaching liquid or chicken stock in a saucepan. Gently simmer until the sauce starts to thicken, then season to taste. Leave to cool and spoon over the salad.

NUTRITION PER SERVING	
Energy	243–162kcals/ 1019–679kJ
Carbohydrate	12–8g
of which sugar	11–7.5g
Fat	8.5–5.5g
of which saturates	1.5–1g
Salt	1.4–0.9g
Fibre	4.5–3g

Bean thread noodle salad

This light yet vibrant summer salad is refreshing and perfect as part of an Asian-inspired meal or buffet lunch.

Low saturated fat

Dairy free

Gluten free

SERVES 4
PREP 20 MINS

200g (7oz) dried Chinese bean thread noodles or thin rice noodles

1 large carrot, shaved using a vegetable peeler

10cm (4in) cucumber, halved lengthways, deseeded, and finely sliced on the diagonal

4 spring onions, white parts only, finely sliced on the diagonal

1 mango, not too ripe, finely julienned

handful of mint leaves, roughly chopped

handful of coriander leaves, roughly chopped

FOR THE DRESSING
juice of 2 limes

2 tbsp white wine vinegar or rice wine vinegar

1 tsp caster sugar

pinch of salt

1 Put the noodles in a large bowl and cover with boiling water from a kettle. Leave for 4 minutes, or according to the packet instructions, until they are soft but still have a bite to them. Stir and separate the strands with chopsticks when you first pour the water over them, and once or twice afterwards. Drain and refresh under cold water, then drain thoroughly.

2 Meanwhile, assemble the rest of the salad ingredients in a bowl, keeping back a few herbs to serve. Preparing the salad vegetables over the bowl means you will capture all the juices. Pat the noodles completely dry with kitchen paper, and add the cold, drained noodles to the bowl.

3 Whisk together the dressing ingredients and toss it through the salad. Serve, scattered with the reserved herbs.

try this....
Prawn and mango salad

In step 2, add 350g (12oz) cooked, peeled **prawns** to the salad ingredients and continue as above.

NUTRITION PER SERVING	
Energy	228kcals/957kJ
Carbohydrate	48g
of which sugar	10g
Fat	0.5g
of which saturates	0.1g
Salt	0.5g
Fibre	3g

Grilled halloumi and roast tomato salad

A perfect balance of rich and fresh flavours. Halloumi is rich in protein, and will melt only at a high temperature. Soak in buttermilk if you find it too salty.

Low carb

Gluten free

SERVES 4
PREP 5 MINS
COOK 15 MINS

200g (7oz) cherry tomatoes, halved

3 tbsp olive oil

salt and freshly ground black pepper

250g (9oz) half-fat halloumi, cut into 5mm- (¼in-) thick slices

3 garlic cloves, finely chopped

small handful of flat-leaf parsley, finely chopped

½ tsp paprika

small handful of fresh basil, roughly chopped

250g (9oz) fresh baby spinach leaves

1 Preheat the oven to 180°C (350°F/Gas 4). Place the tomatoes in a roasting tin, drizzle with 1 tablespoon of the oil and season with salt and pepper. Toss together, then roast in the oven for 15 minutes with the tomatoes sitting skin side down.

2 While they are cooking, put the halloumi, garlic, parsley, paprika, and the remaining oil into a bowl and combine well. Heat a griddle pan until hot, then carefully add a slice of halloumi, letting it drain before adding it to the pan. Repeat, adding the halloumi slices one by one until they are all in the griddle pan. When you have added the last one, go back to the first one and begin turning them over to cook on the other side. They should be golden brown. When you have turned them all, go back to the first one and begin removing them from the griddle pan.

3 Put the halloumi slices back into the bowl with the garlic, herb, and spice mix and stir gently. Add the cooked tomatoes to the mix along with the basil and stir to combine. Add the spinach leaves, toss together, and serve immediately.

NUTRITION PER SERVING	
Energy	264kcals/1105kJ
Carbohydrate	3g
of which sugar	2g
Fat	19g
of which saturates	9g
Salt	1.7g
Fibre	1.5g

Thai-spiced lamb salad with lime dressing

The vibrant colours of this spicy lamb salad really sing out, making it perfect for a summer lunch. The limes disguise the fish flavour of Thai fish sauce.

Dairy free

Gluten free

SERVES 4
PREP 10 MINS
COOK 7–10 MINS,
PLUS RESTING

grated zest and juice of 5 limes

3 tsp palm sugar or Demerara sugar

1 red chilli, deseeded and finely chopped

½ tsp Thai fish sauce

1 tsp tamarind

3 tbsp groundnut oil

500g (1lb 2oz) boneless lamb chump or leg

100g (3½oz) Thai glass noodles, cooked

3 shallots, finely sliced

handful of coriander leaves

12 Thai basil leaves

small handful of mint leaves

50g (1¾oz) roasted peanuts, coarsely ground

1 For the dressing, place the lime zest and juice, sugar, chilli, fish sauce, tamarind, and 1 tablespoon of oil in a small bowl. Mix to combine all the ingredients and dissolve the sugar. Set aside.

2 Cut the lamb into six equal strips. Heat a griddle pan and add the remaining oil. Sear the lamb for about 2 minutes on each side. Do not overcook the lamb – it should be rare. Leave to rest for 3 minutes.

3 Slice the lamb thinly and place in a large bowl. Add the glass noodles, dressing, shallots, herbs, and peanuts, and toss to combine. Divide the salad between four plates and serve immediately.

NUTRITION PER SERVING	
Energy	391kcals/1636kJ
Carbohydrate	12g
of which sugar	5g
Fat	25g
of which saturates	7g
Salt	0.6g
Fibre	1.6g

Watermelon salad with feta and pumpkin seeds

This salad is fast becoming a modern classic. The sweetness of the ripe melon contrasts wonderfully with the salty feta and the nuttiness of the pumpkin seeds.

Low carb

Gluten free

SERVES 4
PREP 10 MINS
COOK 5 MINS

60g (2oz) pumpkin seeds

sea salt and freshly ground
   black pepper

¼ tsp chilli powder

4 tbsp light olive oil

juice of 1 lemon

500g (1lb 2oz) watermelon,
   peeled, deseeded if preferred,
   and cut into 2cm (¾in) squares

½ red onion, finely sliced

4 large handfuls of mixed salad
   leaves, such as watercress,
   rocket, or baby spinach

300g (10oz) feta cheese, cut
   into 1cm (½in) squares

1 Dry-fry the pumpkin seeds for 2–3 minutes until they start to pop. Add a pinch of sea salt and the chilli powder, stir, and cook for another minute. Set aside to cool.

2 In a large bowl, whisk together the oil, lemon juice, and sea salt and pepper to taste. Add the watermelon, red onion, and salad leaves, and toss well to coat with the dressing.

3 Scatter the feta cheese and the seeds over the top of the salad and serve immediately.

NUTRITION PER SERVING	
Energy	419kcals/1742kJ
Carbohydrate	13g
of which sugar	11g
Fat	33g
of which saturates	13g
Salt	2.8g
Fibre	1.8g

Orange salad with olives

Refreshing orange salads are popular in the southern Mediterranean and are served alongside stews and grilled meat or fish.

Low carb

Low saturated fat

Dairy free

Gluten free

SERVES 4
PREP 15–20 MINS,
PLUS STANDING

1 small–medium red
  onion, thinly sliced

2 ripe oranges

8–10 green olives

juice and finely grated zest
  of ½ lemon

2 tbsp fruity olive oil

salt and freshly ground
  black pepper

a few leaves of wild rocket
  (optional)

1 Place the onion in a bowl of cold water. Using a sharp knife, remove the peel and pith from the oranges, and slice thinly.

2 Place the oranges in a shallow serving dish. Drain the onion slices, place on a double layer of kitchen paper, and pat dry. Arrange the slices on the oranges. Scatter the olives on top.

3 In a small cup, combine the lemon juice and zest and the oil. Season to taste and drizzle over the salad. If you like, scatter over the rocket. Leave to stand for 5 minutes before serving.

NUTRITION PER SERVING

Energy	97kcals/406kJ
Carbohydrate	8g
of which sugar	7g
Fat	6.5g
of which saturates	1g
Salt	2g
Fibre	1.6g

Fennel salad

This pretty fennel and peach salad from the French Riviera makes a refreshing starter on a hot summer's day. Peaches contain vitamins A, C, E, and K, plus six B vitamins.

Low carb

Low saturated fat

Gluten free

Low salt

SERVES 4
PREP 15–20 MINS

2 small fennel bulbs, trimmed at the base and very thinly sliced

juice and finely grated zest of ½ lemon

1 tbsp extra virgin olive oil

salt and freshly ground black pepper

2 ripe peaches or nectarines, halved, cored, and sliced

1 tbsp chopped flat-leaf parsley

½ tbsp chopped mint leaves

1 slice of cured ham (about 5mm–1cm/¼in–½in thick), such as prosciutto crudo, Serrano, or Bayonne ham, diced

1 In a shallow bowl, toss the fennel with the lemon juice and zest, oil, and a little salt. Add the peaches or nectarines, sprinkle over half the herbs, and season with pepper. Toss lightly.

2 Arrange on a serving platter. Scatter over the ham and the remaining herbs. Serve immediately.

NUTRITION PER SERVING	
Energy	78kcals/326kJ
Carbohydrate	7g
of which sugar	6.5g
Fat	3.5g
of which saturates	0.5g
Salt	0.3g
Fibre	4g

Swiss chard and sweet potato salad

Here's a different way of serving fibre-rich Swiss chard, which is high in vitamin K and antioxidant carotenoids. Its slightly bitter taste fades with cooking.

Low saturated fat
Dairy free
Low salt

SERVES 4
PREP 5–10 MINS
COOK 25 MINS

1 tbsp olive oil, plus extra to drizzle

2 shallots, finely chopped

1 tsp coriander seeds, crushed

1 chilli, deseeded and finely chopped

2 garlic cloves, crushed

2 large sweet potatoes, peeled and cut into cubes

250g (9oz) Swiss chard, stalks removed and finely chopped, and leaves finely sliced

salt and freshly ground black pepper

1 Heat the olive oil with 1 tablespoon of water in a medium saucepan with a lid. Add the shallots and coriander seeds and cook over a low heat, stirring occasionally, until the shallots have softened.

2 Add the chilli and garlic, and cook for 1 minute. Add the sweet potato and cook over a medium heat for about 5 minutes, adding a dash of water if necessary. Then add the chopped chard stalks, cover, and cook for 10 minutes.

3 When the sweet potato is almost cooked, add the shredded chard leaves, cover, and let them wilt for about 3 minutes. Remove from the heat, season well, drizzle a few drops of olive oil, and serve.

try this....
Pumpkin, spinach, and feta salad

Toss 600g (1lb 5 oz) diced **butternut squash** with 2 tablespoons olive oil, then season with salt, pepper, and **chilli flakes**. Roast at 200°C (400°F/Gas 6) for 20 minutes, or until soft. Leave to cool, then mix with 2 handfuls of **baby spinach**, 1 handful of roughly chopped **almonds**, and 200g (7oz) crumbled **half-fat feta**.

NUTRITION PER SERVING	
Energy	194cals/823kJ
Carbohydrate	33g
of which sugar	9g
Fat	6g
of which saturates	1g
Salt	0.5g
Fibre	5g

Greek salad

A classic, deeply refreshing combination that needs very ripe, flavourful tomatoes. Make sure you use extremely tasty, pungent black or Kalamata olives, and an aromatic, strong extra virgin olive oil.

Low carb

Gluten free

Low salt

SERVES 6–8
PREP 25–30 MINS,
PLUS STANDING

2 small cucumbers

1kg (2½lb) tomatoes

1 red onion

2 green peppers, cored, deseeded, and diced

125g (4½oz) Kalamata or other Greek olives

175g (6oz) feta cheese, cubed

FOR THE HERB VINAIGRETTE

3 tbsp red wine vinegar

salt and freshly ground black pepper

120ml (4fl oz) extra virgin olive oil

3–5 sprigs of mint, leaves picked and finely chopped

3–5 sprigs of oregano, leaves picked and finely chopped

7–10 sprigs of parsley, leaves picked and finely chopped

NUTRITION PER SERVING

Energy	211kcals/883kJ
Carbohydrate	7.5g
of which sugar	7g
Fat	17g
of which saturates	5g
Salt	1g
Fibre	3.5g

1 To make the vinaigrette, whisk together the vinegar, salt, and pepper. Gradually whisk in the oil, so the vinaigrette emulsifies and thickens slightly. Add the herbs, then whisk again and taste for seasoning.

2 Peel the cucumbers and cut each in half lengthways. Scoop out the seeds with a teaspoon. Discard the seeds. Cut the cucumbers lengthways into 2–3 strips, then into 1cm (½in) slices.

3 With the tip of a small knife, core the tomatoes. Cut each one into eight wedges, then cut each wedge in half. Peel and trim the red onion and cut into very thin rings. Gently separate the concentric circles within each ring with your fingers.

4 Put the cucumbers, tomatoes, onion rings, and peppers in a large bowl. Briskly whisk the dressing, pour it over, and toss thoroughly. Add the olives (they may be either left whole or stoned) and feta and gently toss again. Taste for seasoning. Allow the flavours to mellow for about 30 minutes before serving.

Double-decker turkey and avocado sandwiches

Layering a sandwich is an easy way to make it more attractive. Use wholegrain, multigrain bread for the highest fibre content.

High fibre

SERVES 4
PREP 10 MINS

3 heaped tbsp good-quality mayonnaise

1 heaped tsp Dijon mustard

salt and freshly ground black pepper

butter, softened, for spreading

12 large slices of multigrain bread

2 handfuls of salad leaves

150g (5½oz) thinly sliced turkey breast

2 avocados, thinly sliced

½ lemon

1 Mix the mayonnaise and mustard together and season well. Butter eight slices of bread on one side only, and four slices carefully on both sides.

2 Lay four of the single side-buttered slices on a chopping board, buttered-sides up. Top each slice with one-quarter of the salad leaves, pressing them into the bread gently. Lay one-quarter of the turkey on top of each and spread over a thin layer of the mayonnaise.

3 Put a double-side-buttered slice of bread on each sandwich, then layer one-quarter of the avocado over each, drizzle with a little lemon juice, and season well.

4 Top each with a final slice of bread, buttered-side down, and press down well to hold everything together. Carefully trim the crusts off the bread and cut into halves on the diagonal to serve, or pack into a container for transportation.

NUTRITION PER SERVING	
Energy	614kcals/2572kJ
Carbohydrate	55g
of which sugar	4g
Fat	32g
of which saturates	9g
Salt	2g
Fibre	10g

Crayfish panini with herbed mayonnaise

Crayfish is low in fat and a good source of selenium and zinc. Its mild flavour makes a good foil for the strong herbs.

Dairy free

SERVES 4
PREP 15 MINS

1kg (2¼lb) cooked crayfish tails

4 Italian-style crusty bread rolls

1 oakleaf or other butter lettuce, leaves separated

2 fresh peaches, stoned and sliced

FOR THE HERBED MAYONNAISE

120ml (4fl oz) mayonnaise

juice of 1 lime

small handful of fresh coriander, chopped

small handful of fresh mint leaves, chopped

small handful of fresh chives, chopped

1 anchovy fillet in olive oil, drained and chopped

freshly ground black pepper

1 Remove all the meat from the crayfish tails, being careful not to break it up too much. Tear into four even portions, and set aside.

2 To make the herbed mayonnaise, combine the mayonnaise, lime juice, herbs, and anchovy in a bowl. Season with black pepper, and stir through.

3 Slice the rolls in half, but without cutting all the way through. Open up, and spread with the herbed mayonnaise. Arrange some of the leaves over the mayonnaise, then put the crayfish on top of the leaves. Arrange slices of the peaches between the crayfish, then spoon over a little more of the mayonnaise. Close up the rolls, and serve immediately.

NUTRITION PER SERVING

Energy	527kcals/2204kJ
Carbohydrate	38g
of which sugar	8g
Fat	27g
of which saturates	4g
Salt	1.2g
Fibre	4g

Spicy turkey burgers

Turkey is an excellent source of selenium, iron, zinc, and B vitamins. It spoils quickly, so do store it in the fridge after shaping the burgers.

Low saturated fat

Low salt

SERVES 4
PREP 15 MINS,
PLUS CHILLING
COOK 10 MINS

400g (14oz) minced turkey

75g (2½oz) fresh white
   breadcrumbs

1 tbsp sweet chilli sauce

4 spring onions, white part
   only, finely sliced

4 tbsp finely chopped
   coriander leaves

2cm (¾in) fresh root ginger,
   finely grated

1 red chilli, deseeded and
   finely chopped

salt and freshly ground black
   pepper

TO SERVE

4 burger buns

lettuce

tomato

finely sliced red onions

mayonnaise

Greek yogurt

sweet chilli sauce

1 Prepare a barbecue for cooking. In a large bowl, mix together all the ingredients until well combined.

2 With damp hands (to help stop the mixture sticking to your fingers), divide the mixture into four balls and roll each one between your palms until smooth. Flatten each ball out to a large, fat disk, 3cm (1in) high, and pat the edges in to tidy them up. Place the burgers on a plate, cover with cling film, and chill for 30 minutes (this helps them keep their shape on cooking).

3 Cook over a hot barbecue for 6–7 minutes, turning as needed, until the meat is springy to the touch and the edges charred.

4 Serve with a selection of buns and accompaniments, and let everyone build their own burgers.

NUTRITION PER SERVING	
Energy	244kcals/1027kJ
Carbohydrate	16g
of which sugar	2.5g
Fat	7g
of which saturates	3g
Salt	0.5g
Fibre	0.8g

Courgette and pea mini tortillas

Bursting with fresh green summer vegetables, these mini tortillas make a great appetizer. Alternatively, for a packed lunch, wrap them in foil to transport.

Dairy free

Low salt

MAKES 20
PREP 20 MINS
COOK 5 MINS

3 courgettes, grated

50g (1¾oz) baby spinach leaves

grated zest and juice of 1 lemon

250g (9oz) peas (shelled weight)

50g (1¾oz) pine nuts, toasted

salt and freshly ground black pepper

10 wheat tortillas, halved

2 tbsp reduced-fat mayonnaise

large handful of mangetout sprouts

large handful of pea shoots

FOR A GLUTEN-FREE OPTION
use gluten-free tortillas

1 In a large bowl, mix the courgettes, spinach, lemon zest and juice, peas, and pine nuts together. Season well.

2 Heat a frying pan over a high heat. Place two tortilla halves in the pan at a time and heat for 15 seconds on each side. Cover the heated tortillas with a tea towel to keep warm.

3 Brush one of the tortilla halves with mayonnaise. Place a little of the filling in the centre. Arrange some mangetout sprouts and pea shoots on top, so that they stick out at one end, then roll up the tortilla. Repeat to make 20 mini tortillas.

try this....
Carrot and red pepper hummus tortilla

Grate 2 large **carrots**, mix with 300g (10oz) **red pepper hummus**. Heat the tortilla as suggested in step 2. Spread a little of the hummus mixture over 1 tortilla, top with a handful of pea shoots or **watercress**, and then roll. Repeat with the remaining tortilla.

NUTRITION PER SERVING	
Energy	144kcals/602kJ
Carbohydrate	20g
of which sugar	1g
Fat	5g
of which saturates	2g
Salt	0.5g
Fibre	2.5g

Falafel

Dried chickpeas, soaked in advance, will give the best flavour. They are a good source of protein and high in phosphorus, magnesium, and iron.

MAKES 12
PREP 25 MINS, PLUS
SOAKING AND STANDING
COOK 15 MINS

400g (14oz) dried chickpeas, soaked overnight in cold water

1 tbsp tahini

1 garlic clove, crushed

1 tsp salt

1 tsp ground cumin

1 tsp turmeric

1 tsp ground coriander

½ tsp cayenne pepper

2 tbsp finely chopped flat-leaf parsley

juice of 1 small lemon

vegetable oil, for frying

1 Drain the soaked chickpeas and place them in a food processor with the remaining ingredients. Process until finely chopped but not puréed.

2 Transfer the mixture to a bowl and set aside for at least 30 minutes (and up to 8 hours), covered, in the fridge.

3 Wet your hands and shape the mixture into 12 balls. Press down slightly to flatten.

4 Heat 5cm (2in) of oil in a deep pan or wok. Fry the balls in batches for 3–4 minutes, or until lightly golden. Drain on kitchen paper and serve immediately.

NUTRITION PER SERVING	
Energy	162kcals/678kJ
Carbohydrate	21g
of which sugar	2g
Fat	5.5g
of which saturates	1.5g
Salt	0.8g
Fibre	2.3g

Ostrich burgers

A lean alternative to the beef burger, served with savoury ingredients that complement the richness of this low-calorie meat.

SERVES 4
PREP 15 MINS,
PLUS CHILLING
COOK 10 MINS

800g (1¾lb) minced ostrich meat

1 onion, finely chopped

2 tbsp chopped flat-leaf parsley

1 tbsp capers, drained and chopped

4 anchovy fillets, chopped

salt and freshly ground black pepper

FOR A GLUTEN-FREE OPTION
use gluten-free burger buns, mustard, and piccalilli

1 Place all the ingredients in a large bowl, season well, and mix to combine. Divide the meat mixture into four equal-sized balls and gently flatten to make patties. Chill the patties in the fridge for at least 1 hour to help firm them up.

2 Cook the patties on a hot barbecue or a griddle pan for 2 minutes on each side for medium-rare, or reduce the heat and cook for about 5 minutes, on each side, for well done. Do not cook the patties for long over a high heat because they will dry out fast. Serve with burger buns, mustard, and piccalilli.

NUTRITION PER SERVING

Energy	269kcals/1126kJ
Carbohydrate	2.5g
of which sugar	2g
Fat	9g
of which saturates	4g
Salt	0.9g
Fibre	0.7g

Deluxe peanut butter sandwiches

This "dressed-up" version of the popular peanut butter and jelly sandwich makes a nutritious, delicious snack. Marmalade is high in sugar but relatively low-calorie.

Dairy free

SERVES 4
PREP 10 MINS

115g (4oz) creamy or chunky
  peanut butter

2 tbsp orange marmalade

3 ripe bananas

8 slices wholegrain bread, toasted

1 In a small bowl, combine the peanut butter and marmalade until well mixed. Peel the bananas and cut them in half lengthways; then cut each half into two slices.

2 Spread the peanut butter equally over four slices of toast. Top with banana slices, then the second piece of toast.

3 Cut each sandwich in half diagonally, if you like.

NUTRITION PER SERVING

Energy	458kcals/1916kJ
Carbohydrate	53g
of which sugar	21g
Fat	17g
of which saturates	3g
Salt	1g
Fibre	9g

Stuffed ciabatta with grilled vegetables

This is simple to transport, and will easily feed a family of four. Mozzarella contains phosphorus, which helps the body absorb calcium.

SERVES 4
PREP 10 MINS, PLUS CHILLING
COOK 15 MINS, PLUS COOLING

½ aubergine, cut into 1cm (½in) slices

2 courgettes, cut into 1cm (½in) slices

4–6 tbsp olive oil

salt and freshly ground black pepper

1 large beef tomato

1 ciabatta loaf

2 chargrilled red peppers from a jar, drained and sliced

ball of mozzarella, about 125g (4½oz), thinly sliced

handful of basil leaves

1 Preheat a large griddle pan or a grill on its highest setting. Brush the slices of aubergine and courgette on both sides with olive oil and season them well. Either griddle or grill them for 2–4 minutes each side, until they are charred in places and cooked through. Put them on a large plate in a single layer to cool.

2 Slice about 1cm (½in) off each end of the tomato, reserving these pieces. Slice the remaining tomato as thinly as possible.

3 Cut the ciabatta in half, leaving a hinge so you can open it out flat. Drizzle both sides with a little olive oil. Take the offcuts of tomato and rub both sides of the bread with the cut side, to soften and flavour the bread, then discard the offcuts.

4 Cover one side of the loaf with the aubergine, courgette, and red peppers, then top with mozzarella. Sprinkle with the basil, season, then add the tomato.

5 Close the loaf and press down on it hard. Wrap it very tightly in cling film, going round it a few times until it is completely covered and compressed. Leave in the fridge with a weight (such as a chopping board and some cans) on top for at least 4 hours, turning once. Unwrap and slice to serve, or transport in the wrapping and slice at a picnic.

NUTRITION PER SERVING	
Energy	435kcals/1812kJ
Carbohydrate	36g
of which sugar	4g
Fat	25g
of which saturates	6.5g
Salt	1.2g
Fibre	8g

MAINS

Marinated lamb chops with lemon and chilli broccoli

This meal is simplicity itself. The marinade is quick to prepare, and you can leave it to flavour the lamb for as much – or as little – time as you have.

Low carb

Dairy free

Low salt

SERVES 4
PREP 5 MINS, PLUS MARINATING
COOK 30 MINS

4 lean lamb loin chops, fat removed

salt and freshly ground black pepper

handful of fresh rosemary stalks

1 head broccoli, about 300g (10oz),
   florets and stalks chopped fairly small

juice of 1 lemon

pinch of chilli flakes

mint jelly, to serve

FOR THE MARINADE
2 tbsp sherry vinegar, cider vinegar,
   or white wine vinegar

pinch of sugar

splash of dark soy sauce

FOR A GLUTEN-FREE OPTION
use gluten-free tamari to replace
   soy sauce

1 Preheat the oven to 200°C (400°F/Gas 6). First, prepare the marinade. Mix together the vinegar, sugar, and soy sauce, then pour over the lamb. Leave to marinate for 5 minutes, or longer if time permits.

2 Sit the lamb chops in a roasting tin, season well with salt and black pepper, and throw in the rosemary stalks. Roast in the oven for 20–30 minutes until cooked to your liking.

3 While the lamb is cooking, put the broccoli in a pan of boiling salted water, and cook for about 10 minutes until just soft. Drain, keeping the broccoli in the pan, then mash very gently with a fork. Squeeze over the lemon juice, and add the chilli, a pinch of salt, and some black pepper. Put a lid on the pan, and give it a shake. Serve immediately with the roasted lamb chops and a dollop of mint jelly on the side.

NUTRITION PER SERVING	
Energy	258kcals/1079kJ
Carbohydrate	2g
of which sugar	2g
Fat	13g
of which saturates	5g
Salt	0.5g
Fibre	2.5g

Grilled lamb with tomato salsa

Chermoula is a classic North African marinade for seafood, but it also pairs well with grilled meats. In Morocco, it is used liberally in tagines.

Low carb

Dairy free

Gluten free

SERVES 6
PREP 15 MINS,
PLUS MARINATING
COOK 15 MINS

12 lamb cutlets, trimmed

salt and freshly ground black pepper

4 ripe plum tomatoes, chopped

1 tbsp olive oil

1 tbsp balsamic vinegar

coriander leaves, chopped, to garnish

small bunch of mint leaves, chopped, to garnish

FOR THE MARINADE

2–3 garlic cloves, chopped

1 red chilli, deseeded and chopped

1 tsp coarse salt

small bunch of coriander, chopped

small bunch of flat-leaf parsley, chopped

2 tsp ground cumin

1 tsp paprika

4–5 tbsp olive oil

juice of 1 lemon

1 For the marinade, place the garlic, red chilli, and coarse salt in a mortar and pestle and pound, until they form a paste. Add the coriander and parsley, and pound to a coarse paste. Add the cumin and paprika, then pour in the oil and lemon juice. Mix well.

2 Place the cutlets in a dish. Rub the marinade over the lamb, and marinate for 30 minutes.

3 Season the tomatoes, drizzle with the olive oil, balsamic vinegar, coriander, and mint. Set aside.

4 Preheat the grill on its highest setting. Remove the cutlets from the marinade and grill for 5 minutes on each side, or until cooked through and crisp. Serve the lamb with the tomato salad on the side.

NUTRITION PER SERVING

Energy	325kcals/1360kJ
Carbohydrate	2.5g
of which sugar	2.5g
Fat	21g
of which saturates	6.5g
Salt	1.1g
Fibre	0.7g

Calf's liver with sage

The aroma of sage leaves permeates the quickly cooked liver in this classic dish. Replace the lemon juice with balsamic vinegar for a sweet and sour twist. Serve immediately – liver is tender when hot.

Low carb

Low salt

SERVES 4
PREP 15 MINS
COOK 5 MINS

2 tbsp plain flour, seasoned with salt and pepper

450g (1lb) calf's liver, trimmed and sliced

1 tsp olive oil

1 tbsp butter, plus an extra knob of butter

handful of sage leaves

juice of 1 lemon

1 Place the flour in a shallow dish. Add the liver, toss to coat lightly, and shake off any excess.

2 Heat the oil and 1 tablespoon of butter in a large frying pan over a medium–high heat. As the butter starts to foam, add the liver, making sure the pieces do not touch, and cook for about 2 minutes on each side. Do this in batches to avoid overcrowding the pan. Remove the liver from the pan, place on a serving dish, and keep warm.

3 Reduce the heat and add a knob of butter to the pan. Then add the sage leaves and, as soon as they start to fizzle, add the lemon juice.

4 Place the sage leaves over the liver, pour over the buttery juices, and serve hot.

NUTRITION PER SERVING

Energy	206kcals/862kJ
Carbohydrate	6g
of which sugar	0.1g
Fat	11g
of which saturates	4g
Salt	0.3g
Fibre	0.3g

Veal scaloppine with salsa verde

A typical Italian dish, this is traditionally served with salsa verde – a simple sauce that goes well with meat, fish, and vegetables. Try experimenting with different herbs.

Gluten free

SERVES 4
PREP 15–20 MINS
COOK 5 MINS,
PLUS RESTING

4 x 180g (6¼oz) veal sirloin medallions

8 slices Parma ham

12 sage leaves

freshly ground black pepper

2 tbsp unsalted butter

a dash of olive oil (optional)

FOR THE SALSA VERDE

3 tbsp finely chopped flat-leaf parsley

grated zest and juice of 1 small lemon

2 tbsp capers, drained and rinsed, if in salt, and finely chopped

2 garlic cloves, crushed

150ml (5fl oz) olive oil

½ tsp Dijon mustard

sea salt

1 Place the veal between two sheets of cling film and flatten slightly using a rolling pin or mallet. Remove from the cling film and set aside. Spread out two slices of ham on a plate and top with three sage leaves. Place the veal on top of the sage leaves and season with pepper. Wrap the ham around the veal and repeat with each medallion.

2 Meanwhile, for the salsa verde, place the parsley, lemon zest, capers, and garlic in a bowl. Add the lemon juice, oil, and mustard. Toss well to coat, and taste and adjust the seasoning, if needed.

3 Heat the butter in a large frying pan. Add the veal, when the butter starts to foam, and fry until golden on both sides. Add the oil, if required. Leave the veal to rest for 2 minutes and serve with the salsa verde.

NUTRITION PER SERVING	
Energy	541 kcals/2265kJ
Carbohydrate	0.4g
of which sugar	0.1g
Fat	39g
of which saturates	10g
Salt	1.6g
Fibre	0g

Pork steaks with fried apples

A super-quick, tasty meal; the fried apples make a near-instant accompaniment to the pork. Apples and pork are a traditional pairing, still popular even though pork is now available all year round, not just during the autumn.

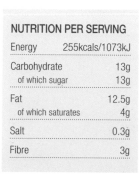

Gluten free

Low salt

SERVES 4
PREP 5 MINS
COOK 15 MINS

4 x 100g (3½oz) boneless pork
  steaks

salt and freshly ground black pepper

2 tbsp olive oil

1 tbsp butter

4 small apples, peeled, cored, and
  quartered

1 tbsp lemon juice

½ tsp caster sugar

1 Season the pork well with salt and pepper. Heat 1 tablespoon of the oil in a large frying pan and fry the pork for 3–5 minutes on each side, depending on thickness, until cooked through. Set it aside, loosely covered in foil to keep it warm.

2 Add the remaining 1 tablespoon of oil and the butter to the pan and allow them to bubble up. Add the apple pieces, pour the lemon juice over, sprinkle with the sugar, and season with salt and pepper.

3 Cook the apples over a medium heat for 5–7 minutes, turning occasionally, until they soften and start to caramelize. Turn them gently using two spatulas, so the pieces don't break up. Serve each pork steak topped with one-quarter of the apples.

NUTRITION PER SERVING	
Energy	255kcals/1073kJ
Carbohydrate	13g
of which sugar	13g
Fat	12.5g
of which saturates	4g
Salt	0.3g
Fibre	3g

Cinnamon and ginger beef with noodles

A quick dish with punchy flavours. Cinnamon and ginger, both from China, have a reputation for health benefits that science is now investigating.

SERVES 4
PREP 10 MINS
COOK 15 MINS

500g (1lb 2oz) lean steak, thinly sliced

2 tsp ground cinnamon

1 tbsp sunflower oil

1 onion, sliced

5cm (2in) piece of fresh ginger, peeled and shredded

1 red chilli, deseeded and finely chopped

2 garlic cloves, finely chopped

1 tbsp fish sauce

1 tbsp sesame oil

200g (7oz) mixed exotic mushrooms, such as oyster, shiitake and hon shimeji, trimmed or chopped

200g (7oz) mangetout

400g (14oz) medium or thick straight-to-wok udon noodles

FOR A GLUTEN-FREE OPTION
use gluten-free noodles

1 Put the steak in a bowl, sprinkle over the cinnamon and stir to coat. Heat the sunflower oil in a wok, add the onion, and stir-fry over a high heat for 1 minute. Add the ginger and chilli and stir-fry for a further minute.

2 Now add the steak, garlic, fish sauce, and sesame oil and continue to cook, stirring, until the meat is no longer pink. Add the mushrooms and mangetout and continue to stir-fry for a further 1–2 minutes.

3 Add the noodles and stir-fry for about 3 minutes until the noodles become sticky. Serve immediately.

NUTRITION PER SERVING	
Energy	378kcals/1584kJ
Carbohydrate	33g
of which sugar	2.5g
Fat	12g
of which saturates	3g
Salt	1.2g
Fibre	2.2g

Wasabi beef and pak choi

Wasabi has anti-bacterial, anti-microbial, and anti-parasitic qualities. Little wonder that the Japanese have cultivated it for thousands of years.

Low carb

Low salt

SERVES 4
PREP 10 MINS
COOK 10 MINS

2 tbsp olive oil

2 tsp wasabi paste

4 sirloin steaks, about 200g (7oz) each

200g (7oz) pak choi, cut lengthways into 8 pieces

5 garlic cloves, grated or finely chopped

1 tbsp dark soy sauce

salt and freshly ground black pepper

FOR A GLUTEN-FREE OPTION
use gluten-free tamari to replace soy sauce

1 Heat the barbecue or charcoal grill until hot. Mix together 1 tablespoon of the olive oil and the wasabi paste. Use to coat the sirloin steaks, ensuring a thin, even covering.

2 Sit the steaks on the barbecue and grill fiercely over a high heat for 3 minutes on each side. Remove to a plate, and leave to rest in a warm place for 5 minutes.

3 Meanwhile, toss the pak choi in the remaining olive oil with the garlic and soy sauce. Grill for 2–3 minutes, or until charred and just wilted. To serve, cut the steak into 1cm (½in) slices, season, and serve with the pak choi.

NUTRITION PER SERVING	
Energy	323kcals/1352kJ
Carbohydrate	2g
of which sugar	1.5g
Fat	14.5g
of which saturates	5g
Salt	0.9g
Fibre	1g

Steak glazed with mustard and brown sugar

Fillet steak is a very lean cut of beef, and has very little fat running through it. This means that it is a very good choice in a balanced diet.

| Low carb |
| Low saturated fat |
| Dairy free |
| Gluten free |
| Low salt |

SERVES 4
PREP 5 MINS
COOK 10 MINS

4 x 100–150g (3½–5½oz) steaks, preferably fillet, about 3cm (1in) thick, at room temperature

1 tbsp olive oil

salt and freshly ground black pepper

1 tbsp Dijon mustard

1 tbsp soft light brown sugar

1 Rub the steaks with the oil and season well with salt and pepper. Fry or chargrill over a high heat until cooked as you like. For rare, allow 2–3 minutes each side; for medium, 3–4 minutes each side; and for well done, 4–5 minutes each side. Allow the meat to rest for about 5 minutes, loosely covered with foil to keep warm.

2 Meanwhile, preheat the grill on its highest setting. Brush each steak on one side with a thin layer of mustard, then sprinkle with an even layer of the sugar.

3 Grill the steaks for a minute or 2 only, until the sugar has melted and caramelized over the top. You don't want to cook them any further, just enough to create a great glazed effect.

NUTRITION PER SERVING	
Energy	184kcals/767kJ
Carbohydrate	4g
of which sugar	4g
Fat	9g
of which saturates	3g
Salt	0.4g
Fibre	0g

Beef with soy and lime, and a grapefruit and ginger salsa

Soy sauce has up to ten times the level of antioxidants found in red wine, chillies have comparatively more vitamin C than citrus fruits, and rump steak is a lean cut of beef. Enjoy!

Low saturated fat

Dairy free

Low salt

SERVES 4
PREP 10 MINS
COOK 15 MINS

1 tbsp groundnut or sunflower oil

1 red onion, cut into 8 wedges

675g (1½lb) rump steak, cut into strips

1 fresh medium-hot red chilli, deseeded and finely sliced into strips

splash of dark soy sauce

juice of 1 lime

1 tbsp clear honey

200g (7oz) chestnut mushrooms, cleaned and sliced

handful of fresh coriander

rice or noodles, to serve

FOR THE GRAPEFRUIT AND GINGER SALSA

2 grapefruit, segmented and chopped

2.5cm (1in) piece of fresh root ginger, grated

1 fresh medium-hot red chilli, deseeded and finely chopped

pinch of sugar (optional)

freshly ground black pepper (optional)

1 First, make the salsa. Put all the ingredients in a bowl, stir, and taste. Add a little black pepper, if you wish. Set aside.

2 Heat the oil in a wok over a high heat until hot. Add the onion, and stir-fry for about 5 minutes until soft, before adding the beef strips and chilli. Continue to stir-fry for another 5 minutes or so, keeping everything moving in the wok. Add the soy, lime juice, and honey, and keep stir-frying.

3 Throw in the mushrooms, and stir-fry for a few minutes until they are soft and begin to release their juices.

4 To serve, pile the coriander on top of the beef, and serve immediately with rice or noodles, and the grapefruit salsa.

NUTRITION PER SERVING	
Energy	326kcals/1365kJ
Carbohydrate	12g
of which sugar	12g
Fat	4g
of which saturates	2.5g
Salt	0.4g
Fibre	2.6g

Dry-rubbed barbecued steak

Rub the steak with this spicy mix and allow it to rest so the flavours permeate the meat.

Low carb

Low saturated fat

Dairy free

Gluten free

Low salt

SERVES 4
PREP 5–10 MINS, PLUS CHILLING
COOK 5–10 MINS, PLUS RESTING

2 tsp smoked paprika

2 tsp mustard powder

1 tsp garlic salt

1 tsp dried thyme

1 tbsp soft light brown sugar

freshly ground black pepper

4 steaks, such as rump or sirloin, about 150g (5½oz) each

1 tbsp olive oil

1 In a mortar and pestle, or a spice grinder, mix the dry ingredients together to form a fine powder.

2 Rub each steak all over with the spice mix and wrap each one with cling film. Leave to rest in the fridge for 4–6 hours. Prepare a barbecue for cooking.

3 Unwrap the steaks and allow them to come to room temperature. Drizzle with a little oil and grill on a hot barbecue for 2–3 minutes on each side if you want medium–rare (3–4 minutes for medium, or 4–5 for well done), turning only after the underside has crusted up.

4 Remove from the heat and allow to rest for 5 minutes, covered with foil, before serving.

NUTRITION PER SERVING	
Energy	226kcals/949kJ
Carbohydrate	4g
of which sugar	4g
Fat	9g
of which saturates	3g
Salt	1.2g
Fibre	0g

Thai-style stir-fried minced beef

If you like Asian flavours but prefer to avoid heat, simply leave out the chilli. Serve with cauliflower rice for a low-carbohydrate option.

Low carb

Dairy free

SERVES 4–6
PREP 5 MINS
COOK 10 MINS

salt

100g (3½oz) broccoli florets, cut very small

2 tbsp sunflower oil

bunch of spring onions, finely chopped

2 garlic cloves, crushed

3cm (1in) fresh root ginger, finely chopped

1 tbsp finely chopped coriander stalks, plus a handful of coriander leaves, roughly chopped

1 red chilli, deseeded and finely chopped (optional)

400g (14oz) minced beef

1 tbsp fish sauce

2 tbsp soy sauce

1 tbsp lime juice

1 tsp caster sugar

rice, to serve

FOR A GLUTEN-FREE OPTION
use gluten-free tamari to replace soy sauce

1 Bring a large pan of salted water to the boil and blanch the broccoli for 1 minute, then drain and refresh it under cold water. Set aside.

2 Heat the sunflower oil in a wok or a large, deep-sided frying pan. Add the spring onions, garlic, ginger, coriander stalks, and chilli (if using), and fry for a couple of minutes until coloured slightly.

3 Add the minced beef and continue to fry over a high heat until the meat is well browned.

4 Return the broccoli and add the fish sauce, soy sauce, lime juice, and sugar. Mix well, cooking for a minute or 2 until the broccoli is piping hot. Stir in the coriander leaves and serve with rice.

NUTRITION PER SERVING	
Energy	300kcals/1244kJ
Carbohydrate	4g
of which sugar	4g
Fat	22g
of which saturates	8g
Salt	2.3g
Fibre	1.5g

Flatbreads topped with lamb and hummus

This tasty Middle Eastern-style recipe is the perfect use for any leftovers from a roast joint of lamb.

Dairy free

Low salt

SERVES 2
PREP 10 MINS
COOK 20 MINS

1 tbsp olive oil, plus extra for drizzling

1 onion, finely chopped

3 garlic cloves, grated or finely chopped

200g (7oz) leftover roast lamb, shredded

pinch of ground allspice

pinch of ground cinnamon

salt and freshly ground black pepper

2 flatbreads or plain naan

handful of pine nuts, toasted

handful of mint leaves, roughly chopped

hummus, to serve

1 Preheat the oven to 200°C (400°F/Gas 6). Heat the oil in a frying pan over a medium heat, add the onion, and cook for about 5 minutes until the onion is soft and translucent.

2 Stir in the garlic and cook for a few more seconds. Now add the leftover lamb and stir through. Sprinkle over the allspice and cinnamon and cook for a few minutes, stirring occasionally. Season with salt and pepper.

3 Lay the flatbreads or naan on a baking tray and drizzle with a little oil. Spoon over the lamb mixture and cook in the oven for about 10 minutes until the lamb is heated through. Scatter over the pine nuts and mint leaves, and top each flatbread or naan with a dollop of hummus. Serve immediately.

NUTRITION PER SERVING	
Energy	624kcals/2611kJ
Carbohydrate	33g
of which sugar	7g
Fat	38g
of which saturates	12g
Salt	0.8g
Fibre	3.5g

Seared duck with raspberry cardamom glaze

The tangy, slightly tart raspberry sauce perfectly complements the rich flavours of the crisp duck breast. Duck fat is relatively healthy, with less saturated fat than butter.

Low carb

Gluten free

Low salt

SERVES 4
PREP 20 MINS
COOK 20 MINS

600g (1lb 5oz) skin-on duck breasts

salt and freshly ground black pepper

FOR THE SAUCE

1 tbsp butter

1 tbsp brown sugar

100g (3½oz) shallots, finely chopped

200g (7oz) fresh raspberries, deseeded and roughly chopped

4 cardamom pods, seeds removed and crushed

1 tbsp red wine vinegar

1 Use a sharp knife to score the skin on the duck breasts. Rub the meat generously with salt and pepper.

2 Place the duck skin-side down in a heavy-based frying pan over a medium-low heat. Allow the duck fat to render for 10–12 minutes. Turn and cook for a further 3–5 minutes on the other side. Set aside to rest. Keep warm.

3 Drain off the duck fat. In the same pan, melt the butter. Add the sugar and shallots and cook until caramelized.

4 Add the raspberries, cardamom, and vinegar. Cook, stirring frequently, for 5–7 minutes. Transfer the duck to a serving plate and serve topped with the raspberry sauce.

NUTRITION PER SERVING	
Energy	429kcals/1794kJ
Carbohydrate	7g
of which sugar	7g
Fat	25g
of which saturates	8g
Salt	trace
Fibre	2g

Venison steak with blackberries

Venison has less fat than most cuts of red meat. This simple method cooks it quickly, and the blackberries provide a tangy accompaniment.

Low carb

Gluten free

Low salt

SERVES 4
PREP 5 MINS
COOK 15 MINS

4 venison haunch steaks, about 200g (7oz) each

salt and freshly ground black pepper

1 tbsp sunflower oil

50g (1¾oz) butter, chilled and diced

4 tbsp blackberry wine or red wine

2 tbsp redcurrant jelly

150g (5½oz) blackberries

1 Pat the steaks dry with kitchen paper to remove any excess blood. Season well. Heat the oil and 1 teaspoon of butter in a heavy-based pan over a medium heat. Place the steaks in the hot pan and cook for 4–5 minutes on each side.

2 Reduce the heat and cook for another 5 minutes, turning once, until well-browned. Remove the meat from the pan, cover with foil, and set aside. Then add the wine, redcurrant jelly, and blackberries to the pan. Bring to the boil, stirring gently to melt the jelly.

3 Once the sauce has thickened, remove from the heat and whisk in the remaining butter. Do not boil the sauce again, or else the butter will separate. Serve the steaks with the sauce poured over.

NUTRITION PER SERVING	
Energy	366kcals/1532kJ
Carbohydrate	6.5g
of which sugar	6.5g
Fat	16g
of which saturates	8.5g
Salt	0.5g
Fibre	1.6g

Spicy chicken meatballs

These are perfect alongside a vegetable and noodle stir-fry. Finely chopped chilli can be added for more heat. Organic chicken has significantly less fat than factory-farmed.

| Low saturated fat |
| Low salt |

SERVES 4
PREP 10 MINS, PLUS CHILLING
COOK 10 MINS

400g (14oz) minced chicken

50g (1¾oz) fresh white breadcrumbs

2 spring onions, finely chopped

1 garlic clove, crushed

2cm (¾in) fresh root ginger, finely grated

1 tbsp finely chopped coriander leaves

1 tbsp sweet chilli sauce

1 tsp lime juice

1 tsp fish sauce

2 tbsp sunflower oil

1 Mix all the ingredients, except the oil, together in a large bowl until evenly incorporated. It's easiest to use your fingers for this; you may prefer to wear plastic food preparation gloves. Cover and refrigerate for at least 30 minutes.

2 With damp hands, shape walnut-sized balls with the chicken mixture, placing them on a plate. At this point, you may cover and chill the meatballs for up to 1 day, if that is more convenient.

3 Heat the sunflower oil in a large frying pan and fry the meatballs over a medium–high heat for about 3–5 minutes, turning to colour all sides, until golden and cooked through (cut one through to the centre to check there is no trace of pink). You may need to do this in batches, depending on the size of the pan. Serve.

NUTRITION PER SERVING	
Energy	211kcals/888kJ
Carbohydrate	11.5g
of which sugar	3g
Fat	7g
of which saturates	1g
Salt	0.8g
Fibre	0.5g

Pad Thai

Originating from road-side food stalls in Thailand, this zingy noodle dish is designed to be quick to cook and easy to assemble – ideal for the time-limited chef! Experiment with different kinds of rice noodles to find your favourite.

Dairy free

Low salt

SERVES 4
PREP 5 MINS
COOK 15 MINS

300g (10oz) medium or thick dried rice noodles

3 tbsp sunflower oil

2 eggs, lightly beaten

1 tsp shrimp paste (optional)

2 hot red chillies, deseeded and finely chopped

3 skinless, boneless chicken breasts, cut into 5mm (¼in) slices

bunch of spring onions, finely chopped

splash of Thai fish sauce, such as nam pla

juice of 1 lime

1 tbsp demerara sugar

salt and freshly ground black pepper

150g (5½oz) unsalted peanuts, toasted in a dry wok or frying pan

handful of coriander leaves, finely chopped

lime wedges, to serve

FOR A GLUTEN-FREE OPTION
use gluten-free noodles

1 Put the noodles in a large bowl, cover with boiling water, and leave for 8 minutes, or until soft. Drain and set aside.

2 Meanwhile, put 1 tablespoon of the oil in a large wok over a high heat and swirl around the pan. Add the beaten egg and swirl it around the wok for about a minute, or until it begins to set – don't let it set completely – then remove, chop, and set aside.

3 Add the remaining 2 tablespoons of oil to the pan, then add the shrimp paste, if using, and chillies, and stir. With the heat still high, add the chicken and stir vigorously for 5 minutes, or until it is no longer pink.

4 Stir through the spring onions, fish sauce, lime juice, and sugar, and toss together well. Cook for a few minutes until the sugar has dissolved, then season well with salt and pepper. Return the egg to the pan.

5 Add the noodles to the pan and toss together to coat with the sauce, then add half the peanuts and half the coriander and toss again. Transfer to a large, shallow warmed serving bowl and scatter over the rest of the peanuts and coriander. Garnish with lime wedges to serve.

NUTRITION PER SERVING	
Energy	740kcals/3092kJ
Carbohydrate	68g
of which sugar	7.5g
Fat	30g
of which saturates	5.5g
Salt	1g
Fibre	0.5g

Spicy stir-fried chicken with vegetables

This dish incorporates three different green vegetables, but it is quite spicy, so to reduce the heat for young palates, reduce the amount of chilli used.

Low carb
Low saturated fat
Dairy free

SERVES 4
PREP 15 MINS, PLUS MARINATING
COOK 10 MINS

3 tbsp soy sauce

2 tbsp rice wine or dry sherry

1 tsp caster sugar

2½ tbsp sunflower oil

400g (14oz) skinless boneless chicken thighs, cut into 1cm (½in) strips

50g (1¾oz) fine green beans, halved

salt

50g (1¾oz) broccoli florets

2 garlic cloves, crushed

3cm (1in) fresh root ginger, finely chopped

1 red chilli, deseeded and finely chopped

bunch of spring onions, cut into 2cm (¾in) pieces

100g (3½oz) sugarsnap peas, halved on the diagonal

1 tbsp oyster sauce

1 Mix 1 tablespoon of the soy sauce, 1 tablespoon of the rice wine, the sugar, and ½ tablespoon of the oil in a bowl. Stir in the chicken, cover, and refrigerate for 30 minutes.

2 Cook the green beans in a pan of boiling salted water for 1 minute. Add the broccoli and cook for a further minute. Drain and refresh under cold water. Set aside.

3 Heat the remaining oil in a wok, add the garlic, ginger, and chilli, and fry for 1 minute. Now add the chicken and stir for 2–3 minutes. Add the spring onions and sugarsnaps, and stir-fry for a further 2–3 minutes. Pour in the remaining soy sauce and rice wine, and the oyster sauce, and bubble up. Tip in the blanched vegetables and heat through to serve.

NUTRITION PER SERVING	
Energy	216kcals/904kJ
Carbohydrate	6g
of which sugar	5g
Fat	10g
of which saturates	1.5g
Salt	2.6g
Fibre	2g

Sweet and sour chicken

A more sophisticated version of the takeaway classic – this one has no pineapple chunks. Try serving with cauliflower rice for a low-calorie option.

Low carb

Low saturated fat

Dairy free

SERVES 4
PREP 15 MINS,
PLUS MARINATING
COOK 10 MINS

FOR THE MARINADE
1 tsp cornflour
1 tbsp soy sauce
1 tbsp rice wine or dry sherry
1 tsp caster sugar

FOR THE CHICKEN
500g (1lb 2oz) skinless boneless chicken breast, cut into 1cm (½in) slices
2 tbsp sunflower oil
2 garlic cloves, finely chopped
2.5cm (1in) fresh root ginger, finely chopped
100g (3½oz) raw, unsalted cashew nuts, roughly chopped

FOR THE SAUCE
2 tbsp rice wine vinegar or white wine vinegar
2 tbsp rice wine or dry sherry
3 tbsp tomato ketchup
2 tbsp soy sauce
100ml (3½fl oz) chicken stock
1 tbsp caster sugar

1 Mix the marinade ingredients in a bowl and turn through the chicken. Cover and refrigerate for at least 30 minutes.

2 Whisk together all the sauce ingredients and set aside.

3 Heat the oil in a wok, add the garlic and ginger, and stir-fry for 1 minute. Add the chicken and stir-fry until it turns pale.

4 Add the sauce and bubble up. Add the nuts and cook for 2–3 minutes until the mixture has thickened and the chicken is coated in a glossy sauce. Serve.

NUTRITION PER SERVING	
Energy	386kcals/1616kJ
Carbohydrate	14g
of which sugar	10g
Fat	19g
of which saturates	3.5g
Salt	2.7g
Fibre	1g

Turkey escalopes stuffed with prunes and pecans

While you can buy ready-prepared turkey escalopes, they are very easy to make from the breasts. Serve these sweetened versions with sautéed potatoes and wilted spinach.

Low saturated fat

Dairy free

Gluten free

Low salt

SERVES 4
PREP 15 MINS
COOK 15–20 MINS

2 skinless turkey breasts, about 400g (14oz) each

large handful of pitted prunes, chopped

handful of roasted pecan nuts, finely chopped

handful of flat-leaf parsley, chopped

1 tbsp olive oil

1 Preheat the oven to 200°C (400°F/Gas 6). Cut each turkey breast in half and sandwich the four pieces between sheets of cling film. Pound them with a meat hammer or the edge of a rolling pin until they are an even thickness of about 5mm (¼in). Remove the cling film and slice the breasts in half so that you now have eight escalopes.

2 Mix the prunes and nuts with the parsley in a bowl, then spoon the mixture into the middle of each turkey escalope. Roll up from one narrow end and secure with a cocktail stick.

3 Sit the turkey rolls in a roasting tin, drizzle with the oil, and roast in the oven for 15–20 minutes, until cooked through. Serve with sautéed potatoes and wilted spinach.

NUTRITION PER SERVING	
Energy	298kcals/1248kJ
Carbohydrate	4.5g
of which sugar	4.3g
Fat	9g
of which saturates	1.3g
Salt	0.3g
Fibre	1.3g

Cajun chicken with sweetcorn salsa

Avocados give the salsa a creamy flavour, which balances the fiery flavour of the chicken.

Low carb

Low saturated fat

Dairy free

Low salt

SERVES 2
PREP 10 MINS
COOK 15 MINS

2 skinless chicken breasts

1 tbsp of Cajun seasoning

1 tbsp olive oil

FOR THE SALSA

1 large fresh corn on the cob, stripped of husks and threads

½ small red onion, finely chopped

½ red pepper, deseeded and diced

1 red chilli, deseeded and finely chopped

1 small Hass avocado, diced

1 tbsp olive oil

juice of 1 lime

1 Put the chicken breasts between two pieces of cling film and pound with a rolling pin until flattened evenly. Mix the Cajun seasoning with the oil and brush over the flattened chicken. Leave to marinate for at least 15 minutes.

2 To make the salsa, add the corn to a large pan of boiling water and cook for 5 minutes, then immediately transfer to a bowl of iced water to cool. Drain well, then, using a sharp knife, scrape off all the kernels. Combine with the remaining salsa ingredients, mix well, and set aside.

3 Heat a griddle pan and cook the chicken for 4–5 minutes on one side, pressing the pieces down on the griddle pan, then turn and cook for 4–5 minutes on the other side, or until cooked through.

4 Spoon the salsa onto serving plates and top with the griddled chicken.

NUTRITION PER SERVING	
Energy	442kcals/1846kJ
Carbohydrate	18g
of which sugar	5g
Fat	23g
of which saturates	4g
Salt	0.3g
Fibre	3.5g

Chicken liver with Marsala

This sauce comes from the Piedmont region of Italy, where wild mushrooms, including truffles grow freely. Mushrooms have good amounts of trace minerals.

Low carb

Gluten free

Low salt

SERVES 4
PREP 15 MINS,
PLUS SOAKING
COOK 10 MINS

60g (2oz) butter

400g (14oz) chicken livers, trimmed

2 shallots, finely chopped

30g (1oz) dried ceps, soaked in water for 30 minutes and the water reserved

1 tsp tomato purée

4 tbsp Marsala

1 Heat the butter in a large saucepan over a medium heat. Add the livers and fry for about 2 minutes. Remove with a slotted spoon, place on a plate lined with kitchen paper, and set aside.

2 Add the shallots to the pan and cook until soft. Then add the ceps and tomato purée and stir to combine. Stir in the Marsala and shake the pan lightly to mix through.

3 Return the livers to the pan and mix well to coat with the sauce. Taste and adjust the seasoning, if needed, and add a little of the reserved soaking water if the sauce seems too thick. Serve hot.

NUTRITION PER SERVING	
Energy	236kcals/988kJ
Carbohydrate	2g
of which sugar	1.7g
Fat	15g
of which saturates	9g
Salt	0.5g
Fibre	1.6g

Cashew nut paella

Cashews are expensive nuts, but they make a delicious paella. Try substituting with chopped cooked chestnuts or even toasted hazelnuts for a change.

SERVES 4
PREP 10 MINS
COOK 25 MINS

large pinch of saffron strands

750ml (1¼ pints) hot vegetable stock

2 tbsp olive oil

1 leek, chopped

1 onion, chopped

2 garlic cloves, crushed

1 red pepper, deseeded and chopped

1 carrot, chopped

250g (9oz) paella rice

150ml (5fl oz) dry white wine

115g (4oz) chestnut mushrooms, sliced

115g (4oz) roasted, unsalted cashew nuts

salt and freshly ground black pepper

115g (4oz) fresh shelled or frozen peas

1½ tbsp chopped thyme

4 tomatoes, quartered

½ tsp smoked paprika

sprig of flat-leaf parsley and lemon wedges, to garnish

FOR A GLUTEN-FREE OPTION
use gluten-free stock

1 Put the saffron in the stock to infuse. Heat the oil in a paella pan or large frying pan and fry the leek, onion, garlic, red pepper, and carrot, stirring, for 3 minutes until softened, but not browned. Add the rice and stir until coated in oil and glistening.

2 Add the wine and boil until it has been absorbed, stirring. Stir in the saffron-infused stock, mushrooms, nuts, and some salt and pepper. Bring to the boil, stirring once, then reduce the heat, cover, and simmer very gently for 10 minutes.

3 Add the peas and thyme, stir gently, then distribute the tomatoes over the top. Cover and simmer very gently for a further 10 minutes until the rice is just tender and has absorbed most of the liquid, but is still creamy.

4 Sprinkle the paprika over and stir through gently, taking care not to break up the tomatoes. Taste and adjust the seasoning, if necessary.

5 Garnish with a sprig of parsley and lemon wedges and serve hot.

NUTRITION PER SERVING	
Energy	582kcals/2435kJ
Carbohydrate	68g
of which sugar	11g
Fat	21g
of which saturates	4g
Salt	1.5g
Fibre	8g

Mixed mushroom and pak choi stir-fry

This dish uses cultivated mushrooms that originate from Japan. They are widely available in supermarkets, but chestnut mushrooms can be substituted, if necessary.

Dairy free

High fibre

SERVES 4
PREP 10 MINS
COOK 8 MINS

250g (9oz) dried soba or brown udon noodles

6 tbsp tamari or 4 tbsp reduced-salt soy sauce

1 tbsp lemon juice

2 tsp grated fresh root ginger

2 garlic cloves, crushed

1 tsp chopped lemongrass or lemongrass purée

1 tbsp caster sugar

¼–½ tsp wasabi paste

225g (8oz) fresh shelled or frozen soya beans

3 tbsp sunflower oil

1 bunch of spring onions, trimmed and sliced

2 celery sticks, cut into matchsticks

100g (3½oz) shiitake mushrooms, sliced

100g (3½oz) oyster mushrooms, sliced

100g (3½oz) enoki mushrooms, trimmed of base and separated

2 heads pak choi (about 200g/7oz), coarsely shredded

2 tbsp sesame seeds, to garnish

1 Cook the noodles according to the packet instructions. Drain and set aside.

2 Whisk the tamari sauce, lemon juice, ginger, garlic, lemongrass, sugar, and wasabi paste in a small bowl with 2 tablespoons water and set aside. Boil the soya beans in water for 3 minutes. Drain and set aside.

3 Heat the oil in a large frying pan or wok. Add the spring onions and celery and stir-fry for 2 minutes. Add all the mushrooms and stir-fry for 3 minutes. Add the pak choi and soya beans and stir-fry for 1 minute.

4 Add the noodles and the bowl of tamari sauce. Toss until everything is hot through and coated. Spoon into bowls and sprinkle with sesame seeds before serving.

NUTRITION PER SERVING	
Energy	460kcals/1925kJ
Carbohydrate	50g
of which sugar	7g
Fat	18g
of which saturates	2.5g
Salt	2g
Fibre	6g

Brown rice stir-fry

Brown rice really comes into its own in this super-healthy stir-fry. It's nutty and deliciously savoury. Brown rice retains the hull and bran, which contains B vitamins and minerals, magnesium and calcium.

Low saturated fat

Dairy free

SERVES 4
PREP 10 MINS
COOK 10 MINS

150g (5½oz) sugarsnap peas, cut into 1cm (½in) pieces

2 asparagus spears, cut into 1cm (½in) pieces

salt

2 tbsp sunflower oil

150g (5½oz) courgettes, cut into 1cm (½in) cubes

4 spring onions, finely sliced

2 garlic cloves, finely chopped

4cm (1½in) piece of fresh root ginger, finely chopped

1 green chilli, deseeded and finely chopped

800g (1¾lb) cooked, cold brown rice

2 tbsp oyster sauce

2 tbsp soy sauce

2 tbsp rice wine or dry sherry

2 tbsp pumpkin seeds

2 tbsp sunflower seeds

1 Blanch the sugarsnap peas and asparagus in a large pan of boiling salted water for 1 minute, then drain and refresh them under cold water.

2 Heat the oil in a large wok and stir-fry the courgettes over a high heat for 2 minutes until they start to colour. Add the spring onions, garlic, ginger, and chilli and cook for a further minute.

3 Add the blanched vegetables and cook for a minute, then add the rice with the remaining ingredients. Stir-fry for a minute or two until everything is well combined and the rice is hot.

NUTRITION PER SERVING	
Energy	441kcals/1856kJ
Carbohydrate	67g
of which sugar	4g
Fat	14g
of which saturates	2g
Salt	2.5g
Fibre	5g

Sweet potato cakes

Spring onion adds a crunchy texture to these cakes.
Sweet potatoes are a rich source of vitamin A.

| Low saturated fat |
| Dairy free |
| Gluten free |
| Low salt |

SERVES 4
PREP 10 MINS
COOK 20 MINS

500g (1lb 2oz) cooked sweet
potato, mashed

5cm (2in) piece of fresh ginger,
peeled and grated

bunch of spring onions,
finely chopped

pinch of freshly grated nutmeg

2 eggs, lightly beaten

salt and freshly ground black
pepper

flour, for dusting

3–4 tbsp polenta

vegetable oil, for shallow frying

lime wedges, to serve

1 Add the sweet potato to a large bowl. Add the ginger,
spring onions, and nutmeg, then add a little of the egg, a
drop at time, reserving plenty for coating, until the mixture
binds together.

2 Season well with salt and black pepper, then scoop up a
handful of the mixture, roll into a ball, then flatten out into
a cake. Repeat until all the mixture is used.

3 Dust the cakes in flour, dip in the reserved egg, then lightly
coat with polenta. Heat the oil in a non-stick frying pan and
add the cakes a couple at a time. Cook for 2–3 minutes or
until the underside turns golden, then carefully flip and cook
for a further 2–3 minutes, or until evenly golden brown. Serve
with lime wedges for squeezing over.

NUTRITION PER SERVING	
Energy	272kcals/1140kJ
Carbohydrate	36g
of which sugar	16g
Fat	12g
of which saturates	2g
Salt	0.2g
Fibre	3.5g

Lentils with leeks and mushrooms

Lentils and mushrooms are both rich ingredients that give this quick vegetarian dish depth and flavour. Use dried puy lentils instead of canned, if you have time.

SERVES 4
PREP 5–10 MINS
COOK 25 MINS

1 tbsp olive oil

1 onion, finely chopped

1 bay leaf

salt and freshly ground black pepper

2 garlic cloves, grated or finely chopped

3 leeks, trimmed and sliced

2 tsp Marmite or Vegemite, or a splash of light soy sauce

225g (8oz) chestnut mushrooms, halved, or quartered if large

400g can green lentils or puy lentils, drained and rinsed

300ml (10fl oz) hot vegetable stock

handful of curly-leaf parsley, leaves picked and finely chopped

NUTRITION PER SERVING

Energy	146kcals/611kJ
Carbohydrate	14g
of which sugar	5g
Fat	4g
of which saturates	0.5g
Salt	1g
Fibre	8g

1 Heat the oil in a frying pan over a low heat. Add the onion, bay leaf, and a little salt, and cook for 5 minutes until the onion is soft and translucent. Add the garlic and leek and stir through the Marmite, Vegemite, or soy sauce. Cook for a further 5 minutes until the leeks begin to soften.

2 Add the mushrooms and cook until they release their juices – you may need to add a little more oil if necessary. Season well with salt and pepper, then stir through the lentils and hot stock. Bring to the boil, reduce the heat, and simmer gently for 15 minutes.

3 Remove from the heat and stir in the parsley. Taste and season again if needed. Serve with some roasted tomatoes and fresh crusty bread.

Mangetout, sweet potato, and cashew nut red curry

Cooking the green vegetables quickly retains their colour and texture. Butternut squash or pumpkin can be substituted for sweet potato, and tofu for cashew nuts.

Dairy free

Gluten free

Low salt

High fibre

SERVES 4
PREP 10 MINS
COOK 20 MINS

2 tbsp sunflower oil

1 bunch spring onions, cut into short lengths

1 sweet potato, about 600g (1lb 5oz), peeled and cut into walnut-sized pieces

1 garlic clove, crushed

1 tsp grated fresh root ginger or galangal

1 tsp finely chopped lemongrass (or lemongrass purée)

3 tbsp Thai red curry paste

400ml can reduced-fat coconut milk

175g (6oz) mangetout, topped and tailed

2 courgettes, cut into batonettes

12 cherry tomatoes

115g (4oz) raw cashew nuts

1 tbsp chopped coriander

squeeze of lime juice

jasmine rice, to serve

1 fat red chilli, deseeded and cut into thin strips, to garnish

1 Heat the oil in a large saucepan or wok. Add the spring onions and stir-fry gently for 2 minutes until softened but not coloured. Add the sweet potato and cook, stirring, for 1 minute.

2 Stir in the garlic, ginger, lemongrass, curry paste, and coconut milk. Bring to a boil, reduce the heat, cover, and simmer gently for 10 minutes, until the sweet potato is tender.

3 Meanwhile, cook the mangetout and courgette batonettes in boiling water for 2–3 minutes until just tender. Drain.

4 Stir the mangetout and courgettes into the curry with the tomatoes, nuts, and coriander. Spike with a squeeze of lime juice and simmer for 2 minutes until the tomatoes are softened slightly but still hold their shape. Spoon the curry over jasmine rice served in bowls and garnish with strips of red chilli.

NUTRITION PER SERVING	
Energy	521kcals/2180kJ
Carbohydrate	44g
of which sugar	16g
Fat	30g
of which saturates	10g
Salt	0.6g
Fibre	10g

Tofu and mushroom stroganoff

Tofu is a complete source of protein, containing all eight amino acids. With no cholesterol, it is also a good source of iron and calcium.

Low carb

Low salt

SERVES 4
PREP 10 MINS
COOK 12–15 MINS

2 tbsp sunflower oil

350g (12oz) tofu, diced

1 red onion, sliced

2 garlic cloves, crushed

1 red pepper, sliced

1 orange pepper, sliced

250g (90z) mixed mushrooms, quartered

2 tsp cornflour

2 tbsp tomato purée

2 tbsp smooth peanut butter

150ml (5fl oz) vegetable stock

200g (7oz) reduced-fat crème fraîche

salt and freshly ground black pepper

handful of chives, finely chopped, to garnish

rice, to serve

FOR A GLUTEN-FREE OPTION
use gluten-free stock

NUTRITION PER SERVING	
Energy	276kcals/1155kJ
Carbohydrate	10g
of which sugar	7g
Fat	20g
of which saturates	6g
Salt	0.4g
Fibre	4g

1 Heat 1 tablespoon of the oil in a large saucepan. Add the tofu and stir-fry over a high heat until golden. Remove from the heat and set aside.

2 Add the remaining oil to the saucepan, reduce the heat, add the onion and garlic, and fry until softened. Add the peppers and mushrooms, and stir-fry for 5 minutes.

3 In a bowl, mix the cornflour with a little water to form a paste and set aside.

4 Add the tomato purée, peanut butter, and tofu to the saucepan. Stir in the vegetable stock and cornflour paste, and cook for 3 minutes. Add the crème fraîche, season to taste, and simmer for 2 minutes. Transfer to a plate, sprinkle with chives, and serve with rice.

Chilli tofu stir-fry

This quick and easy dish plays on tofu's ability to take on the flavour of other ingredients.

Low carb

Low saturated fat

Dairy free

Low salt

SERVES 4
PREP 10 MINS
COOK 15 MINS

2 tbsp sunflower oil

85g (3oz) unsalted cashew nuts

300g (10oz) firm tofu, cubed

1 red onion, thinly sliced

2 carrots, peeled and thinly sliced

1 red pepper, deseeded and chopped

1 celery stick, chopped

4 chestnut mushrooms, sliced

175g (6oz) beansprouts

2 tsp chilli sauce

2 tbsp light soy sauce

1 tsp cornflour

175ml (6fl oz) vegetable stock

FOR A GLUTEN-FREE OPTION
use gluten-free tamari to replace soy sauce

1 Heat the oil in the wok and add the cashews; stir-fry for 30 seconds, or until lightly browned. Drain and set aside.

2 Add the tofu and stir-fry until golden. Drain and set aside. Stir-fry the onion and carrots for 5 minutes, then add the pepper, celery, and mushrooms and stir-fry for 3–4 minutes. Finally, add the beansprouts and stir-fry for 2 minutes. Keep the heat under the wok high, so the vegetables fry quickly, without overcooking.

3 Return the cashews and tofu to the pan and drizzle in the chilli sauce. In a small bowl, mix the soy sauce with the cornflour and pour into the pan, along with the stock. Toss over the heat for 2–3 minutes, or until the sauce is bubbling. Serve with boiled rice or Chinese-style egg noodles.

NUTRITION PER SERVING	
Energy	300kcals/1255kJ
Carbohydrate	14g
of which sugar	8g
Fat	20g
of which saturates	3g
Salt	0.5g
Fibre	5g

Black-eyed bean, spinach, and tomato curry

This curry is both satisfying and cheap. Yogurt adds creaminess to the sauce – just be careful not to overcook it, as it will separate.

Low saturated fat

Low salt

High fibre

SERVES 4
PREP 5 MINS
COOK 15 MINS

3 tbsp sunflower oil

½ tsp mustard seeds

2 garlic cloves, finely chopped

10 curry leaves

1 large onion, chopped

2 green chillies, slit lengthways and deseeded

½ tsp chilli powder

1 tsp ground coriander

½ tsp ground turmeric

3 tomatoes, chopped

100g (3½oz) spinach, chopped

400g can black-eyed beans, rinsed and drained

salt

300g (10oz) plain yogurt

naan breads or rice, to serve

1 Heat the oil in a large saucepan and add the mustard seeds. When they start to pop, add the garlic, curry leaves, and onion. Cook over a medium heat for 5 minutes, or until the onion is soft.

2 Add the green chillies, chilli powder, coriander, and turmeric. Mix well and add the tomato pieces. Stir, then add the spinach. Cook over a low heat for 5 minutes.

3 Finally, add the black-eyed beans and salt to taste. Cook for another minute, or until everything is hot. Remove the pan from the heat and slowly add the yogurt, stirring well. Serve warm with naan breads or rice.

NUTRITION PER SERVING	
Energy	228kcals/956kJ
Carbohydrate	22g
of which sugar	12g
Fat	12g
of which saturates	2.6g
Salt	1.2g
Fibre	7g

Vegetable ramen noodle bowl

Miso paste enhances the flavour of this dish, but omit it if preferred and season with more tamari. Use dashi powder to make the vegetable stock, if it is available.

Low saturated fat

Dairy free

High fibre

SERVES 4
PREP 10 MINS, PLUS SOAKING
COOK 10 MINS

2 × 10cm (4in) pieces wakame

2 heaped tbsp dried shiitake mushrooms

250g (9oz) dried ramen noodles (or brown
  rice noodles)

1 litre (1¾ pints) vegetable stock

2 tbsp tamari or light soy sauce

2 tsp soft light brown sugar

3 tbsp mirin (or dry sherry)

4 spring onions, chopped

1 red pepper, deseeded and finely sliced

2 heads of pak choi, cut into thick shreds

1 courgette, cut into matchsticks

4 radishes, sliced

225g can bamboo shoots, drained

1 tsp crushed dried chillies (optional)

1 tbsp red miso paste

250g block firm tofu, cut into 8 slices

sweet chilli sauce, to drizzle

FOR A GLUTEN-FREE OPTION
use gluten-free noodles

1 Soak the wakame and mushrooms in 300ml (10fl oz) warm water for 30 minutes. Lift out the wakame and cut out any thick stalk, if necessary. If the wakame is large, cut into pieces before returning to the soaking water with the mushrooms.

2 Cook the noodles according to the packet instructions. Drain. Put the stock in a large saucepan with the remaining ingredients, except the miso paste and tofu. Add the wakame, mushrooms, and soaking water. Bring to a boil, reduce the heat, and simmer for 3 minutes.

3 Blend a ladleful of the stock with the miso paste until smooth. Pour back into the pan and stir gently. Taste and add more tamari, if necessary. Make sure the soup is very hot, but not boiling.

4 Divide the noodles between four large open soup bowls. Add two slices of tofu to each bowl and ladle the very hot soup over. Serve at once with sweet chilli sauce to drizzle over, if using.

NUTRITION PER SERVING	
Energy	381kcals/1596kJ
Carbohydrate	61g
of which sugar	14g
Fat	5g
of which saturates	1g
Salt	4g
Fibre	7g

Braised cauliflower with chilli and coriander

A few spices can turn the humble cauliflower into something far more interesting. This dish can be served simply with some buttery basmati rice or as part of an Indian meal.

Low carb

Dairy free

Gluten free

Low salt

SERVES 4
PREP 10 MINS
COOK 10–15 MINS

400g (14oz) cauliflower, outer leaves removed, chopped into small florets

2 dried red chillies

1 tsp cumin seeds

2 tbsp sunflower oil

1 tsp black mustard seeds

½ tsp turmeric

2 garlic cloves, crushed

knob of butter

sea salt

2 tbsp coriander leaves, finely chopped

1 Blanch the cauliflower in salted boiling water for 1–2 minutes, drain, and rinse under cold water.

2 Grind together the chillies and cumin seeds in a mortar and pestle until roughly crushed. Heat the oil in a large, deep frying pan or wok, and add the chilli and cumin seeds, mustard seeds, turmeric, and garlic. Cook gently for 1 minute until the mustard seeds start to pop.

3 Add the cauliflower and enough water so that it covers the bottom of the pan (about 6 tablespoons). Bring the water to the boil and cover the pan or wok. Turn the heat down and simmer the cauliflower for 3–5 minutes, until almost cooked through.

4 Uncover the pan or wok and turn up the heat. Allow the water to cook off, turning the cauliflower all the time. When all the water has evaporated (about 5–6 minutes), add the butter and mix well until it melts. Season with sea salt and sprinkle with coriander before serving.

try this....
Cauliflower with tomatoes, chilli, coriander, and lentils

In step 3, add 200g (7oz) **baby cherry tomatoes** along with the cauliflower. While the cauliflower is cooking, drain 2 cans **brown lentils** and gently heat in a separate pan. At the end of step 4, combine the cauliflower and lentils. Serve with **tzatiki dip**.

NUTRITION PER SERVING	
Energy	102kcals/427kJ
Carbohydrate	4g
of which sugar	3g
Fat	8g
of which saturates	1g
Salt	0.1g
Fibre	2g

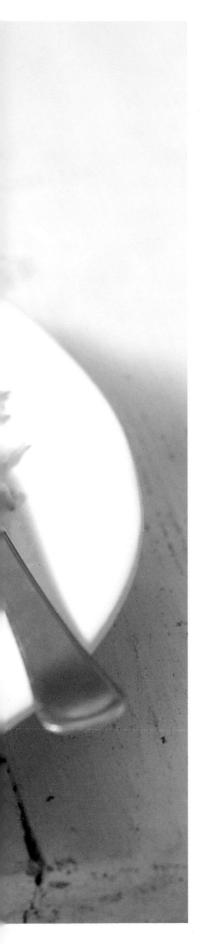

Mediterranean vegetable medley

This summer dish is full of vegetables with antioxidant and anti-inflammatory phytonutrients. Cut the courgettes in larger cubes, to retain their nutrients as they cook.

| Low saturated fat |
| Dairy free |
| Gluten free |
| Low salt |
| High fibre |

SERVES 4
PREP 5–10 MINS
COOK 25 MINS

1 tbsp olive oil

4 shallots, finely chopped

salt and freshly ground black pepper

a pinch of oregano or marjoram

2 red peppers, deseeded and chopped

2 yellow peppers, deseeded and chopped

1 aubergine, chopped

1 courgette, chopped

4 tomatoes, skinned (optional) and chopped

2 garlic cloves, crushed

2 tbsp olive oil

4 tbsp finely chopped parsley leaves, plus extra to garnish

basmati rice, to serve

1 Heat the olive oil in a large, heavy-based saucepan over a medium to low heat. Add the shallots and a pinch of salt, and stir until the shallots begin to turn translucent. Add a dash of water to bring the temperature down and to add moisture to the pan. After 2–3 minutes add the oregano and the peppers. Cook until the peppers have softened.

2 Add the aubergine and the courgette, and when the liquid in the pan has reduced, add the tomatoes. Let the mixture simmer for 15 minutes over a low heat, taking care not to let the vegetables stick to the base of the pan and burn.

3 Add the garlic and a little more olive oil for added flavour and cook for a further 5 minutes. Mix in the chopped parsley and add salt and black pepper to taste. Serve on a bed of brown basmati rice with some parsley scattered on top.

NUTRITION PER SERVING

Energy	158kcals/661kJ
Carbohydrate	12g
of which sugar	12g
Fat	9g
of which saturates	1.5g
Salt	trace
Fibre	7g

try this....
Mediterranean vegetable salad

Follow the above recipe to the end of step 2. Stir in 2 tablespoons **pine nuts**, 2 tablespoons **raisins**, 1 tablespoon **capers**, and ½ can **chickpeas**, rinsed and drained. Chill for at least 30 minutes before serving.

Lemon rice

This is a wonderfully tangy side dish from South India, which can be easily rustled up when you are in a hurry.

Low saturated fat

Dairy free

Gluten free

Low salt

SERVES 4
PREP 10 MINS
COOK 5 MINS

3 tbsp vegetable oil

1 tsp yellow mustard seeds

6 green cardamom pods, split

10 fresh or dried curry leaves

2 red chillies, split lengthways

½ tsp turmeric

1cm (½in) piece of fresh root ginger, finely chopped

1 garlic clove, crushed

3 tbsp lemon juice, or to taste

300g (10oz) cooked, cold white basmati rice

60g (2oz) cashews, lightly toasted

2 tbsp chopped coriander leaves

1 Heat the oil in a large frying pan, add the spices, ginger, and garlic, and fry over a medium heat for 2 minutes, or until aromatic, stirring all the time.

2 Add the lemon juice and cook for 1 minute, then add the rice. Stir until the rice is heated through and coated in the spices.

3 Transfer to a serving dish, scatter with the cashews and coriander, and serve at once.

NUTRITION PER SERVING	
Energy	264kcals/1101kJ
Carbohydrate	24g
of which sugar	1g
Fat	16g
of which saturates	3g
Salt	trace
Fibre	0.7g

Baked tomatoes stuffed with couscous, black olives, and feta

These can be the centrepiece of a meal or can accompany a simple grilled or baked fish dish.

SERVES 2
PREP 20 MINS
COOK 15 MINS,
PLUS RESTING

4–8 beef or other large tomatoes, depending on size

100g (3½oz) couscous

2 tbsp olive oil, plus extra for drizzling

150ml (5fl oz) boiling vegetable stock

2 large spring onions, finely chopped

8 pitted black olives, finely chopped

finely grated zest of ½ lemon

50g (1¾oz) feta cheese, crumbled

2 tbsp finely chopped mint leaves

1 tbsp finely chopped chives

freshly ground black pepper

1 Preheat the oven to 200°C (400°F/Gas 6). Slice the tops from the tomatoes and carefully scoop out and discard the interior flesh, reserving the tops for later.

2 Put the couscous in a wide, shallow dish and rub in 1 tablespoon of the oil with your fingers (to stop the grains sticking together). Pour over the stock, stir briefly, and immediately cover tightly with cling film. Leave for 10 minutes, then uncover. The couscous should be soft and the liquid absorbed. Fluff the couscous with a fork and leave to cool slightly.

3 When the couscous has cooled, add the remaining ingredients, except the tomatoes, with the remaining 1 tablespoon of oil. Season well with pepper (the feta and olives are salty enough), and carefully stuff the tomatoes with the mixture.

4 Place the tomatoes in a small ovenproof dish that fits them tightly, put the reserved tops on, and drizzle with oil. Bake in the hot oven for 15 minutes, until the tomatoes are soft but still hold their shape and the tops are golden. Rest for 5 minutes, then serve.

NUTRITION PER SERVING	
Energy	448kcals/1874kJ
Carbohydrate	50g
of which sugar	28g
Fat	20g
of which saturates	6g
Salt	1.4g
Fibre	10g

Chargrilled prawn and pepper couscous

Omit the prawns for a flavourful vegetable couscous that can also be served as a side dish.

Low saturated fat

Low salt

High fibre

SERVES 4
PREP 15 MINS
COOK 15 MINS

200g (7oz) couscous

240ml (8fl oz) boiling water

1 tbsp butter, softened

4 red peppers

5 tbsp olive oil

salt and freshly ground black pepper

1 leek, white part only, sliced into 5mm (¼in) discs

2 garlic cloves, crushed

175g (6oz) cooked and peeled king prawns

grated zest and juice of 1 lemon

4 tbsp chopped flat-leaf parsley

2 tbsp chopped mint leaves

NUTRITION PER SERVING	
Energy	413kcals/1728kJ
Carbohydrate	45g
of which sugar	7.5g
Fat	18g
of which saturates	4g
Salt	0.5g
Fibre	6g

1 Put the couscous in a large bowl. Add the boiling water and the butter, and stir to combine. Cover the bowl with cling film, and set aside for 5–10 minutes. Using a fork, separate and fluff up the grains. Set aside.

2 Heat the barbecue or charcoal grill until hot. Cut off and discard the tops of the peppers, then cut the peppers in half lengthways. Remove all the seeds. Put the peppers in a shallow dish, add 3 tablespoons of the oil, and season with salt and black pepper. Mix until the peppers are well coated in the oil. Grill the peppers over a high heat for about 10 minutes until they are charred all over and softened. Allow to cool a little. Peel off the skin and reserve the pepper halves.

3 Heat the remaining olive oil in a frying pan over a low heat. Add the leeks, and sweat gently, stirring occasionally, for about 5 minutes. Tip in the garlic, and cook for a further 30 seconds. Remove from the heat.

4 To finish, cut or tear the pepper halves into strips, and put in the bowl with the couscous. Add the prawns, the leek and garlic mixture, lemon zest and juice, parsley, and mint. Stir through well, and serve.

Kale with soba buckwheat noodles

Kale is the ultimate leafy vegetable, full of antioxidants and omega-3 fatty acids that benefit the heart. It is best cooked lightly for a minimal amount of time.

Low saturated fat

Dairy free

High fibre

SERVES 4
PREP 10 MINS
COOK 20 MINS

400g (14oz) soba buckwheat noodles

2 tbsp walnut oil, plus extra for sprinkling

pinch of salt (optional)

1 red chilli, deseeded and finely diced

2 garlic cloves, crushed

2 tbsp tamari soy sauce

600g (1lb 5oz) fresh kale, cut into strips with the spines removed

2 tbsp fresh orange juice

4 tbsp walnut pieces, toasted, to garnish

FOR A GLUTEN-FREE OPTION
use gluten-free noodles

1 Cook the soba noodles according to the packet instructions. Add a dash of walnut oil and a pinch of salt to the water before you add the noodles, if you like.

2 Meanwhile, place a large heavy-based saucepan with a lid over a moderate heat and add the walnut oil with 2 tablespoons of water. When the oil has warmed, add the chilli and crushed garlic, and stir. Add the tamari soy sauce, followed by the kale, and stir to coat the leaves in the other ingredients.

3 Add the orange juice, put the lid on, and let the kale steam for 2–3 minutes or until it is just cooked. Stir occasionally as it cooks, to stop it sticking to the base of the pan, and add a dash of water if necessary. Remove from the heat. Arrange the soba noodles on a warmed serving dish, pile the kale on top, and scatter over the toasted walnuts. Sprinkle a few drops of walnut oil over the dish and serve.

NUTRITION PER SERVING	
Energy	556kcals/2326kJ
Carbohydrate	71g
of which sugar	8g
Fat	20g
of which saturates	2g
Salt	2.5g
Fibre	7g

Tomato, bean, and courgette stew

Packed with vitamins, this hearty stew makes for a perfect dinner on a chilly winter evening.

Low saturated fat

Dairy free

Low salt

High fibre

SERVES 4
PREP 10 MINS
COOK 20 MINS

3 tbsp olive oil

1 large onion, finely chopped

2 courgettes, chopped into chunky pieces

3 garlic cloves, finely sliced

400g can borlotti beans, drained and rinsed

3 fresh tomatoes, diced

1 tsp paprika

1 tsp dried oregano

salt and freshly ground black pepper

chilli oil, to garnish (optional)

crusty bread, to serve

1 Heat the oil in a deep-sided frying pan, add the onion, and cook over a medium heat for 3 minutes. Add the courgettes and cook for a further 5 minutes, stirring constantly.

2 Add the garlic and beans, cook for 1 minute, then add the tomatoes, paprika, and oregano. Cook for 10 minutes, stirring occasionally, then season with salt and black pepper. Drizzle with chilli oil (if using), and serve with some fresh crusty bread.

NUTRITION PER SERVING

Energy	168kcals/696kJ
Carbohydrate	15g
of which sugar	5.5g
Fat	9g
of which saturates	1.5g
Salt	0.1g
Fibre	7g

Mixed root tempura

Root vegetables and leeks are given a Japanese treatment in this quick tempura recipe. Serve to your guests with sweet chilli sauce for dipping.

Low saturated fat

Dairy free

Low salt

High fibre

SERVES 6
PREP 10 MINS
COOK 20 MINS

1 parsnip, cut into short fingers

½ small swede

½ small celeriac, cut into small chunks

1 large carrot, cut into short fingers

1 leek, cut into thick slices

2 tbsp cornflour

sunflower oil, for deep-frying

FOR THE BATTER

85g (3oz) self-raising flour

85g (3oz) cornflour

200ml (7fl oz) sparkling mineral water

2 tsp sunflower oil

½ tsp salt

¾ tsp cumin seeds

1 Bring a large saucepan of water to the boil. Carefully add the vegetables and cook for about 2 minutes until blanched. Remove from the heat and drain using a colander.

2 Transfer the vegetables onto kitchen paper, pat dry, and transfer to a large bowl. Sprinkle over the cornflour, toss to coat well, and set aside.

3 For the batter, place all the ingredients in a separate bowl and using a balloon whisk, mix until well combined.

4 Heat the oil in a large wok over a high heat. Dip the vegetables in the batter, a few at a time, to coat lightly, shaking off any excess. Then deep-fry for 2–3 minutes, turning occasionally, until golden.

5 Using a slotted spoon, remove the tempura from the pan and drain on double layer of kitchen paper. Serve immediately.

NUTRITION PER SERVING	
Energy	313kcals/1310kJ
Carbohydrate	36g
of which sugar	6g
Fat	16g
of which saturates	2g
Salt	0.7g
Fibre	6g

WHOLESOME PASTAS

Spaghetti with garlic, oil, and red chilli

This vibrant Sicilian sauce is inexpensive and ready in minutes. So it is the go-to recipe for anyone late home and hungry. Arguably, it is better served without cheese.

Low saturated fat

Low salt

SERVES 4
PREP 10 MINS
COOK 10 MINS

salt and freshly ground black pepper

400g (14oz) dried spaghetti

100ml (3½fl oz) olive oil

2 garlic cloves, crushed

1 small red chilli, deseeded and finely chopped

3 tbsp snipped flat-leaf parsley

freshly grated ricotta salata, pecorino, feta, or Parmesan cheese, to serve (optional)

1 Bring a large saucepan of lightly salted water to the boil, then add the spaghetti and cook until al dente, or according to the packet instructions.

2 Meanwhile, heat 5 tablespoons of the oil in a large sauté pan or non-stick frying pan and cook the garlic and chilli over a low heat, stirring frequently, until the garlic turns golden. Add 4 tablespoons of spaghetti water. Remove from the heat, stir, and set aside until the spaghetti is cooked.

3 Drain the spaghetti into a colander. On a high heat, stir the garlic sauce until emulsified and tip in the spaghetti. Stir in the remaining oil and the parsley. Toss until thoroughly coated. Adjust the seasoning. Serve immediately, with grated ricotta salata or other cheese, if you like.

NUTRITION PER SERVING	
Energy	526kcals/2201kJ
Carbohydrate	72g
of which sugar	2g
Fat	19g
of which saturates	3g
Salt	0g
Fibre	5g

Chanterelles and chillies with pasta

Kamut is an ancient grain related to modern wheat. It contains gluten but has been found to be more easily digestible for people intolerant to wheat.

| Low salt |
| High fibre |

SERVES 4
PREP 10 MINS
COOK 15–20 MINS

400g (14oz) fresh chanterelle mushrooms, sliced

4 tsp olive oil

2–3 garlic cloves, crushed

1–2 small chillies, deseeded and finely chopped

5 tbsp soured cream

salt and freshly ground black pepper

500g (1lb 2oz) pasta, such as tagliatelle or spaghetti, made from kamut wheat

1 tbsp finely chopped flat-leaf parsley leaves, to garnish

1 Place the mushrooms in a saucepan and dry-fry them over a low heat, shaking the pan gently, until their juices run. Then, turn the heat up so the liquid evaporates and the mushrooms are soft, but reasonably dry. Add 3 teaspoons of the olive oil to coat the mushrooms, then add the garlic, chillies, and soured cream, and let the mixture simmer over a low heat for 2–6 minutes. Season with salt and black pepper to taste.

2 Meanwhile, cook the pasta according to the packet instructions until it is al dente, adding the last teaspoon of olive oil to the cooking water to prevent it boiling over and to enhance the flavour of the pasta. Drain and transfer to a warmed serving dish. Spoon the sauce over the pasta, garnish with the parsley, combine the ingredients well, and serve with a green salad.

try this....
Mushrooms, spring onions, and chillies with pasta

Replace the chanterelles with **oyster mushrooms**. Add 1 bunch of finely chopped **spring onions** with the garlic and chilli. Once the mushrooms are cooked, stir in 300g (10oz) **white crabmeat** and then continue with step 2.

NUTRITION PER SERVING	
Energy	557kcals/2330kJ
Carbohydrate	90g
of which sugar	3.5g
Fat	11g
of which saturates	4g
Salt	0.3g
Fibre	6g

Farfalle with spinach, avocado, and tomatoes

Slow-roasted tomatoes are sold in vacuum packs. Sun-dried tomatoes, drained of oil, may be used instead.

Dairy free

Low salt

High fibre

SERVES 4
PREP 10 MINS
COOK 16 MINS

400g (14oz) dried farfalle pasta

2 tbsp olive oil

4 spring onions, chopped

1 garlic clove, finely chopped

1 tsp crushed dried chillies

350g (12oz) baby spinach leaves

150ml (5fl oz) vegetable stock

4 slow-roasted tomatoes, chopped

175g (6oz) baby plum tomatoes, halved

30g (1oz) sliced black olives

1½ tbsp pickled capers

2 avocados, peeled, stoned, and diced

squeeze of lemon juice

salt and freshly ground black pepper

3 tbsp pumpkin seeds

lemon wedges and a few torn basil leaves, to garnish

1 Cook the pasta according to the packet instructions. Drain. Heat the oil in a deep-sided sauté pan or wok. Add the spring onions and garlic and fry, stirring gently, for 1 minute. Stir in the chillies.

2 Add the spinach and stock and simmer, turning over gently for about 2 minutes until beginning to wilt. Gently fold in the pasta and the remaining ingredients. Simmer for 3 minutes until most of the liquid has been absorbed.

3 Pile into warmed, shallow bowls. Garnish with lemon wedges and a few torn basil leaves.

NUTRITION PER SERVING	
Energy	680kcals/2845kJ
Carbohydrate	79g
of which sugar	7g
Fat	29g
of which saturates	6g
Salt	0.5g
Fibre	11g

try this....
Brown rice and prawns

Replace the farfalle with 300g (10oz) **brown basmati rice**, cooked according to the packet instructions. In step 1, add 300g (10oz) cooked, peeled **prawns**.

Spaghetti with chilli, broccoli, and spring onion

This is a simple way to enjoy fresh greens at their best. You can use other pasta instead if you prefer – try the sauce with bucatini or the large, flat pappardelle for a change.

Low saturated fat

Low salt

High fibre

SERVES 4
PREP 10 MINS
COOK 12 MINS

350g (12oz) dried spaghetti

salt and freshly ground black pepper

200g (7oz) sprouting broccoli or broccoli rabe

5 tbsp olive oil

bunch of spring onions, trimmed and chopped

1 tsp dried chilli flakes

1 tbsp lime juice

Parmesan cheese, grated, to serve

FOR A GLUTEN-FREE OPTION
use gluten-free pasta

1 Cook the spaghetti in boiling salted water according to the packet's instructions. Drain and return to the pan.

2 Meanwhile, trim the broccoli, cut the heads into small florets, and chop the stalks.

3 Heat the oil in a large frying pan or wok. Add the broccoli and spring onions and stir-fry for about 4 minutes until just tender.

4 Tip the contents of the pan into the spaghetti. Add the chilli, lime juice, and seasoning to taste. Toss gently, pile onto plates, and serve with plenty of Parmesan cheese.

try this....
Spaghetti with broccoli, capers, and smoked salmon

Replace white spaghetti with **wholemeal spaghetti**. At the end of step 3, combine the broccoli and spaghetti, then stir in 300g (10oz) roughly chopped **smoked salmon**, 2 tablespoons **capers**, 100ml (3½fl oz) **half-fat crème**, and **zest** from 1 **lemon**.

NUTRITION PER SERVING	
Energy	462kcals/1933kJ
Carbohydrate	64g
of which sugar	3g
Fat	16g
of which saturates	2g
Salt	0g
Fibre	6g

Pasta with asparagus and courgettes

This pasta dish is an easy and delicious way to get plenty of green vegetables – and thus plenty of fibre and antioxidants – into your diet.

Low saturated fat

Low salt

High fibre

SERVES 4
PREP 10 MINS
COOK 20 MINS

1 tbsp olive oil

1 onion, finely chopped

salt

4 small courgettes, 2 diced and 2 grated

3 garlic cloves, grated or finely chopped

1 bunch fine asparagus spears, trimmed and stalks cut into 3

1 small glass of white wine

1–2 tsp capers, rinsed and chopped

zest of 1 lemon

350g (12oz) penne

handful of fresh flat-leaf parsley, finely chopped

Parmesan cheese, grated, to serve

FOR A GLUTEN-FREE OPTION
use gluten-free pasta

1 Heat the oil in a large frying pan, add the onion and a pinch of salt, and cook over a low heat for 5 minutes or until soft and translucent. Add all the courgettes, and cook for 10 minutes or until they have cooked down and softened. Don't allow them to brown.

2 Stir in the garlic and asparagus. Add the wine, raise the heat, and allow to boil for 2–3 minutes, then return to a simmer. Cook for 2–3 minutes, or until the asparagus has softened, then stir in the capers and lemon zest.

3 Meanwhile, cook the pasta in a large pan of boiling salted water for 10 minutes or until it is cooked but still has a bit of bite to it. Drain, keeping back a tiny amount of the cooking water. Return the pasta to the pan and toss together. Add the courgette mixture and parsley, then toss again. Sprinkle with Parmesan and serve.

NUTRITION PER SERVING	
Energy	392kcals/1661kJ
Carbohydrate	68g
of which sugar	6g
Fat	5g
of which saturates	0.8g
Salt	0.3g
Fibre	7g

Pasta with peas and pancetta

This tasty pasta relies on just a few storecupboard essentials to make a quick meal. Replace the pancetta with thinly sliced ham for a leaner cut of pork.

High fibre

SERVES 4
PREP 10 MINS
COOK 15 MINS

300g (10oz) dried shell pasta, such as conchigliette

salt and freshly ground black pepper

200g (7oz) frozen peas or petits pois

2 tbsp olive oil

100g (3½oz) pancetta lardons

2 garlic cloves, crushed

50g (1¾oz) finely grated Parmesan cheese, plus extra for serving

FOR A GLUTEN-FREE OPTION
use gluten-free pasta

1 Cook the pasta in boiling salted water according to the packet instructions. A minute or two before the end of cooking, throw the peas in with the pasta to cook through. Drain (reserving a ladleful of the cooking water) and return it to the pan with the reserved water.

2 Meanwhile, heat the oil in a large frying pan. Cook the pancetta for 3–5 minutes over a medium heat until crispy. Add the garlic and cook for a further minute, then remove from the heat.

3 Toss the garlicky pancetta through the pasta and peas, and follow with the Parmesan cheese. Season well to taste and serve with extra Parmesan cheese.

try this....
Pea and prawn pasta

Omit the pancetta and Parmesan cheese. In step 2, add 300g (10oz) cooked, peeled **prawns**. In step 3, add the **juice** and **zest** of 1 small **lemon** and season to taste.

NUTRITION PER SERVING	
Energy	507kcals/2121kJ
Carbohydrate	60g
of which sugar	3g
Fat	19g
of which saturates	6.5g
Salt	1.2g
Fibre	6g

Pasta with crab and lemon

Rich in omega 3, crab is a good source of protein and the minerals chromium and selenium.

Low saturated fat

Dairy free

Low salt

SERVES 4
PREP 5 MINS
COOK 10 MINS

1 tbsp olive oil

1 large onion, cut into quarters, then finely sliced

salt and freshly ground black pepper

2 garlic cloves, finely sliced

grated zest and juice of 1 lemon

handful of fresh flat-leaf parsley, finely chopped

200g (7oz) fresh or canned white crabmeat

350g (12oz) linguine or spaghetti

chilli oil, to serve (optional)

FOR A GLUTEN-FREE OPTION
use gluten-free pasta

1 Heat the oil in a large frying pan, add the onion and a pinch of salt, and cook over a low heat for 5 minutes, or until soft and translucent. Stir in the garlic and lemon zest, and cook for a few seconds more.

2 Stir through the parsley and crabmeat, then season well with salt and lots of black pepper. Add lemon juice to taste.

3 Meanwhile, cook the pasta in a large pan of boiling salted water for 6–8 minutes, or until it is cooked but still has a bit of bite to it. Drain, keeping back a tiny amount of the cooking water. Return the pasta to the pan and toss together. Add the crab sauce, toss again, drizzle with chilli oil (if using), and serve.

NUTRITION PER SERVING	
Energy	415kcals/1739kJ
Carbohydrate	66g
of which sugar	4g
Fat	6g
of which saturates	1g
Salt	0.4g
Fibre	5g

Trofie with pesto

The original pasta of Genoa, trofie is often dressed with pesto and is particularly good with green beans and, surprisingly, diced potato.

| Low saturated fat |
| Low salt |
| High fibre |

SERVES 4–6
PREP 10 MINS
COOK 15–20 MINS

sea salt and freshly ground black pepper

200g (7oz) small green beans, topped, tailed, and cut into 3cm (1½in) segments

2 waxy potatoes, peeled and diced

450g–500g (1lb–1lb 2oz) dried trofie

handful of small basil leaves, to garnish

2 tbsp Parmesan shavings, to garnish

FOR PESTO GENOVESE

3–4 garlic cloves

5–6 tbsp pine nuts

3–4 large handfuls of basil leaves, torn

2 tbsp coarsely grated Parmesan or pecorino cheese

4–6 tbsp fruity olive oil

FOR A GLUTEN-FREE OPTION
use gluten-free pasta

1 For the pesto, crush the garlic using a mortar and pestle. Add the pine nuts and pound well until creamy. Add the basil and a little salt. Pound until you get a rough, fragrant purée. Add the cheese and pound until mixed. Work in the oil, a little at a time, working in the same direction, until you get a thick, sloshy, bright green sauce. Season and cover with cling film.

2 Bring a large saucepan filled with water to the boil over a high heat. Season with salt, add the beans, and boil for 4–6 minutes, until just tender. Remove the beans with a slotted spoon, refresh under cold running water, then drain and set aside.

3 Add the potatoes to the saucepan and return to the boil. Add the trofie and cook, as per the packet instructions, until al dente. Meanwhile, put the pesto in a serving bowl and pour over with 3 tablespoons of the boiling cooking liquid.

4 Drain the pasta and potato. Tip into the bowl with the pesto, add the beans, and toss gently. Adjust the seasoning with pepper, and scatter over the basil and Parmesan.

NUTRITION PER SERVING	
Energy	769–512kcals/ 3234–2156kJ
Carbohydrate	100–68g
of which sugar	5–3g
Fat	31–20.5g
of which saturates	6–4g
Salt	0.4–0.2g
Fibre	8–6g

Prawn and garlic courgetti

Also known as "zoodles" (zucchini noodles), the spaghetti-like ribbons of courgette in this quick and enticing dish offer a healthy, carb- and gluten-free alternative to pasta.

Low carb

Low saturated fat

Dairy free

Gluten free

Low salt

SERVES 4
PREP 20 MINS
COOK 5 MINS

6 courgettes

1 tbsp olive oil, plus extra for drizzling

1 garlic clove, crushed

1 red chilli, deseeded and chopped

300g (10oz) raw tiger prawns, shelled and deveined

2 tbsp chopped fresh dill

salt and freshly ground black pepper

squeeze of lemon juice

1 Feed the courgettes through a spiralizer to make spaghetti-style spirals, discarding the cores.

2 Heat the oil in a large frying pan. Add the garlic, chilli, and prawns, and sauté until the prawns are pink and cooked through. Remove from the heat. Stir in 1 tablespoon dill.

3 While the prawns are cooking, blanch (briefly boil) the courgetti. Place enough water to cover the courgetti in a large saucepan. Add a pinch of salt and bring to the boil. Then add the courgetti, cook for 1 minute, and remove. Plunge the courgetti into a bowl of ice water to stop the cooking process.

4 Drain the courgetti and place on a serving dish. Drizzle over 1 tablespoon oil, season to taste, and add a squeeze of lemon juice. Toss to mix, top with the prawns, sprinkle over the remaining dill, and serve.

try this....
Pesto, cherry tomatoes, and garlic courgetti

For a vegetarian option, omit the prawns, stir through some **pesto sauce**, and top with halved **cherry tomatoes**.

NUTRITION PER SERVING	
Energy	131kcals/548kJ
Carbohydrate	3g
of which sugar	3g
Fat	7g
of which saturates	1g
Salt	0.3g
Fibre	2g

FISH

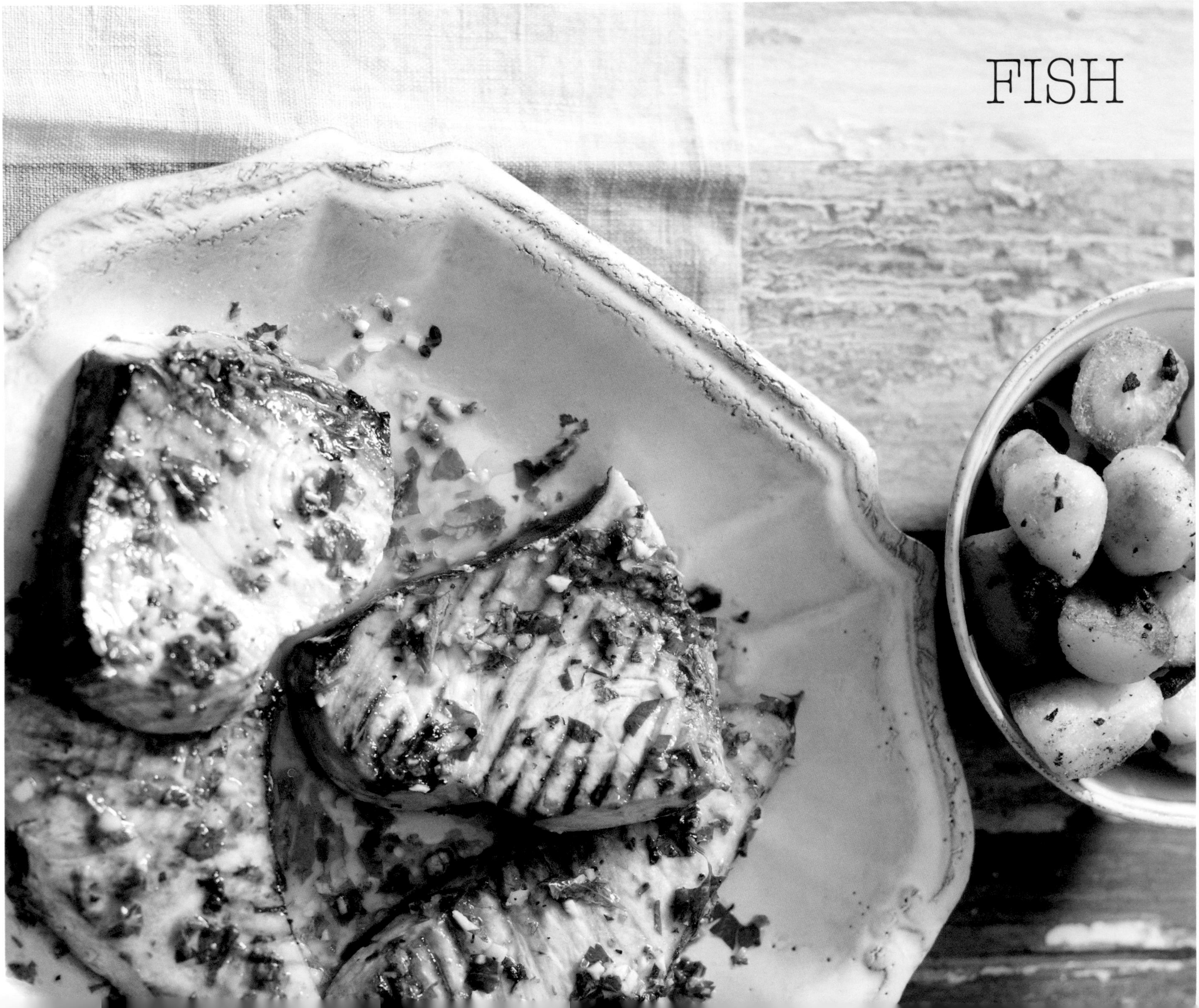

Swordfish in salmoriglio

Swordfish has long been caught off the coasts of Sicily where it is very popular. Use only sustainable swordfish. Its firm meaty texture makes it perfect for grilling and griddling.

Low carb

Low saturated fat

Dairy free

Gluten free

Low salt

SERVES 4
PREP 10 MINS,
PLUS MARINATING
COOK 8 MINS

2 swordfish steaks, at least
   2.5cm (1in) thick, about
   675g (1½ lb) total weight

1 tbsp snipped herbs, such
   as parsley, oregano, or mint,
   to finish

FOR THE SALMORIGLIO SAUCE

finely grated zest and juice of
   1 lemon

1 tbsp snipped flat-leaf parsley

1–2 garlic cloves, crushed

½ tbsp chopped fresh oregano,
   or 1 tsp dried oregano

½ tsp chilli pepper

salt and freshly ground black
   pepper

6 tbsp olive oil

1 For the sauce, place the lemon zest and juice, parsley, garlic, oregano, and chilli pepper in a bowl, mix well, and season. Whisk in 2 tablespoons of cold water and the oil. Brush the steaks with half the sauce and leave to marinate for 5 minutes.

2 Preheat the grill to high, or preheat a griddle pan. Grill or griddle the steaks for 3–4 minutes only on each side, or until just cooked through but still moist in the centre, as swordfish tends to get dry quickly.

3 To serve, cut each steak in half and spoon over the remaining sauce. Season with a little extra pepper, scatter over the snipped herbs, and serve immediately.

NUTRITION PER SERVING	
Energy	353kcals/1469kJ
Carbohydrate	0g
of which sugar	0g
Fat	24g
of which saturates	4g
Salt	0.6g
Fibre	0g

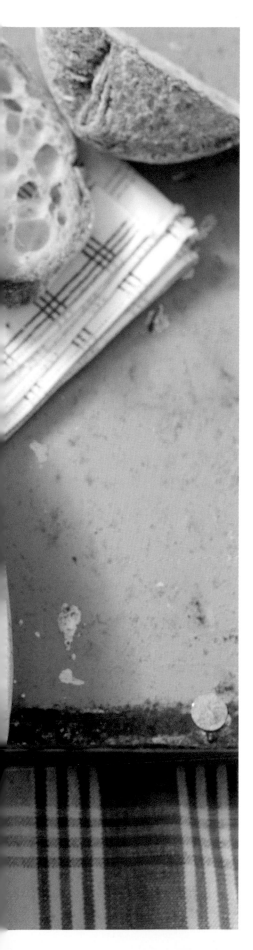

Marinated tuna

Briefly frying or poaching fish, then marinating it to finish the cooking and add flavour, is a favourite Mediterranean cooking method.

| Low carb |
| Low saturated fat |
| Dairy free |
| Gluten free |
| Low salt |

SERVES 4–6
PREP 10 MINS,
PLUS CHILLING
COOK 10–15 MINS

90ml (3fl oz) olive oil

450g (1lb) fresh boneless tuna or other fish fillet cut into 1cm (½in) thick slices

1 large mild onion, cut into thin rings, rings halved

salt and freshly ground black pepper

2 garlic cloves, crushed

1 tsp smoked pimentón (Spanish paprika)

1 scant tsp ground cumin or coriander

1 tbsp snipped flat-leaf parsley

a few sprigs of thyme

1 lemon, thinly sliced

3 tbsp white wine vinegar

1 Heat 1 tablespoon of the oil in a frying pan. Add the tuna slices and sear over a medium heat for 2 minutes on each side, until coloured and a little stiff. Place the slices in a non-metallic dish.

2 Add 2 tablespoons of the oil to the pan, stir in the halved onion rings, season, and cook for 3–5 minutes over a medium heat. Add the garlic, paprika, and cumin. Fry for a further 2 minutes, stirring occasionally. Spoon the contents of the pan over the fish and spread with the back of a spoon to coat evenly. Season again lightly and stir.

3 Scatter over the parsley and thyme. Cover the tuna with the slices of lemon. Mix the remaining oil with the vinegar and pour over the fish. Cover with cling film and refrigerate overnight or for 24 hours. Serve as a starter, chilled, or at room temperature.

try this....
Swordfish and orange escabeche

Replace the tuna with **4 swordfish steaks** and replace the lemon with **orange**.

NUTRITION PER SERVING	
Energy	189kcals/791kJ
Carbohydrate	2g
of which sugar	1.5g
Fat	11g
of which saturates	1.7g
Salt	0.1g
Fibre	0.5g

Seared tuna with cucumber and fennel

This tuna is served very rare, so use the freshest possible fish. Avoid bluefin tuna, which is endangered.

Low carb

Low saturated fat

Dairy free

Gluten free

Low salt

SERVES 4
PREP 15 MINS, PLUS COOLING
COOK 6 MINS

6 tbsp olive oil, plus extra for brushing

4 x 150g (5½oz) tuna steaks

salt and freshly ground black pepper

1 fennel bulb, sliced

2 shallots, finely chopped

1 cucumber, deseeded, skinned, and finely chopped

30g (1oz) mint, parsley, and chervil leaves, torn and mixed

juice of 1 lemon

8 anchovy fillets

lemon wedges, to serve

1 Rub 2 tablespoons of oil over the tuna steaks and sprinkle with lots of black pepper. Set aside.

2 Heat 2 tablespoons of olive oil and sauté the fennel for 4–5 minutes, or until just tender. Season with salt and pepper. Tip the fennel into a large bowl and set aside to cool a little.

3 Add the shallots, cucumber, and herbs to the fennel. Stir in the lemon juice and remaining oil.

4 Heat a heavy frying pan or grill pan until smoking. Lightly brush the tuna steaks with oil, then pan-fry for 30 seconds. Brush the top with a little more oil, turn over, and cook for a further 30 seconds.

5 Place a tuna steak on each serving plate, with the salad piled on top, and two anchovies draped over. Drizzle with the remaining lemon and oil from the bowl, and serve with a wedge of lemon. This dish is good with a salad of warm parsley-buttered new potatoes.

try this....
Seared tuna with mango salsa

Prepare and cook the tuna as above and serve with a salsa made from 1 diced **mango**, 1 **red pepper**, and 1 **red onion**, mixed with a handful of chopped **coriander leaves**.

NUTRITION PER SERVING	
Energy	370kcals/1548kJ
Carbohydrate	2g
of which sugar	2g
Fat	21.5g
of which saturates	3g
Salt	1.2g
Fibre	2.4g

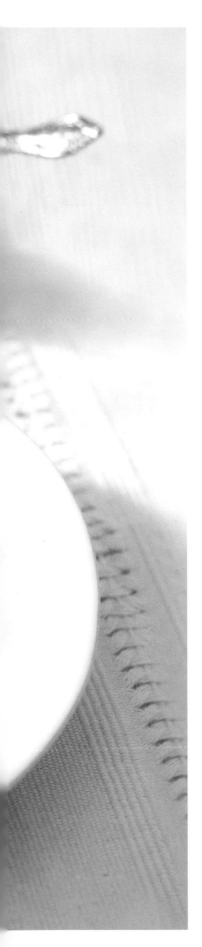

Tuna steaks with onion and cucumber relish

Tuna is fabulous to cook on a barbecue; its robust texture holds together well. Yellowfin tuna is not endangered.

Low carb

Low saturated fat

Dairy free

Gluten free

SERVES 4
PREP 10 MINS, PLUS MARINATING
COOK 10 MINS

15cm (6in) piece of cucumber

2 tbsp rice wine or white wine vinegar

1 tsp caster sugar

pinch of chilli flakes

pinch of salt

¼ red onion, finely sliced

4 tuna steaks, about 100g (3½oz) each

1 tbsp olive oil

1 tsp smoked paprika

salt and freshly ground black pepper

lemon or lime wedges, to serve

1 Prepare a barbecue for cooking. Slice the cucumber in half lengthways and scoop out the seeds with a spoon. Slice each half again lengthways to make four long, thin pieces. Slice thinly on the diagonal.

2 In a bowl, whisk together the vinegar, sugar, chilli flakes, and salt. Mix through the sliced cucumber and red onion, cover, and leave in the fridge to rest for 30 minutes (this helps soften the taste of the raw onion).

3 Rub each tuna steak on both sides with a little oil and smoked paprika, and season them well. Cook the tuna on the hot barbecue for 2–3 minutes on each side for medium, or 3–4 minutes for well done (and less for rare tuna, but serve it this way only if it is very fresh). It is easy to see if the tuna has cooked on one side, as the fish will turn opaque from the bottom upwards when looked at from the side. Remember that the fish will continue to cook when removed from the barbecue.

4 Serve with the cucumber relish and a wedge of lemon or lime to squeeze over.

NUTRITION PER SERVING	
Energy	174kcals/729kJ
Carbohydrate	2g
of which sugar	1.5g
Fat	7.5g
of which saturates	1.5g
Salt	0.4g
Fibre	0.8g

try this....
Tuna steaks with black-eyed beans and avocado salsa

Serve with a salsa made from 400g **canned black-eyed beans**, rinsed and drained, 1 diced **avocado**, and 1 finely chopped **onion** mixed with handful of chopped **coriander leaves**.

Red mullet in rakı sauce

A favourite fish of the Romans, red mullet is one of the most prized fish in the eastern Mediterranean. In this recipe, the fish is doused in rakı, Turkey's national spirit that is often served with mezze and fish.

Low carb

Low saturated fat

Dairy free

Gluten free

Low salt

SERVES 4
PREP 5 MINS
COOK 12 MINS

4 fresh red mullet, gutted
   and cleaned

2–3 tbsp olive oil

salt and freshly ground black
   pepper

about 150ml (5fl oz) rakı
   or ouzo

small bunch of flat-leaf parsley,
   finely chopped

1 lemon, cut into quarters

1 Preheat the grill. Brush the fish with oil on both sides and season. Line a grill pan with aluminium foil and place the fish on top.

2 Place the grill pan under the grill and cook the fish for 5–6 minutes on each side, allowing the skin to buckle and brown. Remove from the grill and place the fish on a serving dish. Splash the rakı or ouzo over, set it alight, and wait until the flames die down before serving.

3 To serve, garnish with a sprinkling of parsley and serve each fish with a drizzle of rakı or ouzo and a wedge of lemon to squeeze over.

NUTRITION PER SERVING

Energy	309kcals/1293kJ
Carbohydrate	0g
of which sugar	0g
Fat	13g
of which saturates	0.8g
Salt	0.5g
Fibre	0g

Grey mullet with herb crust

This recipe works well with fish that have a slightly earthy taste, such as grey mullet. Improve its flavour by soaking in water with some lemon juice or vinegar.

Low salt

SERVES 4
PREP 15 MINS
COOK 12–15 MINS

4 grey mullet fillets, about 175g (6oz) each, skinned

1 tbsp olive oil

1 tbsp chopped flat-leaf parsley

juice of ½ lemon

salt and freshly ground black pepper

a few sprigs of sage, to garnish

lemon wedges, to garnish

FOR THE CRUST

8 tbsp fresh breadcrumbs

15g (½oz) melted butter

1 tbsp chopped sage

1 tbsp snipped chives

grated zest of ½ lemon

1 Preheat the oven to 200°C (400°F/Gas 6). Arrange the fish on a baking sheet. Mix the oil, parsley, and lemon juice, and season with salt and plenty of pepper.

2 To make the crust, mix together the breadcrumbs, melted butter, sage, chives, and lemon zest. Season lightly and sprinkle over the fish, pressing to stick to the butter.

3 Roast in the oven for 12–15 minutes, or until the fish is cooked – it will be firm, white, and opaque.

4 Transfer to a warmed serving dish, garnish with the sage and lemon wedges, and serve with green beans.

try this....
A Parmesan, olive, and sun-dried tomato crust

Mix 8 tablespoons fresh breadcrumbs with 2 tablespoons grated **Parmesan cheese**, 1 tablespoon chopped, pitted **black olives**, and 4 finely chopped **sun-dried tomatoes**, and continue as above.

NUTRITION PER SERVING	
Energy	363kcals/1519kJ
Carbohydrate	22g
of which sugar	1.5g
Fat	13g
of which saturates	4g
Salt	0.7g
Fibre	0.3g

Baked fish with a herby crust

This easy recipe looks amazing, with its vivid green crust, and is pleasingly aromatic. White fish are low in fat.

Low carb

Low saturated fat

Dairy free

Low salt

SERVES 4
PREP 5 MINS
COOK 10 MINS

50g (1¾oz) fresh breadcrumbs

2 tbsp roughly chopped basil leaves

2 tbsp roughly chopped flat-leaf parsley leaves

2 tbsp roughly chopped chives

finely grated zest of ½ lemon

salt and freshly ground black pepper

4 tbsp olive oil, plus extra for brushing

4 fillets firm-fleshed, white, sustainable fish, such as cod or haddock, about 150g (5½ oz) each

FOR A GLUTEN-FREE OPTION
use gluten-free breadcrumbs

1 Preheat the oven to 220°C (425°F/Gas 7). In a small food processor, whizz the breadcrumbs, herbs, lemon zest, and seasoning, until the breadcrumbs are bright green.

2 Add the oil in a slow stream, with the food processor running, until it forms a thick, bright green paste.

3 Brush the fish fillets with a little oil on both sides and season them well. Press the herby crust onto the top (or skinless side) of the fillets, packing it down well. Place on a non-stick baking tray and bake in the top of the oven for 10 minutes, or until cooked through and turning crispy on top.

NUTRITION PER SERVING	
Energy	290kcals/1214kJ
Carbohydrate	9g
of which sugar	0g
Fat	15g
of which saturates	2g
Salt	0.5g
Fibre	0.5g

Sea bream with tomato sauce

Make sure you use well-flavoured tomatoes, as they make all the difference. You can make the tomato sauce 2–3 days in advance and store in the fridge.

| Low carb |
| Low saturated fat |
| Dairy free |
| Gluten free |
| Low salt |

SERVES 4
PREP 10 MINS
COOK 25 MINS

4 small sea bream, about 350g (12oz) in total, scaled, gutted, and trimmed

1 tbsp buckwheat flour

salt and freshly ground black pepper

5 tbsp extra virgin olive oil

1 onion, finely chopped

2 celery sticks, finely sliced

2 garlic cloves, chopped

8 plum tomatoes, roughly chopped

5 tbsp dry white wine

pinch of sugar

2 tbsp chopped flat-leaf parsley

1 Preheat the oven to 190°C (375°F/Gas 5). Slash the sea bream 3–4 times on each side with a sharp knife. Mix the flour with some salt and pepper and dust it over the fish. Arrange in a baking tray.

2 Heat the oil in a pan over a low heat, add the onion, celery, and garlic, and cook for 2–3 minutes, until the vegetables soften. Add the tomatoes and wine, and cook for 3–4 minutes, until the juices run. Season with salt and pepper and add the sugar.

3 Spoon the tomato sauce over the fish and bake in the oven for 15–20 minutes, or until cooked. The flesh will be white and opaque.

4 Slide the fish onto a large, warmed serving dish, sprinkle with parsley, and serve immediately.

NUTRITION PER SERVING	
Energy	282kcals/1180kJ
Carbohydrate	11g
of which sugar	8g
Fat	17g
of which saturates	2g
Salt	0.3g
Fibre	3g

Barbecued mackerel with fennel and tomato salad

The strong flavours of mackerel are complemented well by this robust marinade and the bright, zingy salad.

Low carb

Dairy free

Gluten free

Low salt

SERVES 4
PREP 20 MINS,
PLUS MARINATING
COOK 6 MINS

1 hot red chilli, deseeded and finely chopped

1 tbsp small capers, rinsed, dried, and chopped

2 tbsp olive oil, plus extra for brushing

juice of 1 lemon, plus extra lemon wedges to serve

4 large skin-on mackerel fillets

salt and freshly ground black pepper

FOR THE SALAD

1 bulb fennel, thinly sliced

250g (9oz) cherry tomatoes, halved

2 red chillies, deseeded and thinly sliced lengthways

½ bunch chives, snipped into 2.5cm (1in) lengths

large handful of flat-leaf parsley, chopped

4 sprigs of dill, chopped

2 tbsp olive oil

juice of ½ lemon

1 garlic clove, crushed

1 Mix together the chilli, capers, olive oil, and lemon juice in a shallow bowl. Add the mackerel fillets, and season well on both sides. Rub the mixture over the fish, cover, and marinate in the fridge for 1 hour.

2 Prepare a barbecue for cooking, and brush the bars with oil. Cook the fish, skin-side down, for 2–3 minutes, or until the skin is golden brown. Turn it gently, brush with the marinade, and cook for a further 2–3 minutes. Remove from the heat and divide between four serving plates.

3 Put the salad ingredients in a bowl, toss gently, then serve with the fish, with lemon wedges for squeezing.

NUTRITION PER SERVING	
Energy	504kcals/2089kJ
Carbohydrate	3g
of which sugar	2.5g
Fat	40g
of which saturates	7g
Salt	0.6g
Fibre	2.1g

Grilled halibut with green sauce

A fresh-tasting dish that is easy to prepare and cooks in minutes. The high water content of halibut makes it a mild-flavoured, low-calorie fish.

Low carb
Low saturated fat
Dairy free
Gluten free
Low salt

SERVES 6
PREP 10 MINS, PLUS CHILLING
COOK 4 MINS

FOR THE SAUCE
45g (1½oz) mixed herbs, such as parsley, chives, mint, tarragon, and chervil

2 garlic cloves

8 tbsp olive oil

1 tbsp tarragon vinegar

salt and freshly ground black pepper

pinch of caster sugar

FOR THE FISH
6 x chunky halibut fillets, 140g (5oz) each

1 tbsp olive oil

lemon wedges, to serve

1 Place all the ingredients for the sauce in a food processor, process until smooth, and season to taste with salt and pepper, and the pinch of caster sugar. Chill until needed.

2 Preheat the grill on its highest setting or a barbecue to hot. Lightly brush the halibut with oil, and season to taste with salt and pepper. Cook the fish for 2 minutes on each side, and serve with the green sauce and lemon wedges to squeeze over.

try this....
Halibut with a cherry tomato sauce

Prepare and cook the halibut as in step 2. To make the tomato sauce, first slice 2 punnets **cherry tomatoes** in half. Heat 1 tablespoon olive oil in a pan, then add the tomatoes and cook over a low heat for 5 minutes. Add 1 teaspoon **balsamic vinegar** and 100g (3½oz) **vegetable stock**, and simmer until the liquid starts to thicken.

NUTRITION PER SERVING	
Energy	294kcals/1230kJ
Carbohydrate	0.3g
of which sugar	0.3g
Fat	19g
of which saturates	3g
Salt	0.2g
Fibre	0g

Oriental halibut en papillote

Each diner opens a paper case and savours the aroma as it is freshly released. Though the flavourings are Chinese, the method of cooking food in paper parcels is French.

Low carb

Low saturated fat

Dairy free

SERVES 4
PREP 15–20 MINS
COOK 10–12 MINS

salt

125g (4½oz) mangetout, trimmed

4 garlic cloves, finely chopped

2.5cm (1in) piece fresh root ginger, finely chopped

2 tbsp black bean sauce

3 tbsp reduced-salt light soy sauce

2 tbsp dry sherry

½ tsp granulated sugar

1 tbsp sesame oil

2 tbsp vegetable oil

1 egg

4 x 175g (6oz) skinned halibut fillets or steaks

4 spring onions, thinly sliced

1 Half-fill a saucepan with salted water and bring to the boil. Add the mangetout and simmer for 1–2 minutes. Drain.

2 Combine the garlic, ginger, black bean sauce, soy sauce, sherry, sugar, and sesame oil in a bowl. Stir well to mix, then set aside.

3 Fold a sheet of baking parchment (about 30x34.5cm/12x15in) in half and draw a curve with a pencil to make a heart shape when unfolded. It should be large enough to leave a 7.5cm (3in) border around a fish fillet. Cut out the heart shape with scissors. Repeat to make four paper hearts. Open each out and brush with the vegetable oil, leaving a border about 2.5cm (1in) wide at the edges.

4 Put the egg and ½ tsp salt in a small bowl and beat together. Brush this egg glaze evenly on the border of each of the paper hearts.

5 Preheat the oven to 200°C (400°F/Gas 6). Rinse the fish fillets and pat dry with kitchen paper. Arrange a quarter of the mangetout on one side of each paper heart and set a halibut fillet on top. Spoon a quarter of the seasoning on top of each fillet and sprinkle with a quarter of the spring onions. Fold the paper over the fish and run your finger along the edge to stick the two sides together. Make small pleats to seal the edges.

6 Twist the 'tails' of each paper case to seal them. Lay the cases on a baking sheet and bake for 10–12 minutes, until puffed and brown. Transfer to warmed plates, allowing each guest to open the package.

NUTRITION PER SERVING	
Energy	319kcals/1335kJ
Carbohydrate	5g
of which sugar	4g
Fat	13g
of which saturates	2g
Salt	2.4g
Fibre	1.4g

Lemon sole with herbs

One serving of lemon sole will meet almost half of an adult's daily requirement for protein while also being low in calories. It is a good source of B vitamins.

Low carb

Low saturated fat

Dairy free

Gluten free

Low salt

SERVES 4
PREP 10 MINS
COOK 20 MINS

3 tbsp extra virgin olive oil

1 tbsp white wine vinegar

1 tsp Dijon mustard

small handful of fresh mixed herbs, such as parsley, thyme, and dill

salt and freshly ground black pepper

4 lemon sole fillets or other flat fish fillets, such as plaice or brill, about 175g (6oz) each

1 Preheat the oven to 200°C (400°F/Gas 6). To make the dressing, whisk together the oil and vinegar in a jug. Add the mustard and herbs, and mix well. Season well with salt and black pepper, and mix again.

2 Lay out the fish in a roasting tin, then cover with about 5mm (¼in) water. Season well with salt and black pepper. Bake in the oven for 15–20 minutes, until the fish is cooked through and the water has almost evaporated.

3 Using a fish slice or spatula, carefully lift the fish onto a serving dish or individual plates. Spoon over some of the herb dressing. Serve hot with sautéed potatoes and broccoli.

NUTRITION PER SERVING	
Energy	222kcals/930kJ
Carbohydrate	0g
of which sugar	0g
Fat	11g
of which saturates	1.5g
Salt	0.5g
Fibre	0g

Chinese-style steamed bass

This restaurant-style dish is surprisingly easy to prepare. Sea bass offers high levels of protein but does contain mercury, so eat it only occasionally.

Low carb

Dairy free

SERVES 2
PREP 15 MINS
COOK 10–12 MINS

3 tbsp reduced-salt soy sauce

4 tbsp Chinese rice wine or dry sherry

3 tbsp thinly sliced fresh root ginger

2 small sea bass, gutted and rinsed

1 tbsp sesame oil

½ tsp salt

2 spring onions, trimmed and thinly sliced

2 tbsp sunflower oil

2 garlic cloves, chopped

1 small red chillies, deseeded and thinly sliced

thinly sliced zest of 1 lime

1 Prepare a steamer, or position a steaming rack in a wok with water so it doesn't touch the water. Bring to the boil.

2 Stir together the soy sauce, rice wine, and 2 tablespoons of ginger, and set aside. Using a sharp knife, make slashes in the fish, 2.5cm (1in) apart and not quite as deep as the bone, on both sides. Rub the fish inside and out with the sesame oil and salt.

3 Scatter one-quarter of the spring onions over a heatproof serving dish that will hold two fish and fit in the steamer or on the steaming rack. Place the fish on the dish and pour the sauce over.

4 Place the dish in the steamer or on the rack, cover, and steam for 10–12 minutes, or until the fish is cooked through and flakes easily when tested with a knife.

5 Meanwhile, heat the sunflower oil in a small saucepan over a medium–high heat until shimmering. Scatter the fish with remaining spring onions and ginger, and the garlic, chilli, and lime zest. Drizzle the hot oil over the fish and serve.

NUTRITION PER SERVING	
Energy	553kcals/2314kJ
Carbohydrate	5g
of which sugar	2.5g
Fat	36g
of which saturates	6.5g
Salt	3.5g
Fibre	0.7g

Roast hake with remoulade

Remoulade is similar to tartare sauce and both work equally well with deep-fried, pan-fried, or roasted white fish.

Low carb

Low saturated fat

Gluten free

Low salt

SERVES 4
PREP 5–10 MINS
COOK 6–8 MINS

4 hake fillets, about 175g (6oz) each, pinboned and skinned

1 tbsp extra virgin olive oil

salt and freshly ground black pepper

4 small sprigs of thyme

sprigs of watercress, to serve

lemon wedges, to serve

FOR THE REMOULADE

5 tbsp mayonnaise

5 tbsp half-fat crème fraîche

1 tsp Dijon mustard

2 tsp chopped capers

2 tsp chopped gherkins

1 tbsp chopped tarragon

1 tbsp chopped chervil, or flat-leaf parsley

½–1 tsp anchovy essence, to taste

1 Preheat the oven to 200°C (400°F/Gas 6). To make the remoulade, mix all the ingredients in a small bowl and season to taste with anchovy essence and pepper.

2 Brush the hake with the olive oil and season lightly. Arrange on a baking sheet and put the thyme on top. Bake in the oven for 6–8 minutes, or until cooked; it will be opaque and the flesh white and firm. Lift out the fish and drain well on kitchen paper.

3 Lift the fish onto a warmed serving dish and garnish with the watercress and lemon wedges. Serve the remoulade separately.

NUTRITION PER SERVING	
Energy	347kcals/1452kJ
Carbohydrate	1.5g
of which sugar	1g
Fat	24g
of which saturates	4g
Salt	0.6g
Fibre	0g

Hake in green sauce

Add extra vegetables, such as lightly cooked peas or asparagus tips, to the sauce in keeping with its green theme.

Low carb

Low saturated fat

Dairy free

Low salt

SERVES 4
PREP 10 MINS
COOK 14–16 MINS

2 tbsp olive oil

2 garlic cloves, finely chopped

2 tbsp plain flour

150ml (5fl oz) dry white wine

175ml (6fl oz) fish stock

4 tbsp chopped flat-leaf parsley leaves

salt and freshly ground black pepper

4 skin-on hake fillets, about 150g (5½oz) each

sautéed potatoes and green beans, to serve

1 Heat the oil in a large, non-stick frying pan over a medium heat. Gently fry the garlic for 1 minute.

2 Sprinkle the flour into the pan and stir thoroughly with a wooden spoon. Cook for 2 minutes, stirring until smooth. Gradually add the wine, followed by the stock, stirring constantly.

3 Stir in the parsley and simmer very gently over a low heat for about 5 minutes.

4 Season the fish and add to the pan, skin-side down. Spoon some sauce over and cook for 2–3 minutes. Turn and cook for a further 2–3 minutes, or until cooked through.

5 Transfer to warmed plates and serve immediately with sautéed potatoes and green beans.

NUTRITION PER SERVING	
Energy	238kcals/998kJ
Carbohydrate	6g
of which sugar	0.3g
Fat	9g
of which saturates	1.5g
Salt	0.8g
Fibre	0.3g

Keralan fish curry

The flavour and aroma of this curry is beautifully subtle and fragrant, so try it with any firm white fish. Tamarind paste offers a slight sourness.

Low saturated fat

Dairy free

Low salt

SERVES 4
PREP 10 MINS
COOK 15 MINS

800g (1¾lb) skinless haddock fillets, cut into bite-sized pieces

2 tsp ground turmeric

salt and freshly ground black pepper

1 tbsp vegetable oil

1 large onion, finely sliced

1 tsp black mustard seeds

5 curry leaves

4cm (1½in) fresh root ginger, finely chopped

2 tbsp tamarind paste

200ml (7fl oz) coconut milk

150ml (5fl oz) fish stock

2 spring onions, finely sliced

1 red chilli, deseeded and finely chopped (optional)

basmati rice and chopped coriander leaves, to serve

FOR A GLUTEN-FREE OPTION
use gluten-free stock

1 Place the haddock in a bowl, sprinkle with the turmeric, season, and stir to coat. Set aside.

2 Heat the oil in a large, non-stick frying pan over a medium heat, and add the onion, black mustard seeds, and curry leaves. Fry gently for 10 minutes, stirring occasionally, until the onion is lightly brown.

3 Add the ginger and cook for 1 or 2 minutes, then add the tamarind paste, coconut milk, and stock, and stir well. Heat the sauce to a gentle simmer.

4 Add the fish and simmer gently for 3–4 minutes or until it is just cooked. Stir in the spring onions and chilli (if using).

5 Serve the curry with basmati rice, sprinkled with chopped coriander leaves.

NUTRITION PER SERVING	
Energy	213kcals/905kJ
Carbohydrate	5.5g
of which sugar	5g
Fat	4.5g
of which saturates	0.5g
Salt	0.8g
Fibre	0.8g

Barbecued sardines in harissa

Very fresh sardines have a sweet and delicate flavour.
And they're a rich source of calcium and potassium.

Low carb

Dairy free

Gluten free

Low salt

SERVES 4
PREP 25 MINS
COOK 2–3 MINS

12–16 sardines, scaled, gutted,
  and trimmed

1–2 tbsp olive oil

salt and freshly ground black
  pepper

1 tsp ground coriander

FOR THE HARISSA DRESSING
2 tbsp extra virgin olive oil

2 tbsp harissa paste

2 tsp runny honey, to taste

grated zest and juice of 1 lime

FOR THE SALAD
large handful of coriander leaves

2 Little Gem lettuces, finely sliced

grated zest and juice of 1 lemon

pinch of sugar

3 tbsp extra virgin olive oil

1 Preheat a barbecue until the coals are glowing and grey in appearance.

2 Cut three slashes in either side of each sardine. Brush with olive oil and season generously with salt, pepper, and ground coriander. Set aside.

3 To make the dressing, whisk together the oil, harissa, honey, and lime zest and juice, then season, and add more honey if necessary to balance the acidity of the lime. Set aside.

4 Prepare the salad: toss the coriander with the lettuce and pile into a large, flat serving dish. Whisk together the lemon zest, juice, sugar, and olive oil. Season and drizzle over the salad.

5 Cook the sardines on the barbecue (or under a preheated grill) for 2–3 minutes or until the flesh is white and opaque. Brush with the harissa paste and barbecue the other side for a further 30 seconds. Pile onto the coriander salad and serve at once.

NUTRITION PER SERVING	
Energy	303kcals/1263kJ
Carbohydrate	3.5g
of which sugar	3.5g
Fat	21.5g
of which saturates	4g
Salt	0.5g
Fibre	0g

Grilled sardines

Ensure you use sustainable sardines for this delightful Mediterranean dish. You don't need to descale or brush the fish with oil. Sardines are one of the best sources of omega-3 fatty acids.

Low carb

Low saturated fat

Dairy free

Gluten free

SERVES 4
PREP 15–20 MINS
COOK 4–8 MINS

500g (1lb 2oz) fresh sardines

1 tbsp salt

lemon quarters, to serve

1 Gut the sardines – or have the fishmonger do this for you – leaving the heads and scales in place. Gutting is easily done by pushing your index finger through the soft belly and scooping the innards from the cavity. Sprinkle the flanks with salt.

2 Heat a heavy-based metal pan, grill, or barbecue until it is really hot. Grill the sardines fiercely, turning them once, until the skin blisters and turns black. Cook for 2–4 minutes on each side, depending on the thickness of the fish. Serve with quartered lemons.

NUTRITION PER SERVING	
Energy	206kcals/864kJ
Carbohydrate	0g
of which sugar	0g
Fat	11.5g
of which saturates	3.5g
Salt	3.3g
Fibre	0g

Blackened salmon

A spice rub, rather than a marinade, is useful to have in your barbecue repertoire, and works for meat and fish. Organic or wild salmon offers optimum nutrition.

Low carb

Low saturated fat

Dairy free

Gluten free

Low salt

SERVES 4
PREP 5 MINS, PLUS RESTING
COOK 10 MINS

1 tsp cayenne pepper

1 tsp celery salt

2 tsp dried oregano

1½ tbsp soft light brown sugar

freshly ground black pepper

4 skinless salmon fillets, about 150g (5½oz) each

1 tbsp olive oil

lemon or lime wedges, to serve

1 Prepare a barbecue for cooking. Grind all the dry ingredients together in a mortar and pestle to a fine consistency.

2 Rub all sides of the salmon fillets with the spice rub, cover, and rest in the fridge for 1 hour to let the flavours soak into the fish. Drizzle each piece of fish with a little oil and rub it gently all over.

3 Grill the salmon on the barbecue for 2–3 minutes on each side, until brown and crispy, but still moist. Serve with lemon or lime wedges to squeeze over.

try this....
Salmon baked with maple syrup and mustard

Mix 1 tablespoon **maple syrup** with 2 tablespoons **grainy mustard**, then brush over the salmon and proceed as above.

NUTRITION PER SERVING

Energy	316kcals/1316kJ
Carbohydrate	5.5g
of which sugar	5.5g
Fat	19g
of which saturates	3g
Salt	1.2g
Fibre	0g

Cajun-spiced salmon

This simple, Louisiana-inspired rub livens up any fish, and it's particularly good with salmon. Serve the salmon with a thinly sliced onion, avocado, and cherry tomato salad for a light, flavoursome meal.

| Low carb |
| Low saturated fat |
| Dairy free |
| Gluten free |
| Low salt |

SERVES 4
PREP 10 MINS
COOK 10 MINS

1 tsp smoked paprika

1 tsp cayenne pepper

1 tsp garlic powder

½ tsp dried thyme

1 tsp soft light brown sugar

½ tsp salt

4 skinless salmon fillets, about 150g (5½oz) each

2 tbsp olive oil

thinly sliced onion, avocado, and cherry tomato salad, to serve

1 Combine the spices, thyme, sugar, and salt in a mortar and pestle or a spice grinder. Grind to a fine powder.

2 Rub the mixture over both sides of the fish, cover with cling film, and leave to rest in the fridge while you prepare the grill.

3 Preheat the grill on its highest setting and line a grill pan with foil. Brush the fish with a little oil on both sides, being careful not to dislodge the spice rub. Grill for 3–4 minutes on each side, depending on its thickness.

4 Once done, serve the grilled salmon on a plate with onion, avocado, and cherry tomato salad.

try this....
Tandoori salmon

Mix 3 tablespoons **tandoori curry paste** with 200g (7oz) **2% fat Greek yogurt**. Place the fish in the yogurt mixture and continue as above from step 2.

NUTRITION PER SERVING	
Energy	324kcals/1348kJ
Carbohydrate	1g
of which sugar	1g
Fat	22g
of which saturates	3.5g
Salt	0.8g
Fibre	0g

Baked salmon with cucumber dill sauce

Equally good with salmon steaks or fillets, this simple summery dish is quick to make and very healthy.

Low carb

Gluten free

Low salt

SERVES 4
PREP 10 MINS,
PLUS STANDING
COOK 10 MINS

½ cucumber

salt and freshly ground black pepper

250g (9oz) plain yogurt

2 tsp Dijon mustard

1 spring onion, finely chopped

1 tbsp chopped dill

4 salmon steaks or fillets, skinned

2 tsp olive oil

juice of ½ lemon

1 Finely dice the cucumber and place in a sieve over a bowl. Sprinkle with salt and leave to drain for 1 hour. Rinse with cold water and pat dry with kitchen paper. Stir the drained cucumber into the yogurt and add the mustard, spring onion, and dill. Season to taste with salt and pepper. Set aside.

2 Preheat the oven to 200°C (400°F/Gas 6). Arrange the salmon fillets in a shallow baking dish, brush with oil, and season to taste with salt and pepper.

3 Sprinkle the salmon with lemon juice and roast for 8–10 minutes, depending on the thickness, until just cooked through but still moist inside. Remove from the oven and stir the juices from the dish into the cucumber sauce.

4 Serve the salmon hot or cold, with the sauce spooned over it.

try this....
Baked salmon with freekeh, cherry tomatoes, and capers

Prepare the salmon as in steps 2 and 3. While the salmon is cooking, heat 2 x 250g packs **ready-to-eat freekeh** according to pack instructions. Turn the freekeh into a large bowl and stir in 200g (7oz) halved **cherry tomatoes**, 1 bunch finely chopped **spring onions**, 5 tablespoons finely chopped fresh **parsley**, 2 tablespoons roughly chopped **capers**, and the **zest** and **juice** of 1 **lemon**.

NUTRITION PER SERVING	
Energy	339kcals/1418kJ
Carbohydrate	5g
of which sugar	5g
Fat	19g
of which saturates	4.5g
Salt	0.3g
Fibre	0.3g

Steamed trout in lettuce

Steaming is a good way to enjoy trout while keeping it low in fat. Cooked lettuce is a slightly bitter revelation.

Low carb

Gluten free

Low salt

SERVES 2
PREP 15 MINS
COOK 10 MINS

8 large Iceberg lettuce leaves

4 trout fillets, pinboned and skinned

salt and freshly ground black pepper

1 tbsp sunflower oil

4 spring onions, finely sliced

8 shiitake mushrooms, finely sliced

2 tbsp chopped tarragon

splash of lemon juice

FOR THE DRESSING

150ml (5fl oz) Greek yogurt

1 tbsp chopped capers

2 tbsp chopped parsley

1 shallot, finely chopped

1 Blanch the lettuce leaves in boiling water for 20–30 seconds. Rinse under running cold water and pat dry with kitchen paper. Trim out the thick centre veins so it is possible to lay the leaves flat. Overlap two leaves together, arrange a trout fillet on each, and season.

2 Heat the oil in a small saucepan, add the spring onions and mushrooms, and fry over a brisk heat for 3–4 minutes until cooked. Add the tarragon and lemon juice, then cool.

3 Divide the mushroom mixture over each trout fillet. Fold the lettuce over to encase.

4 Lift the trout onto a large bamboo steamer. Do not allow the parcels to touch. Steam for 5–6 minutes, until the fish flakes to the touch.

5 Meanwhile, mix the yogurt, capers, parsley, and shallot together and season lightly. Lift the fish parcels onto a large serving dish and serve the dressing separately.

NUTRITION PER SERVING	
Energy	429kcals/1795kJ
Carbohydrate	6g
of which sugar	5g
Fat	24g
of which saturates	8g
Salt	0.7g
Fibre	1.5g

Thai red curry with snapper

Home-made curry paste adds a delicious fragrance and warmth to the curry. Snapper is a low-calorie and lean source of protein.

Low carb

Dairy free

SERVES 4
PREP 10 MINS
COOK 20 MINS

2 tbsp sunflower oil

2 tsp shrimp paste

1 large onion, finely chopped

2 garlic cloves, crushed

1 tbsp palm sugar, or dark brown sugar

4 tomatoes, deseeded and diced

400g can reduced-fat coconut milk

300ml (10fl oz) Thai fish or shellfish stock

1–2 tbsp fish sauce, to taste

juice of ½–1 lime

4 snapper fillets, about 175g (6oz) each, scaled, pinboned, and halved

3 tbsp roughly chopped coriander leaves

steamed rice, to serve

FOR THE CURRY PASTE

4 red chillies, deseeded and chopped

1 red pepper, grilled, skin removed

1 tbsp ground coriander

2 stalks lemongrass, roughly chopped

2 tbsp grated galangal or fresh root ginger

1 tbsp Thai fish sauce

1 tsp shrimp paste

1 tsp palm sugar

FOR A GLUTEN-FREE OPTION
use gluten-free stock

1 Place all the ingredients for the curry paste in a food processor and whizz to a paste.

2 Heat the oil in a wok, add the shrimp paste, and stir over a low heat for 1–2 minutes. Add the onion and cook for a further 2 minutes, then add the garlic, palm sugar, tomatoes, and curry paste. Stir for 2 minutes, then add the coconut milk and stock. Bring to the boil and simmer for 4–5 minutes; season with fish sauce and lime juice.

3 Add the snapper, return to the boil, then reduce the heat and simmer for 5–6 minutes or until the fish is just cooked; it will be white and beginning to flake. Sprinkle over the coriander and serve with steamed rice.

NUTRITION PER SERVING	
Energy	357kcals/1494kJ
Carbohydrate	14g
of which sugar	12g
Fat	16g
of which saturates	8g
Salt	2.5g
Fibre	2.8g

Asian style soy and sesame fish bites

A great way to get children to eat fish, these sweet and sticky fish bites look and taste delicious.

Low carb

Low saturated fat

Dairy free

SERVES 4
PREP 10 MINS, PLUS
COOLING AND
MARINATING
COOK 10 MINS

4 tbsp soy sauce

4 tbsp rice wine or dry sherry

2 tbsp rice vinegar or white wine vinegar

1 tbsp soft light brown sugar

1 tbsp runny honey

2 tsp sesame oil

500g (1lb 2oz) firm white-fleshed fish fillets, cut into 2cm (¾in) cubes

2 tbsp sesame seeds

FOR A GLUTEN-FREE OPTION
use gluten-free tamari to replace soy sauce

1 Combine the soy sauce, rice wine, vinegar, sugar, honey, and oil in a small, heavy-based saucepan and bring it to the boil.

2 Reduce the heat to a simmer and cook, uncovered, for 5 minutes, until the sauce has reduced. Allow it to cool.

3 Turn the fish in the cooled sauce to coat, cover, and marinate in the fridge for 1 hour.

4 Preheat the grill on its highest setting. Line a baking tray or grill pan with foil and spread out the marinated fish in a single layer. Sprinkle half the sesame seeds evenly over the fish.

5 Grill the fish for 3–4 minutes, until it is beginning to turn crispy at the edges, then turn it over carefully, sprinkle with the remaining sesame seeds, and grill for a further 3–4 minutes.

NUTRITION PER SERVING	
Energy	210kcals/881kJ
Carbohydrate	8.5g
of which sugar	8.5g
Fat	7g
of which saturates	1g
Salt	2.9g
Fibre	1g

SEAFOOD

Pilpil prawns

In this speciality of the tapas bars of Andalucia, freshly caught raw prawns are cooked to order in little earthenware *cazuela*. They contain more protein than chicken, for fewer calories and less fat.

Low carb

Low saturated fat

Dairy free

Low salt

SERVES 2
PREP 5 MINS
COOK 1–2 MINS

150g (5½oz) raw peeled prawns

3–4 tbsp olive oil

1–2 garlic cloves, thickly sliced

4–5 small dried chillies, whole but deseeded

sea salt

soft-crumbed bread, to serve

FOR A GLUTEN-FREE OPTION
use gluten-free bread

1 Clean the prawns and devein them, if necessary.

2 Heat the oil in an earthenware *cazuela* or a small frying pan. Add the prawns, garlic, and chillies, sprinkle with a little salt, and fry for 1–2 minutes, until the prawns change colour and become opaque.

3 Serve immediately with cocktail sticks or wooden forks, and plenty of soft-crumbed bread for mopping up the juices.

NUTRITION PER SERVING	
Energy	259kcals/1072kJ
Carbohydrate	0g
of which sugar	0g
Fat	23g
of which saturates	3.5g
Salt	0.4g
Fibre	0g

Moroccan-style prawns

Originally from Morocco and also found in Provence, this easy dish tastes as good as it smells. Serve with a salad for a quick lunch, or tapas-style with cocktail sticks.

Low carb

Low saturated fat

Dairy free

Gluten free

Low salt

SERVES 4–6
PREP 5 MINS
COOK 5 MINS

500g (1lb 2oz) uncooked shelled gambas or large prawns (defrosted if frozen)

4 tbsp olive oil

½ tsp harissa paste or hot paprika

1 tsp ground ginger

1 tsp ground cumin

½ tsp ground coriander

3 garlic cloves, crushed

1 tbsp snipped flat-leaf parsley

1 tbsp snipped coriander

1 Drain the gambas on a double layer of kitchen paper. Heat the oil in a large frying pan, tip in the spices and garlic, and stir for a minute to release the flavours.

2 Add the gambas and cook for 1–2 minutes over a medium-high heat until they turn a little pink, then turn over. Cook until the gambas are pink all over, stirring frequently. Stir in the herbs and serve hot.

NUTRITION PER SERVING	
Energy	194–130kcals/ 810–540kJ
Carbohydrate	0–0g
of which sugar	0–0g
Fat	12–8g
of which saturates	1.7–1.1g
Salt	0.6–0.4g
Fibre	0–0g

Pan-fried prawns in garlic butter

The prawns can be peeled or not; provide finger bowls and plenty of paper napkins if you leave the shell on. Parsley is rich in antioxidants.

Low carb

Gluten free

Low salt

SERVES 4
PREP 5 MINS
COOK 10 MINS

25g (scant 1oz) unsalted butter

juice of 1 lemon, plus more to serve

2 garlic cloves, crushed

2 tbsp finely chopped flat-leaf parsley, plus extra, to serve

salt and freshly ground black pepper

2 tbsp olive oil

16–20 raw tiger prawns, peeled, deveined, and butterflied

lemon wedges, to garnish

1 Mix the butter, lemon juice, garlic, and parsley together, and season to taste with salt and plenty of pepper.

2 Heat the oil in a large frying pan, add half the prawns and pan-fry over a medium heat for 2 minutes, or until they have lost their translucency and turned pink. Lift onto a large serving platter and keep warm while you cook the remaining prawns in the same way.

3 Wipe out the frying pan if necessary and add the garlic butter. Heat until hot and foaming and the garlic is soft, but not brown. Add a splash of lemon juice to stop the cooking and immediately pour over the prawns.

4 Garnish with parsley and lemon wedges and serve at once.

NUTRITION PER SERVING	
Energy	173kcals/724kJ
Carbohydrate	0g
of which sugar	0g
Fat	11g
of which saturates	4g
Salt	0.7g
Fibre	0g

Spinach and coconut prawn curry

This mild, creamy curry flavoured with coconut makes a low-calorie and fragrant supper dish that is easy to prepare.

Low carb

Dairy free

Low salt

High fibre

SERVES 4
PREP 15 MINS
COOK 15–20 MINS

2 tbsp sunflower oil

2 red onions, finely chopped

4 garlic cloves, finely chopped

5cm (2in) piece of fresh root ginger, finely grated

¼–½ tsp chilli powder

½ tsp turmeric

2 tsp ground cumin

1 tsp ground coriander

4 large tomatoes, skinned and finely chopped

400ml (14fl oz) reduced-fat coconut milk

10 fresh or dried curry leaves (optional)

150g (5½oz) spinach, shredded

400g (14oz) raw king prawns, shelled and deveined

½ tsp caster sugar

salt

basmati rice, warmed naan bread, and lime wedges, to serve

FOR A GLUTEN-FREE OPTION
use gluten-free naan bread

1 Heat the oil in a large, deep-sided frying pan or wok. Add the onions, garlic, and ginger and cook for 2–3 minutes over a low heat until softened, but not browned. Add the spices and cook for a further 1 or 2 minutes to release the flavours.

2 Add the tomatoes and continue to cook over a low heat for another 2 minutes, until the tomato flesh starts to break down. Add the coconut milk and curry leaves (if using), and bring to the boil. Mix in the spinach and reduce the heat, continuing to cook until the spinach has collapsed. Baby spinach will take 1 or 2 minutes, bigger leaves up to 4 minutes.

3 Add the prawns, sugar, and a pinch of salt, and cook for a further 2 minutes over a high heat, or until the prawns turn a bright pink colour. Serve with basmati rice, warmed naan bread, and lime wedges on the side.

NUTRITION PER SERVING	
Energy	271kcals/1134kJ
Carbohydrate	12g
of which sugar	9g
Fat	15g
of which saturates	7g
Salt	0.9g
Fibre	4g

Laksa lemak

This Malaysian dish is rich with coconut milk. This is high in fat, although mostly in a form that is converted to energy and not stored in the body.

Dairy free

SERVES 4
PREP 20 MINS
COOK 10–15 MINS

400g can reduced-fat coconut milk

450ml (15fl oz) low salt shellfish stock

1 stalk lemongrass

4 kaffir lime leaves

2.5cm (1in) piece galangal or fresh root ginger, peeled and finely sliced

450g (1lb) mahi mahi fillets, pinboned, skinned, and cut into large chunks

12 raw tiger prawns, peeled and deveined, tails left on

450g (1lb) mussels, prepared

2 squid, gutted, cleaned, and cut into rings

350g (12oz) vermicelli, to serve

lime wedges, to serve

FOR THE CURRY PASTE

2 tsp vegetable oil

splash of sesame oil

2 tsp palm sugar

3 garlic cloves, halved

½ bunch of spring onions, roughly chopped

1 tsp shrimp paste

2 red chillies, deseeded and chopped

1 large bunch of coriander (with roots, if possible)

1 tsp cumin

1 tsp turmeric

½ tsp salt

FOR A GLUTEN-FREE OPTION

use gluten-free stock

1 Put all the ingredients for the curry paste in a food processor and whizz. Blend in half the coconut milk to make a smooth paste.

2 Heat a large wok, add the paste and cook over a low heat for 1 minute. Add the remaining coconut milk and the stock, bring to a boil, and add the lemongrass, lime leaves, and galangal; simmer for 5 minutes. Add the fish, prawns, and mussels; cook for 3–4 minutes. Add the squid.

3 Meanwhile, cook the vermicelli according to packet instructions. Divide between four bowls and ladle the laksa on top. Serve with lime wedges.

NUTRITION PER SERVING

Energy	606kcals/2536kJ
Carbohydrate	66g
of which sugar	6g
Fat	14g
of which saturates	7.5g
Salt	2.6g
Fibre	5g

Simple Italian roast lobster

This Neapolitan dish is easy to prepare and the lobster offers significant amounts of protein and zinc.

Low carb

Low saturated fat

Dairy free

Low salt

SERVES 4
PREP 15 MINS
COOK 15 MINS

2 cooked lobsters, preferably rock lobsters, split and prepared

4 tbsp Italian extra virgin olive oil

4 tbsp finely chopped flat-leaf parsley, plus extra sprigs, to serve

2 garlic cloves, crushed

3–4 tbsp fresh breadcrumbs

salt and freshly ground black pepper

lemon wedges, to serve

FOR A GLUTEN-FREE OPTION
use gluten-free breadcrumbs

1 Preheat the oven to 190°C (375°F/Gas 5). Put the split lobsters onto a large baking tray or baking dish.

2 Heat the olive oil in a small saucepan, add the parsley and garlic, and sizzle for 30 seconds, then stir in the breadcrumbs and season well.

3 Spoon the mixture over the cut lobster flesh. Bake in the oven for 7–10 minutes, or until the lobsters are piping hot. Remove from the oven and arrange on a large, warmed serving dish with lemon wedges.

NUTRITION PER SERVING	
Energy	233kcals/975kJ
Carbohydrate	8g
of which sugar	0.5g
Fat	13g
of which saturates	2g
Salt	0.9g
Fibre	0g

Moules marinières

This classic French recipe – mussels in wine, garlic, and herbs – translates as "in the fisherman's style". Offering an important source of vitamins and minerals, mussels are also sustainable and cheap.

SERVES 4
PREP 15–20 MINS
COOK 15 MINS

40g (1½oz) butter

2 onions, finely chopped

3.6kg (8lb) mussels, prepared

2 garlic cloves, crushed

600ml (1 pint) dry white wine

4 bay leaves

2 sprigs of thyme

salt and freshly ground black pepper

2–4 tbsp chopped flat-leaf parsley

1 Melt the butter in a large, heavy saucepan, add the onions, and fry gently until lightly browned. Add the mussels, garlic, wine, bay leaves, and thyme. Season to taste. Cover, bring to the boil, and cook for 5–6 minutes, or until the mussels have opened, shaking frequently.

2 Remove the mussels with a slotted spoon, discarding any that remain closed. Transfer them to warmed bowls, cover, and keep warm.

3 Strain the liquor into a pan and bring to the boil. Season to taste, add the parsley, pour over the mussels, and serve at once.

NUTRITION PER SERVING	
Energy	415kcals/1736kJ
Carbohydrate	1g
of which sugar	1g
Fat	14g
of which saturates	6g
Salt	2g
Fibre	0g

Spicy stir-fried squid

A traditional Thai recipe, although such recipes are legion in many countries and regions across Asia.

Low carb

Low saturated fat

Dairy free

Gluten free

SERVES 4
PREP 20 MINS
COOK 5–6 MINS

8 small squid, gutted and cleaned

1 tbsp vegetable oil

1 stalk lemongrass, split into 4 lengthways

2 kaffir lime leaves

1 yellow or orange pepper, deseeded and diced

handful of basil leaves, preferably Thai, shredded

salt and freshly ground black pepper

FOR THE PASTE

3 garlic cloves, chopped

2 shallots, roughly chopped

1 tbsp grated fresh root ginger

1–2 red chillies, to taste (deseeded for a milder result)

50g (1¾oz) chopped coriander, preferably both leaves and roots

large splash of vegetable oil

1 tbsp palm sugar or dark brown sugar

1 tbsp Thai fish sauce

1 Score the squid tubes and set aside with the tentacles.

2 To make the paste, put the garlic, shallots, ginger, chilli, coriander, vegetable oil, palm sugar, and fish sauce into a food processor. Whizz to form a finely chopped green paste.

3 Heat the 1 tablespoon vegetable oil in a large wok, add the paste, and fry over a low to medium heat for 2–3 minutes or until it smells aromatic. Add the squid, lemongrass, lime leaves, and pepper. Stir-fry, tossing over a brisk heat until the squid is opaque and coated in the other ingredients. (Avoid overcooking the squid, as it will become tough.)

4 Stir in the basil and adjust the seasoning, then remove the lemongrass and lime leaves before serving.

NUTRITION PER SERVING	
Energy	170kcals/711kJ
Carbohydrate	6g
of which sugar	6g
Fat	5.5g
of which saturates	1g
Salt	1.5g
Fibre	1.1g

Scallops with bacon

Bacon, chorizo, and pancetta are all excellent to serve with pan-fried scallops.

Low carb

Dairy free

Gluten free

Low salt

SERVES 4
PREP 5–10 MINS
COOK 15 MINS

4 rashers rindless smoked streaky bacon, sliced

12 king scallops

1 tbsp chopped flat-leaf parsley

squeeze of lemon juice

salt and freshly ground black pepper

handful of rocket, to serve

1 Heat a frying pan and add the bacon. Cook over a medium heat until the bacon is brown and frazzled. Lift onto a plate.

2 Remove the roe from the scallops. Fry the scallops in the bacon fat for 1–2 minutes on each side or until golden brown. Do not put too many in the pan at once, as they will not brown. Lift onto a plate.

3 Reduce the heat in the pan and fry the roes; these are likely to pop in the hot fat. They are cooked when they are firm.

4 Return the scallop muscles and bacon to the pan, add the parsley and the lemon juice. Season, and serve with rocket leaves.

NUTRITION PER SERVING	
Energy	75kcals/314kJ
Carbohydrate	6.2g
of which sugar	0.5g
Fat	3g
of which saturates	1.5g
Salt	0.9g
Fibre	0.6g

Cured mackerel sashimi with salad

In spring and summer, mackerel has quite a soft texture; curing it firms the flesh.

SERVES 4
PREP 30 MINS

2 very fresh mackerel (preferably still with rigor mortis), filleted, cured, and pinboned

FOR THE SALAD

60g (2oz) rocket, washed

2 Baby Gem lettuces, washed and torn into strips

large handful of cress, washed

handful of cherry tomatoes, halved

½ small cucumber, peeled and thinly sliced

1 ripe avocado, diced

2 tbsp chopped pickled sushi ginger

Japanese soy sauce, to serve

wasabi paste, to serve

FOR THE DRESSING

1 tsp runny honey

1 tbsp mirin

1 tbsp rice wine vinegar

1 tsp sesame oil

2 tbsp sunflower oil

FOR A GLUTEN-FREE OPTION

use gluten-free tamari to replace soy sauce

1 Slice the mackerel very thinly, and set aside.

2 Put the salad ingredients into a big bowl and toss together. Put the dressing ingredients into a bowl, whisk to blend, then add to the salad, and toss together.

3 Pile the salad onto a large platter and arrange the sliced mackerel on top. Serve with the dark soy sauce and wasabi in small dishes on the side.

NUTRITION PER SERVING	
Energy	281kcals/1166kJ
Carbohydrate	8.5g
of which sugar	8g
Fat	22g
of which saturates	4g
Salt	0.2g
Fibre	3g

Sesame sushi rolls

Colourful and nutty, these little sushi rolls have contrasting textures, which make them so appealing to eat.

Low carb

Low saturated fat

Dairy free

MAKES 24
PREP 30 MINS
COOK 3 MINS

3 tbsp sesame seeds

125g (4½oz) medium prawns

2 sheets of nori, halved

1 quantity sushi rice (see p259)

½ tsp wasabi paste

½ cucumber, seeded and julienned

6 tbsp shoyu (Japanese soy sauce), to serve

1 Toast the sesame seeds in a dry saucepan over low heat for 3 minutes until nutty and golden. Set aside to cool. Cut the prawns in half lengthways.

2 Cut one sheet of cling film just larger than half of a nori sheet. Place half of a nori, smooth side down, on a sushi mat or a square of heavy-duty foil. Moisten your fingers with water, then spread a quarter of the rice in an even layer on the nori. Cover with the cling film.

3 Pick up the nori, carefully turn it over, and place on the mat, cling film side down. The nori should now be facing up. Spread a thin line of wasabi lengthways along the centre of the nori with your fingers.

4 Arrange a quarter of the prawns, cucumber, and 1 teaspoon sesame seeds on top, making sure the fillings extend completely to each end. Pick up the mat and cling film and tightly roll the rice around filling, pressing down firmly as you roll. Unroll the mat and cling film.

5 Gently roll the rice roll in half of the remaining sesame seeds. Roll up tightly in cling film, twisting the ends to secure. Repeat with remaining nori, rice, wasabi, prawns, cucumber, and sesame seeds.

6 Trim the ends of each roll, then cut each rice roll into six equal-sized pieces with a moist knife. Remove cling film from the cut pieces. Serve at room temperature with shoyu for dipping.

NUTRITION PER SERVING	
Energy	62kcals/259kJ
Carbohydrate	10g
of which sugar	0.5g
Fat	1g
of which saturates	0.2g
Salt	0.8g
Fibre	0.3g

Nori maki

You will need a bamboo mat to make these California-style rolls. Crabmeat is a low-calorie source of protein, B vitamins, omega-3 fats, and minerals.

Dairy free

Gluten free

MAKES 16
PREP 5 MINS

splash of rice vinegar

4 sheets nori seaweed, halved

⅓ recipe sushi rice (see p259)

a little wasabi paste

½ avocado, thinly sliced

115g (4oz) white crabmeat, or 4 pieces of surimi (ocean sticks), halved

1 Lay a bamboo mat on a board. Have to hand a bowl of tepid water mixed with the vinegar.

2 Lay a half piece of nori seaweed on the bamboo mat, shiny side down. Using wet hands, take a small handful of rice and spread it on the nori, pressing gently, and leaving a 2.5cm (1in) border at one end. Don't use too much water, or the nori will become wet and tough.

3 If using a single ingredient, use a little more rice to fill the rolls. Make an indentation down the centre of the rice, spread on a little wasabi paste, the avocado, and crab or surimi.

4 Roll up the sushi, pressing on the bamboo mat to help keep the roll even.

5 To cut the roll, use a very sharp, wet knife and do not saw, but pull the knife towards you. Cut the roll in half, then in half again and stand each upright. Wipe the knife between cuts.

6 Arrange the cut sushi on a large tray to serve. Serve with dark soy sauce or gluten-free tamari, pickled sushi ginger, pickled daikon, and wasabi paste.

NUTRITION PER SERVING

Energy	367kcals/1536kJ
Carbohydrate	69g
of which sugar	8g
Fat	4.5g
of which saturates	1g
Salt	0.9g
Fibre	2g

Seafood ceviche

A brief pickling for raw fish conserves its freshness and brings out the true flavour. The pimentón lends the dish its red colour.

Low carb

Dairy free

Gluten free

Low salt

SERVES 4
PREP 20 MINS,
PLUS FREEZING
AND MARINATING

450g (1lb) very fresh,
   firm-fleshed fish fillets,
   pinboned and skinned

1 red onion, finely sliced

juice of 2 lemons or limes

1 tbsp olive oil

½ tsp pimentón piccante

1 chilli, finely chopped

salt and freshly ground
   black pepper

2 tbsp finely chopped
   flat-leaf parsley

1 Wrap the fish in cling film or foil, and put it in the freezer for 1 hour to firm up the flesh. This will make it easier to slice. With a sharp knife, slice the fish into very thin slivers.

2 Spread the onion evenly in the bottom of a shallow, non-metallic dish. Pour over the lemon juice and olive oil, then sprinkle with the pimentón and chilli.

3 Place the fish on the onion, gently turning to coat with the marinade. Cover and marinate in the refrigerator for at least 20 minutes, preferably more than 1 hour. Season and sprinkle with parsley.

try this....
Seafood ceviche with avocado and fennel

Peel and dice 2 ripe **Hass avocados**, finely slice 1 small bulb of **fennel**, and mix them with the fish.

NUTRITION PER SERVING

Energy	125kcals/525kJ
Carbohydrate	2g
of which sugar	1.5g
Fat	3.5g
of which saturates	0.5g
Salt	0.2g
Fibre	0.5g

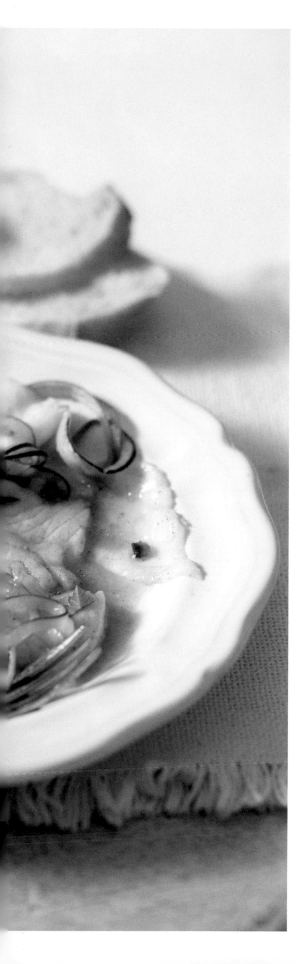

Chirashi sushi

This type of sushi requires no rolling and is very easy to make. Daikon is low in calories but high in vitamin C. Its enzymes help digest raw fish.

Low saturated fat

Dairy free

SERVES 4
PREP 20 MINS,
PLUS COOLING
COOK 20 MINS,
PLUS STEAMING

FOR THE SUSHI RICE

300g (10oz) short-grain sushi rice

1 small strip of kombu (dried seaweed)

4 tbsp Japanese rice vinegar

2 tbsp sugar

½ tsp salt

ANY SELECTION OF THE FOLLOWING

shredded daikon

thinly sliced cucumber

1 fillet sashimi-grade tuna, thinly and evenly sliced

1 fillet sashimi-grade salmon, thinly and evenly sliced

1 fillet sashimi-grade kingfish, thinly and evenly sliced

8–12 prepared and cooked tiger prawns

1 cured mackerel fillet, thinly sliced

1 thin squid tube, scored and cut into pieces

wasabi, to serve

Japanese dark soy sauce, to serve

FOR A GLUTEN-FREE OPTION

use gluten-free tamari to replace soy sauce

1 In a sieve, rinse the rice until the water runs clear. Put the rice, kombu, and 300ml (11fl oz) water in a heavy saucepan, and cover with a lid. Bring to the boil, then simmer for 11–12 minutes. Remove from the heat and leave to steam, with the lid on, for 10 minutes.

2 Put the vinegar, sugar, and salt into a saucepan and heat slowly until the grains have dissolved.

3 Turn the rice onto a shallow dish. Drizzle the vinegar mixture over, then turn to gloss the rice. Leave to cool.

4 Serve the rice on the dish or in four bowls, arranging the vegetables and fish on top. Serve with wasabi and dark soy sauce.

NUTRITION PER SERVING	
Energy	449kcals/1879kJ
Carbohydrate	69g
of which sugar	8g
Fat	6g
of which saturates	1g
Salt	0.8g
Fibre	1g

Quinoa salmon cakes

The peppers and quinoa add a fresh take to this quick and easy-to-make recipe for fishcakes. Serve with a light tossed salad for a delicious and filling meal.

Low carb

Low saturated fat

Dairy free

Low salt

SERVES 4
PREP 10 MINS,
PLUS CHILLING
COOK 20 MINS

2 x 213g cans salmon, drained, flaked, and pin boned

100g (3½oz) prepared quinoa

2 eggs, beaten

2 garlic cloves, crushed

grated zest of 1 lemon

40g (1½oz) green peppers, deseeded and finely chopped

1 tsp freshly ground black pepper

sea salt

2–3 tbsp olive oil

1 lemon, cut into wedges, to serve

1 Place the salmon, quinoa, eggs, garlic, lemon zest, green peppers, and black pepper in a large bowl. Season to taste with sea salt and mix well until fully incorporated.

2 Divide the mixture into eight equal-sized portions. Gently form each portion into a patty-like shape. Place the cakes on a plate and chill in the fridge for about 15 minutes.

3 Heat the oil in a large frying pan over a medium heat. Gently place the cakes in the pan and fry for 4 minutes on each side, until golden brown and cooked through. Do this in batches to avoid overcrowding the pan. Remove from the heat and serve hot with lemon wedges and a watercress salad.

NUTRITION PER SERVING	
Energy	171kcals/715kJ
Carbohydrate	8g
of which sugar	0.6g
Fat	13g
of which saturates	2.5g
Salt	1.4g
Fibre	1g

Prawn and asparagus stir-fry with polenta

In this quick and easy dish, prawns and asparagus are stir-fried in a light white wine sauce and served over creamy, cheesy polenta. Asparagus is a good source of fibre and also of folate.

Gluten free

SERVES 4
PREP 10 MINS
COOK 20 MINS

2 tbsp extra virgin olive oil

3 garlic cloves, crushed

6–8 spring onions, white and green parts, finely chopped

450g (1lb) asparagus, ends removed and cut into 2.5cm (1in) pieces

450g (1lb) prawns, peeled and deveined

60ml (2fl oz) white wine

salt and freshly ground black pepper

150g (5½oz) uncooked polenta

100g (3½oz) freshly grated Asiago or Parmesan cheese, plus extra to garnish

1 lemon, sliced, to serve

1 Heat the oil in a large frying pan over a medium heat. Add the garlic, spring onions, and asparagus. Cook for 5 minutes, stirring occasionally, until the onions have softened. Then add the prawns and cook for 3 minutes, stirring, until just beginning to turn pink.

2 Pour in the wine and stir to combine. Cook for a further 2–3 minutes or until the prawns are cooked through and pink. Remove from the heat and season to taste, if needed.

3 Meanwhile, place 750ml (1¼ pints) water and ¼ teaspoon salt in a large saucepan and bring to the boil. Stir in the polenta and reduce the heat to medium-low. Cook for about 5 minutes, stirring occasionally. Remove from the heat and stir in the cheese.

4 Divide the polenta evenly between four plates and top with one-quarter of the prawn and asparagus stir-fry. Garnish with cheese and serve hot with lemon slices.

NUTRITION PER SERVING	
Energy	412kcals/1724kJ
Carbohydrate	30g
of which sugar	3g
Fat	15g
of which saturates	6g
Salt	2.2g
Fibre	4g

Cherry and pistachio freekeh pilaf

This dish is made with warming, aromatic spices and mixes freekeh with dried cherries and pistachios, creating an unusual savoury and sweet pilaf.

Low saturated fat

Dairy free

Low salt

SERVES 4
PREP 5 MINS
COOK 20–25 MINS

200g (7oz) uncooked freekeh

8 cardamom pods

8 whole cloves

1 tbsp oil

1 onion, finely chopped

1 tsp ground cinnamon

pinch of salt

100g (3½oz) dried cherries, roughly chopped

100g (3½oz) pistachios, roughly chopped

FOR THE DRESSING

3 tbsp olive oil

2 tbsp lemon juice

pinch of salt

1 Place the freekeh in a large saucepan, cover with 1 litre (1¾ pints) of water, and place over a medium heat. Add the cardamom and cloves and simmer for 20 minutes or until all the water has been absorbed. Drain any remaining water and remove and discard the cardamom and cloves. Set aside.

2 Meanwhile, heat the oil in a large frying pan over a medium heat. Add the onions and cook for 5–10 minutes, stirring occasionally, until softened and translucent. Then add the cinnamon and cook for a further 2 minutes.

3 For the dressing, place all the ingredients in a small bowl and mix to combine. Add the freekeh to the onion mixture, season with the salt, and stir to mix. Then add the cherries and pistachios and stir until evenly distributed. Remove from the heat. Serve hot with the dressing drizzled over.

NUTRITION PER SERVING	
Energy	506kcals/2112kJ
Carbohydrate	55g
of which sugar	18g
Fat	24g
of which saturates	3g
Salt	0.6g
Fibre	2.5g

Tabbouleh and cacik

Warmed pitta bread makes a fitting and delicious accompaniment to these mezze salads. Mezze are little dishes of vegetables, salads, olives, and such like that are common all over the Middle East.

SERVES 4
**PREP 30–35 MINS, PLUS
SOAKING AND CHILLING**

100g (3½oz) bulgur wheat

1 small cucumber

salt and freshly ground black pepper

250g (9oz) tomatoes, peeled, deseeded, and chopped

2 spring onions, trimmed and chopped

small bunch of flat-leaf parsley, leaves chopped

3 tbsp lemon juice

4 tbsp olive oil

1 bunch of mint, leaves chopped

1 large garlic clove, finely chopped

¼ tsp ground coriander

¼ tsp ground cumin

250ml (9fl oz) natural yogurt

3–4 pitta breads

1 Put the bulgur wheat in a large bowl and pour over enough cold water to cover generously. Let it soak for 30 minutes, then drain through a sieve and squeeze out any remaining water with your fist.

2 Trim the ends from the cucumber, cut in half lengthways, and scoop out the seeds with a teaspoon. Dice the cucumber halves, put in a colander, sprinkle with salt, and stir to mix. Leave for 15–20 minutes, to draw out the bitter juices, then rinse under cold, running water and drain.

3 For the tabbouleh, in a large bowl, combine the bulgur, tomatoes, spring onions, parsley, lemon juice, oil, two-thirds of the mint, and plenty of salt and pepper. Mix and taste for seasoning, then cover and chill in the fridge for at least 2 hours.

4 To make the cacik, put the cucumber in a bowl and add the garlic, remaining mint, ground coriander, ground cumin, and salt and pepper. Pour in the yogurt. Stir to combine and taste for seasoning. Chill in the fridge for at least 2 hours, to allow the flavours to blend.

5 Warm the pitta breads in a low oven for 3–5 minutes, then remove and cut into strips. Take the salads from the fridge and allow to come to room temperature, then arrange them in separate bowls with the warm pitta bread fingers alongside.

NUTRITION PER SERVING	
Energy	436kcals/1833kJ
Carbohydrate	63g
of which sugar	10g
Fat	14.5g
of which saturates	3g
Salt	0.9g
Fibre	3g

Beef and edamame stir-fry

In this quick recipe, sirloin steak is stir-fried with a home-made sauce and fresh vegetables. Served over wholegrain freekeh, it is a healthy alternative to the traditional beef stir-fry.

> Low saturated fat

> Dairy free

SERVES 4
PREP 10 MINS
COOK 25 MINS

225g (8oz) uncooked freekeh

1 tbsp light olive oil

450g (1lb) beef sirloin steak, cut into strips

225g (8oz) carrots, shredded

225g (8oz) frozen shelled edamame

175ml (6fl oz) low-sodium soy sauce

60ml (2fl oz) beef stock

60ml (2fl oz) rice vinegar

½ tbsp cornflour, mixed with a little warm water

1 tsp freshly grated root ginger

½ tsp freshly ground black pepper

handful of chopped spring onions, to garnish

1 Place the freekeh and 750ml (1¼ pints) of water in a large, lidded saucepan over a medium heat. Bring to the boil, then reduce the heat to a simmer. Cover and cook for 20–25 minutes, until almost all the water has been absorbed. Remove from the heat, drain any excess water, and set aside.

2 Meanwhile, heat the oil in a large, lidded frying pan over a medium heat. Add the beef and cook for about 1 minute, stirring occasionally. Remove with a slotted spoon and set aside. Add the carrots and edamame to the pan, cover, and cook for about 5 minutes, stirring occasionally.

3 Place the soy sauce, beef stock, rice vinegar, cornflour, ginger, and pepper in a bowl. Whisk until well combined. Pour the liquid mixture into the pan. Then add the beef, stir well to combine, and bring to the boil. Cook, stirring frequently, for a further 10–12 minutes, or until the sauce thickens slightly. Remove from the heat. Divide the freekeh between four serving bowls and top with the stir-fry. Serve hot, garnished with spring onions.

NUTRITION PER SERVING	
Energy	540kcals/2259kJ
Carbohydrate	61g
of which sugar	6g
Fat	13g
of which saturates	3g
Salt	4g
Fibre	4.5g

Millet cashew stir-fry with chilli and lime sauce

This simple stir-fry is light, yet full of flavour and colour. The lime gives it an added zing that contrasts with the sweetness of the toasted cashews and crunchy vegetables.

Dairy free

Low salt

High fibre

SERVES 2
PREP 20 MINS
COOK 20 MINS

100g (3½oz) uncooked millet

50g (1¾oz) cashew nuts

2 tbsp light olive oil

110g (3¾oz) carrot, roughly chopped

110g (3¾oz) cabbage, roughly chopped

100g (3½oz) bean sprouts

85g (3oz) red onion, thinly sliced

FOR THE SAUCE

juice of 1 lime and grated zest of ½ lime

2 tbsp soy sauce

2 tbsp honey

1 red chilli, deseeded and finely chopped

FOR A GLUTEN-FREE OPTION
use gluten-free tamari to replace soy sauce

1 Place the millet in a large saucepan. Cover with 125ml (4¼fl oz) of water and simmer for about 10 minutes or until all the water has been absorbed. Then remove from the heat and set aside.

2 Heat a large wok or frying pan over a high heat. Add the cashew nuts and toast until lightly coloured. Remove from the heat and roughly chop. Add the oil to the pan. Then add the carrots, cabbage, bean sprouts, and onions. Cook, stirring frequently, for about 5 minutes or until lightly cooked.

3 Meanwhile, for the sauce, place all the ingredients in a bowl and mix to combine. Add the millet to the vegetables and mix well. Pour over the chilli and lime sauce, mix well, and cook for 1–2 minutes. Remove from the heat and serve hot.

NUTRITION PER SERVING	
Energy	544kcals/2268kJ
Carbohydrate	66g
of which sugar	25g
Fat	25g
of which saturates	4g
Salt	2.8g
Fibre	6g

Polenta with tomato, mozzarella, pesto, and Parma ham

As a healthy alternative to fried bread, polenta is the perfect foundation for this light lunch or supper dish. The salty Parma ham is complemented by the creamy mozzarella.

SERVES 4
PREP 15 MINS,
COOK 10 MINS

1 tbsp light olive oil

8 x 1cm (½in) thick slices of baked polenta or precooked, shop-bought polenta, about 300g (10oz) in total

2 tomatoes, cut into 8 slices

8 x 1cm (½in) thick slices mozzarella cheese, about 300g (10oz) in total

8 slices Parma ham

85g (3oz) ready-made basil pesto

1 Heat the oil in a large frying pan set over a medium heat. Add the polenta and fry for about 5 minutes on each side, until golden brown. Remove from the pan.

2 Divide the polenta slices between four plates. Top each one with a slice of tomato and mozzarella. Place a slice of ham on each stack and drizzle evenly with the pesto. Serve immediately.

NUTRITION PER SERVING	
Energy	432kcals/1799kJ
Carbohydrate	3g
of which sugar	1.5g
Fat	32g
of which saturates	12g
Salt	1.5g
Fibre	0.7g

SIDES

Anchoïade

There are many versions of this powerful, versatile anchovy paste. Typically French, it has a moreish salty taste, and used sparingly it goes a long way.

Low carb

Low saturated fat

Dairy free

SERVES 6–8
PREP 5 MINS

12 anchovy fillets in oil or brine

2 garlic cloves, crushed

1 spring onion, white part only, chopped

90ml (3fl oz) olive oil

juice and grated zest of ½ small unwaxed lemon

freshly ground black pepper

1 Drain the anchovies. If using anchovies in oil, pat dry between layers of kitchen paper, and if in brine, rinse in cold water before patting dry.

2 Chop the anchovies. Place in the bowl of a food processor, add the garlic, spring onion, and a little oil, and whizz to make a coarse paste. If you prefer, use a mortar and pestle.

3 Trickle in the rest of the oil, a little at a time, with the motor running. Add the lemon juice and zest, and whizz until you have a coarse, thick purée.

4 Adjust the seasoning with a little pepper and serve immediately. Any leftovers can be kept in the fridge for up to 5 days.

NUTRITION PER SERVING	
Energy	84kcals/351kJ
Carbohydrate	0.3g
of which sugar	0.2g
Fat	9g
of which saturates	1.5g
Salt	0.7g
Fibre	0.1g

Roasted red pepper, almond, and chilli pesto

As well as stirring it through pasta, try spreading this zingy pesto on bruschetta and topping it with tomatoes and basil. It also works well on pizza bases.

Low carb

Low saturated fat

MAKES 1 SMALL JAR (ABOUT 175G/6OZ)
PREP 10 MINS

1 red pepper, roasted, deseeded and roughly chopped

4 semi-dried tomatoes in oil, drained

1–2 fat red chillies, deseeded and roughly chopped

2 garlic cloves, lightly crushed

30g (1oz) ground almonds

30g (1oz) grated Parmesan cheese

2 tbsp tomato oil from the jar

salt and freshly ground black pepper

4 tbsp extra virgin olive oil

1 Place the red pepper in a food processor with the semi-dried tomatoes, chillies, garlic, almonds, cheese, tomato oil, and a generous sprinkling of salt and pepper. Run the machine until well blended, stopping and scraping down the sides as necessary. With the machine running, trickle in 2 tablespoons olive oil until you have a glistening paste.

2 Alternatively, put the red pepper, tomatoes, chillies, and garlic in a mortar and pound with a pestle. Gradually add the almonds and salt and pepper. Work in a little of the cheese, then add a little each of the tomato oil and olive oil. Continue until the cheese, tomato oil, and 2 tablespoons olive oil are used up and you have a glistening paste.

3 Spoon into a clean, sterilized jar, top with the remaining olive oil to prevent air getting in, screw the lid on, and store in the refrigerator. Use within 2 weeks.

NUTRITION PER SERVING	
Energy	83kcals/347kJ
Carbohydrate	0.8g
of which sugar	0.7g
Fat	8g
of which saturates	1.5g
Salt	trace
Fibre	0.3g

Hummus

This dip is one of the most widely recognized of all Middle Eastern dishes. It tastes brilliant with warm pitta bread and sticks of carrot, cucumber, celery, and sweet pepper.

Low saturated fat

Dairy free

Gluten free

SERVES 4
PREP 10 MINS

400g can chickpeas

3 tbsp tahini

juice of 3 lemons

3 garlic cloves, chopped

½ tsp salt

pimentón (Spanish paprika), for sprinkling

olive oil, to drizzle

1 Drain and rinse the chickpeas, reserving 4–6 tablespoons of the liquid from the can. Place the chickpeas in a blender or food processor with 3 tablespoons of liquid.

2 Add the tahini, lemon juice, and garlic, then blend until smooth. Add more liquid from the can, if required.

3 Season to taste with salt. Transfer the hummus to a small bowl, sprinkle with paprika, and drizzle with oil. Serve.

NUTRITION PER SERVING

Energy	152kcals/636kJ
Carbohydrate	10g
of which sugar	0.3g
Fat	8g
of which saturates	1g
Salt	0.6g
Fibre	4.5g

try this....
Red pepper hummus

Add 3 skinned, roasted **red peppers** with the other ingredients in step 2.

VEGETABLES

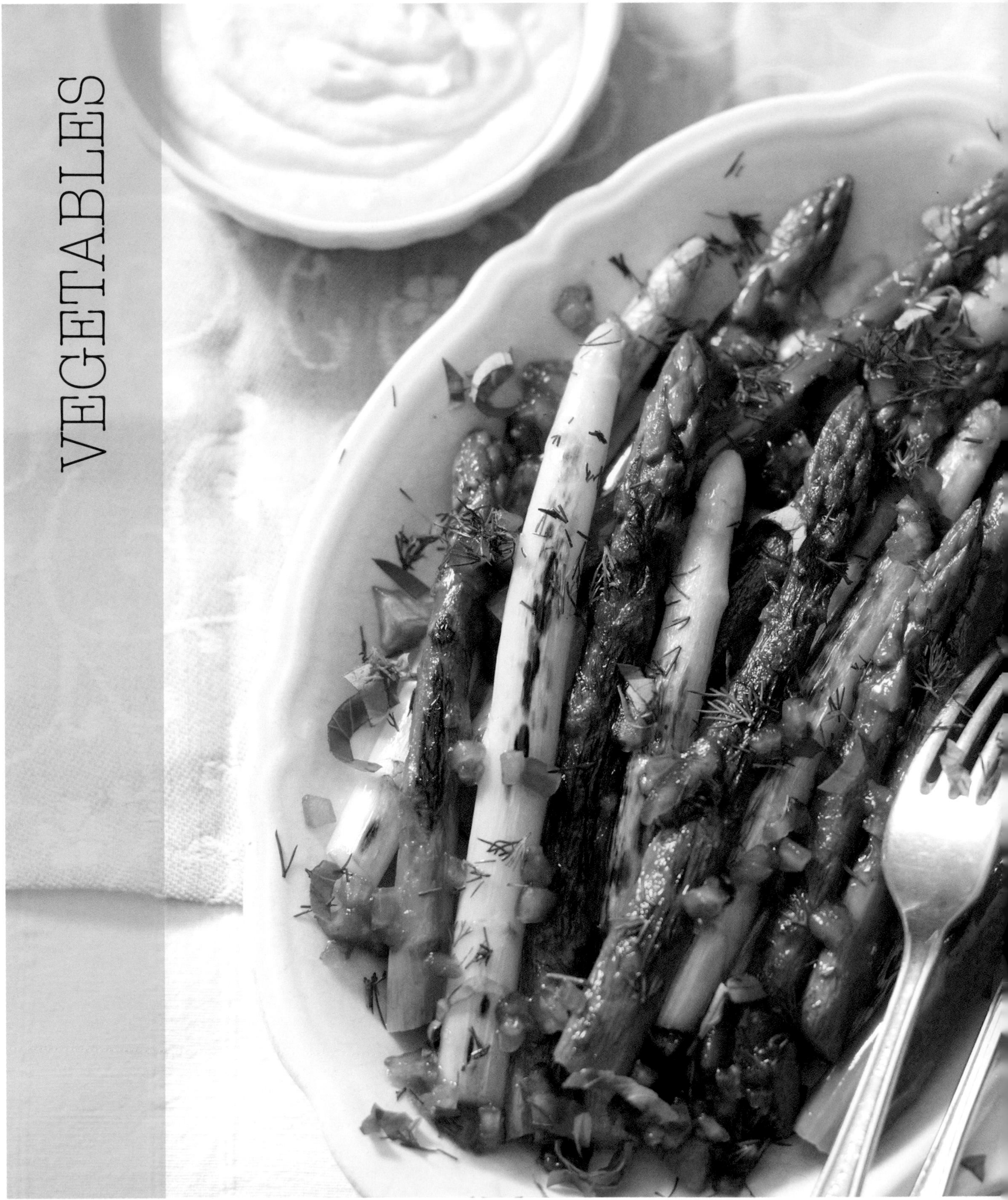

Roasted asparagus with aïoli sauce

Celebrate the first of the new season's asparagus with this easy starter. You can use only green asparagus, or include white and purple spears.

SERVES 4
PREP 10 MINS
COOK 20 MINS

24 asparagus spears, including at least 12 green spears

salt and freshly ground black pepper

3 tbsp olive oil

about 6 tbsp aïoli

1 tbsp finely snipped basil

1 tbsp finely snipped dill

1 tomato, blanched, peeled, deseeded, and finely chopped

1 Trim the asparagus. In a large frying pan, add water to a depth of 5cm (2in) and bring to the boil. Reduce the heat to medium–high and add a little salt. Blanch the asparagus, starting with the white and purple spears, if using, for 7 minutes. Then add the green spears and cook for a further 3 minutes. Drain and refresh under cold running water.

2 Dry the pan and add the oil. Fry the asparagus in a single layer, in batches, for 5 minutes, until a little charred. Remove from the pan and arrange them on plates.

3 Place a generous tablespoon of aïoli on each plate and scatter over the basil, dill, and tomato. Season with a little pepper and serve immediately.

NUTRITION PER SERVING	
Energy	268kcals/1121kJ
Carbohydrate	3.5g
of which sugar	3.5g
Fat	26g
of which saturates	2.6g
Salt	0.1g
Fibre	3g

Spring vegetable stew

Serve this with simple grilled chicken or fish.
The stew brings a lovely garlic flavour of its own.

Low carb

Gluten free

Low salt

High fibre

SERVES 4
PREP 10 MINS
COOK 5 MINS

salt and freshly ground
  black pepper

8–10 asparagus stalks, woody
  ends broken off, chopped
  into 2cm (¾in) lengths, tips
  and stalks kept separate

100g (3½oz) frozen petits pois

1 tbsp butter

1 tbsp olive oil

2 small courgettes, quartered
  lengthways, cut into 1cm
  (½in) cubes

4 large spring onions,
  white part only, cut into
  1cm (½in) pieces

1 garlic clove, finely chopped

3–4 tbsp white wine

100ml (3½fl oz) single cream

1 tbsp finely chopped mint
  leaves

1 In a large pan of boiling salted water, blanch the asparagus stalks together with the petits pois for 1 minute. Add the asparagus tips and cook for a further 1 minute. Drain the vegetables and refresh immediately in a large bowl of cold water, then drain again.

2 In the same pan, melt the butter with the oil. Add the courgettes and spring onions and fry for 2–3 minutes until they start to brown at the edges. Add the garlic and cook for a further minute. Add the wine (it will bubble up and almost evaporate), then the cream, and season well.

3 Add the blanched vegetables to the pan and cook for a further 1–2 minutes over a high heat until the sauce has reduced and thickened. Stir in the mint to serve.

NUTRITION PER SERVING	
Energy	163kcals/672kJ
Carbohydrate	6g
of which sugar	4g
Fat	11.5g
of which saturates	5.5g
Salt	trace
Fibre	4g

Steamed broccoli with bagna càuda

In Italy, this warm, garlicky dip is traditionally served with raw vegetables, like baby carrots and radishes, but it is also good with lightly steamed sprouting broccoli.

Low carb

Gluten free

High fibre

SERVES 4, MAKES ABOUT 150ML (5FL OZ) DIPPING SAUCE
PREP 10 MINS
COOK 10 MINS

500g (1lb 2oz) purple sprouting or young broccoli spears, trimmed

4 chopped anchovies

2 garlic cloves, crushed

100ml (3½fl oz) extra virgin olive oil

25g (scant 1oz) cold butter

1 tsp lemon juice

sea salt and freshly ground black pepper

1 Steam the broccoli for no more than 5 minutes until it is just al dente.

2 Put the anchovies into a mortar and pestle, and grind them to a paste. Put them in a small saucepan along with the garlic and oil, and heat gently for 2 minutes until the garlic is lightly coloured, but not brown.

3 Remove the pan from the heat and use a wire whisk to add the cold butter in small pieces, beating well between additions.

4 Add the lemon juice and continue to whisk until the mixture emulsifies slightly, then season to taste. Serve the dipping sauce warm with the broccoli.

NUTRITION PER SERVING	
Energy	270kcals/1130kJ
Carbohydrate	4g
of which sugar	2.5g
Fat	24g
of which saturates	6g
Salt	0.6g
Fibre	5g

Roasted asparagus and prosciutto bundles

This easy but elegant dish makes a great starter, and each bundle is one perfect serving.

Low carb

Low saturated fat

Dairy free

Gluten free

Low salt

SERVES 4
PREP 10 MINS
COOK 15 MINS

24 fine asparagus spears

2 tbsp olive oil

salt and freshly ground black pepper

4 prosciutto slices

1 Preheat the oven to 230°C (450°F/Gas 8). Trim the asparagus spears of their woody ends, put them on a plate, and rub with 1 tablespoon of olive oil. Season well.

2 Lay a slice of the prosciutto on a board and put one-quarter of the asparagus spears in the middle. Carefully wrap the prosciutto around the asparagus to make a neat parcel, leaving the tips exposed. Lay it on a baking tray with the join of the meat facing down. Repeat to make four parcels. Brush the prosciutto with the remaining olive oil.

3 Bake at the top of the hot oven for 15 minutes, until the prosciutto is crispy and the asparagus cooked through. Serve as it is, or with a Hollandaise sauce, or a poached egg.

NUTRITION PER SERVING	
Energy	119kcals/492kJ
Carbohydrate	2g
of which sugar	2g
Fat	9g
of which saturates	3g
Salt	0.2g
Fibre	2.5g

Green beans with parsley

Very fine French green beans are best for this recipe, but the dressing also works well on larger beans. The cooking time varies depending on the size of the beans.

- Low carb
- Low saturated fat
- Dairy free
- Gluten free
- Low salt

SERVES 4
PREP 10 MINS
COOK 15 MINS

500g (1lb 2oz) fine green beans, topped and tailed

sea salt and freshly ground black pepper

FOR THE PERSILLADE

2 tbsp chopped flat-leaf parsley

1 garlic clove, crushed

2½ tbsp extra virgin olive oil

1 In a large saucepan of lightly salted boiling water, add the beans and cook for 8–10 minutes, or until tender but not soft. Drain well and refresh under cold running water. Keep warm.

2 Meanwhile, combine the parsley, garlic, and oil in a small bowl. Season well.

3 Tip the beans into a serving bowl, stir to coat with the persillade, and serve warm.

NUTRITION PER SERVING	
Energy	100kcals/418kJ
Carbohydrate	4g
of which sugar	2.5g
Fat	7.5g
of which saturates	1g
Salt	0g
Fibre	4g

Barbecued corn on the cob with lime and chilli butter

This butter can also flavour grilled meat or fish. It freezes well for up to six months.

> Gluten free

> Low salt

SERVES 4
PREP 10 MINS
COOK 10 MINS

40g (1½oz) unsalted butter, softened

finely grated zest of 1 lime

½ tsp chilli powder or cayenne pepper

½ tsp sea salt

freshly ground black pepper

4 sweetcorn cobs

a little olive oil

1 Prepare a barbecue for cooking. In a small bowl, mash the butter with the lime zest, chilli powder, sea salt, and black pepper.

2 Cut a square of greaseproof paper, about 15cm (6in) square. Put the butter in the middle of one edge of the paper and shape it like a sausage. Roll the butter sausage up in the paper, then twist the ends like a Christmas cracker so the butter forms a tight shape. Leave in the freezer for at least 30 minutes before use (or freeze until needed).

3 Cook the sweetcorn cobs in a large pan of boiling water for up to 5 minutes until the corn is tender (this will depend on the size and age of the cobs). Drain well, rub them in a little oil, and grill for 6 minutes over a hot barbecue, turning them frequently, until they are lightly charred on all sides.

4 Serve the sweetcorn with a 1cm- (½in-) thick disk of the chilled butter on top to melt.

NUTRITION PER SERVING	
Energy	139kcals/582kJ
Carbohydrate	8g
of which sugar	2g
Fat	10g
of which saturates	5g
Salt	0.2g
Fibre	2g

Barbecued aubergine with garlicky yogurt

These Middle Eastern-inspired aubergine slices are a good vegetarian option at a barbecue.

Low carb

Low saturated fat

Gluten free

Low salt

SERVES 3–4
PREP 10 MINS
COOK 15 MINS

4 tbsp olive oil

1 tbsp chopped coriander leaves

½ tsp ground cumin

2 garlic cloves, crushed

3 tbsp chopped mint leaves

salt and freshly ground black pepper

2 large aubergines, cut into 2cm (¾in) slices

150g (5½oz) Greek yogurt

1 Prepare a barbecue for cooking. In a small bowl, mix together the oil, coriander, cumin, one of the crushed garlic cloves, and 1 tablespoon of the mint, and season well.

2 Brush the slices of aubergine with the herby oil and grill them over a hot barbecue for 3–5 minutes on each side until soft and charred in places.

3 Meanwhile, make the sauce by mixing together the Greek yogurt, remaining crushed garlic clove, and remaining 2 tablespoons of mint. Season well and serve in a bowl alongside the aubergine slices.

NUTRITION PER SERVING	
Energy	164kcals/677kJ
Carbohydrate	4g
of which sugar	3.5g
Fat	15g
of which saturates	4g
Salt	0.1g
Fibre	3g

Savoy cabbage with onions and garlic

This delicious cabbage is the perfect accompaniment to mashed potato and a warming winter stew.

Low carb

Low saturated fat

Gluten free

Low salt

SERVES 4
PREP 5 MINS
COOK 20 MINS

2 tbsp olive oil

1 tbsp butter

1 onion, finely sliced

1 garlic clove, crushed

400g (14oz) Savoy cabbage, shredded

salt and freshly ground black pepper

1 Heat the oil and butter in a large flameproof casserole or heavy-based saucepan with a lid. Add the onion, cover, and cook over a medium heat, stirring frequently, for 10 minutes, until it is well softened, but not brown. Add the garlic and cook for a further minute.

2 Add the cabbage, seasoning, and 4 tablespoons of water. The water will practically sizzle away. Mix it all together and cover. Cook over a low heat for 10 minutes, stirring occasionally, until the cabbage is cooked through.

NUTRITION PER SERVING	
Energy	237kcals/998kJ
Carbohydrate	7g
of which sugar	1.5g
Fat	6g
of which saturates	0.8g
Salt	trace
Fibre	4.5g

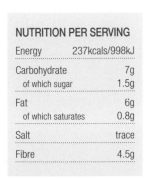

Peas with lettuce

This traditional French dish is often made with tinned petit pois when fresh tender baby peas are not available. Peas are a good source of protein.

SERVES 6
PREP 10 MINS
COOK 10 MINS

250g (9oz) button onions

25g (scant 1oz) butter, softened

500g (1lb 2oz) shelled peas or frozen petit pois

120ml (4fl oz) ham stock or water

1 tsp sugar

salt and freshly ground black pepper

1 tbsp plain flour

2 tbsp finely chopped mint or flat-leaf parsley

2 lettuce hearts, such as Little Gem, trimmed and finely shredded

FOR A GLUTEN-FREE OPTION
use gluten-free flour, and water instead of ham stock

1 Put the onions in a bowl and cover with boiling water. Drain, and remove the skins, keeping the roots intact.

2 Melt 50g (1¾oz) of the butter in a large saucepan and add the onions. Cook over a medium heat for 2 minutes.

3 Add the peas and stock and bring to the boil. Skim off any sediment, then add the sugar and season to taste with salt and pepper. Lower the heat and simmer for a further 5–8 minutes.

4 Mix the remaining butter to a smooth paste with the flour. Gradually add this mixture to the peas, stirring to thicken the sauce. Stir continuously until it has been completely incorporated and there are no lumps.

5 Stir in the mint or parsley and the shredded lettuce hearts, transfer to a serving dish, and serve immediately.

NUTRITION PER SERVING	
Energy	145kcals/607kJ
Carbohydrate	15g
of which sugar	5.5g
Fat	5g
of which saturates	2.7g
Salt	0.1g
Fibre	6g

Glazed carrots with nutmeg

The nutmeg and tiny amount of sugar really bring out the flavour of the carrots, which are full of the antioxidant beta-carotene.

Low carb

Low saturated fat

Gluten free

Low salt

SERVES 4

PREP 5 MINS

COOK 10 MINS

300g (10oz) thin, young carrots, peeled weight, cut into 1cm (½in) rounds

salt and freshly ground black pepper

1 tbsp butter

½ tsp caster sugar

pinch of nutmeg

1 Cook the carrots in plenty of boiling salted water for about 7 minutes until they are quite soft. Drain well.

2 Put the butter in the pan in which you cooked the carrots and allow it to melt over a low heat. Stir in the sugar and nutmeg and cook gently until the sugar dissolves. Return the carrots, season well, and turn them in the butter until well glazed.

try this....
Glazed carrots with garlic and ginger

Sauté the cooked carrots with 1 teaspoon grated fresh **ginger** and 1 crushed **garlic clove** in a little **sesame oil** instead of butter. Sprinkle over 1 teaspoon **black sesame seeds** before serving.

NUTRITION PER SERVING	
Energy	56kcals/233kJ
Carbohydrate	6g
of which sugar	6g
Fat	3.5g
of which saturates	2g
Salt	0.1g
Fibre	2.5g

Courgettes with garlic and mint

Courgettes, when eaten small, are sweet and juicy. The secret to cooking them well is in this recipe. Low in calories, courgettes are high in fibre.

Gluten free

Low salt

SERVES 4

PREP 5 MINS

COOK 5 MINS

2 tbsp olive oil

1 tbsp butter

300g (10oz) small courgettes, sliced into 1cm (½in) rounds

1 garlic clove, crushed

1 tbsp finely chopped mint

salt and freshly ground black pepper

1 Melt the oil and butter in a large flameproof casserole, or heavy-based saucepan with a lid, ideally one that will fit the courgettes in a single layer.

2 Add the courgettes and stir them around so that as many as possible are touching the bottom of the pan. Cover and cook over a medium-high heat for 3 minutes.

3 Remove the lid, stir in the garlic and mint, and season well. Cover again and cook for a further 2 minutes, shaking occasionally, until the courgettes are just cooked and golden brown in places.

try this....
Courgettes with gnocchi, prawns, and cherry tomatoes

To make this into a main course dish, cook 600g (1lb 5oz) **gnocchi** according to packet instructions. Prepare the courgettes as above, but in step 2 add 300g (10oz) cooked, peeled **prawns**. Combine the cooked courgettes with the gnocchi and 200g (7oz) halved **cherry tomatoes**.

NUTRITION PER SERVING	
Energy	91kcals/373kJ
Carbohydrate	1.5g
of which sugar	1g
Fat	9g
of which saturates	3g
Salt	trace
Fibre	1g

Treviso-style radicchio

Radicchio has a slightly bitter flavour and is refreshing in salads. In this Italian recipe, it is cooked and gently caramelized until richly bitter-sweet.

Low carb

Low saturated fat

Dairy free

Gluten free

Low salt

SERVES 4
PREP 5 MINS
COOK 20 MINS

3 tbsp olive oil

white part of 1 large spring onion, chopped

1 garlic clove, crushed

4 heads of radicchio, trimmed at the base and quartered

salt and freshly ground black pepper

1 tbsp balsamic vinegar

1–2 tsp caster sugar

1 In a frying pan, heat the olive oil, add the spring onion and garlic, and cook over a medium heat, until softened and golden.

2 Spread the radicchio in the pan. Cook for 3 minutes, then turn it over using tongs, and cook for a further 3 minutes. Season. Add about 3–4 tablespoons of cold water, cover, and simmer for 10 minutes.

3 Remove the lid, increase the heat, then add the balsamic vinegar and sugar. Cook for 2–3 minutes, turn the radicchio over, and cook for a further 2 minutes. Serve hot.

NUTRITION PER SERVING	
Energy	107kcals/448kJ
Carbohydrate	5.5g
of which sugar	3.3g
Fat	9g
of which saturates	1.5g
Salt	trace
Fibre	1.5g

Sweet potato salad

In Morocco and Tunisia, sweet potatoes are often cooked in tagines, with herbs and spices, and served as a side dish or salad. The combination of green olives and preserved lemon is typically Moroccan.

Low carb

Low saturated fat

Dairy free

Gluten free

Low salt

SERVES 4
PREP 15 MINS
COOK 20 MINS

3–4 tbsp olive oil

1 onion, coarsely chopped

1 tsp cumin seeds

25g (scant 1oz) fresh root ginger, peeled and finely chopped

500g (1lb 2oz) sweet potatoes, peeled and cut into bite-sized cubes

½ tsp Spanish paprika

salt and freshly ground black pepper

8–10 pitted green olives

peel of 1 preserved lemon, finely chopped

juice of ½ lemon

small bunch of flat-leaf parsley, finely chopped

small bunch of coriander, finely chopped

1 Heat the oil in a tagine pot or heavy-based pan. Stir in the onion and cook for 1–2 minutes, until it begins to colour. Add the cumin and ginger, and fry until fragrant.

2 Toss in the sweet potatoes along with the paprika and pour in cold enough water to just cover the base of the pot. Cover and cook gently for 10–12 minutes, until tender but firm, and the liquid has reduced.

3 Season to taste and add the olives, lemon, and lemon juice. Cover and cook for a further 5 minutes to let the flavours combine.

4 Stir in half the herbs and transfer the mixture to a serving dish. Garnish with the rest of the herbs and serve warm or at room temperature.

NUTRITION PER SERVING	
Energy	227kcals/950kJ
Carbohydrate	28g
of which sugar	9g
Fat	11g
of which saturates	1.5g
Salt	0.3g
Fibre	5g

SNACKS AND QUICK BITES

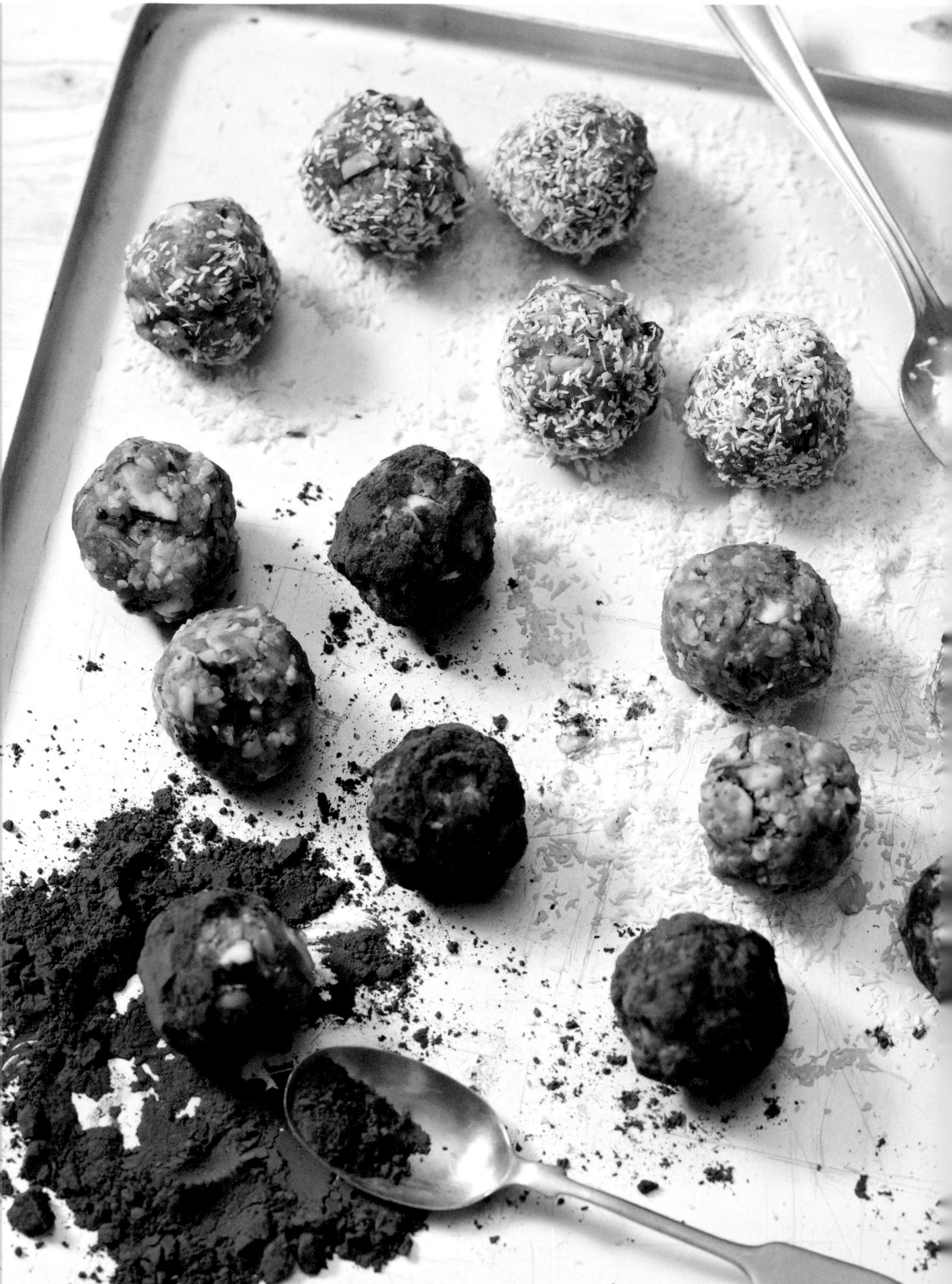

Almond and apricot energy balls

Peanut butter and almonds are both high in monounsaturated fat, and they also offer good amounts of protein and fibre as well as vitamin E.

| Low saturated fat |
| Dairy free |

MAKES 20
PREP 5 MINS

200g (7oz) skin-on almonds

280g (9½oz) ready-to-eat dried apricots

4 tbsp rolled oats

8 tbsp smooth peanut butter

2 tbsp desiccated coconut or cocoa power, to decorate

FOR A GLUTEN-FREE OPTION
use gluten-free oats

1 Place the almonds, apricots, oats, and peanut butter in a blender and whizz until combined.

2 Turn the mixture out onto a clean work surface. With damp hands, shape the mixture into walnut-sized balls.

3 Roll the balls in either desiccated coconut or cocoa powder. Store for up to 3 days in an airtight container.

try this....
Ginger, almond, and apricot energy balls

If you like ginger, add 50g (1¾oz) **crystallized ginger** to the mixture in step 1, and continue as above from step 2.

NUTRITION PER SERVING

Energy	156kcals/653kJ
Carbohydrate	8g
of which sugar	6g
Fat	11g
of which saturates	3g
Salt	0.1g
Fibre	2.5g

Courgette and saffron bruschetta

These gorgeous little bruschettas have a herby flavour. Adding lemon juice and zest brings out the tastes of summer, and may cut down the need for salt.

Dairy free

MAKES 20
PREP 10 MINS
COOK 10–15 MINS

1 small baguette

1 tsp olive oil, plus extra to drizzle

2 garlic cloves, peeled

2 courgettes

pinch of saffron threads

1 tbsp lemon juice, or to taste

salt and freshly ground black pepper

TO GARNISH
grated lemon zest

handful of basil or mint leaves

1 Preheat griddle or grill. Slice the baguette thinly on an angle, drizzle with olive oil, and grill until crisp on both sides.

2 Use one garlic clove to rub gently over the crisp bread.

3 Dice the courgettes and chop the other garlic clove finely. Heat a little oil in a pan and sauté courgette and garlic for 5 minutes.

4 Add a pinch of saffron and cook until vegetables start to turn golden. Add 1 tablespoon lemon juice or more to taste, then season and use to top the crisp bruschetta. Garnish with lemon zest and basil leaves scattered over.

NUTRITION PER SERVING

Energy	52kcals/220kJ
Carbohydrate	8g
of which sugar	0.6g
Fat	1.5g
of which saturates	0.2g
Salt	0.2g
Fibre	0.7g

Crostini napolitana

A classic Italian appetizer, these crostini are best prepared using fresh mozzarella, slightly squishy ripe tomatoes, and Gaeta olives. They are easy to make at home and are traditionally enjoyed with soup.

MAKES 4
PREP 15 MINS
COOK 4–5 MINS

2 large, very ripe tomatoes

175g (6oz) fresh buffalo mozzarella

4 thick slices of focaccia, ciabatta, or toasting bread

4 anchovy fillets, drained and patted dry

freshly ground black pepper

2–3 tbsp fruity olive oil, plus extra for greasing

6 pitted black olives, to finish

leaves from a few sprigs of fresh oregano

1 Blanch the tomatoes in a pan of boiling water for 1–2 minutes, then drain and refresh in cold water. Peel the skins, then quarter, remove the seeds, and finely chop.

2 Preheat the oven to 230°C (450°F/Gas 8) or the grill to high. Cut the mozzarella and arrange evenly on each slice of bread and cover with a layer of tomato. Place the anchovies between two layers of kitchen paper or cling film and flatten lengthways with a rolling pin. Cut each fillet crossways. Place two halved fillets on each slice of bread. Season generously with pepper.

3 Lightly grease a baking sheet. Place the slices of bread on the sheet and drizzle with oil. Bake for 7–8 minutes, or grill for 2–3 minutes, until the mozzarella is melting and bubbling. The crostini should be crisp outside but soft inside. Place three olive halves on top, scatter over the oregano, and allow to cool for 5 minutes before serving.

NUTRITION PER SERVING	
Energy	292kcals/1222kJ
Carbohydrate	71g
of which sugar	3g
Fat	17g
of which saturates	7g
Salt	1.5g
Fibre	2.3g

Fennel-marinated feta and olive skewers

Tasting fresh and clean, this recipe is a delicious vegetarian option. Fennel seeds, which range from yellow to greenish-brown, help with digestion.

Low carb

Gluten free

MAKES 20
PREP 10 MINS,
PLUS CHILLING
COOK 5 MINS

2 tbsp sesame seeds

1 tbsp fennel seeds

200g (7oz) feta cheese

grated zest of 1 lemon

1 tbsp lemon juice

2 tbsp olive oil

1½ tsp cracked black pepper

15g (½oz) mint, finely chopped

½ cucumber, peeled
  and seeded

20 mint leaves

10 pitted black olives, halved

1 Toast the seeds in a dry pan over low heat until nutty and golden for 3 minutes. Cool.

2 Gently rinse the feta in cold water. Drain on paper towels.

3 Cut the feta into 2cm (¾in) cubes. Toss the feta together with the toasted sesame and fennel seeds, lemon zest and juice, oil, and pepper to coat each cube well. Cover and refrigerate for 4 hours to allow the flavours to combine.

4 Sprinkle the feta with chopped mint and toss to coat each cube well.

5 Cut the cucumber into 20 cubes (1cm/½in).

6 Thread one mint leaf, one olive half, one cucumber cube, and one feta cube onto each skewer. Serve chilled or at room temperature.

NUTRITION PER SERVING	
Energy	51kcals/211kJ
Carbohydrate	0.3g
of which sugar	0.3g
Fat	5g
of which saturates	1.8g
Salt	0.4g
Fibre	0.3g

Baked Parmesan and rosemary crisps

The addition of Parmesan and rosemary transforms a simple wrap into a gourmet snack in mere minutes. Parmesan is aged for an average of two years.

Low salt

SERVES 4
PREP 5 MINS
COOK 5–7 MINS

4 large wraps

2 tbsp olive oil

2 tsp rosemary leaves, finely chopped

4 tbsp finely grated Parmesan cheese

freshly ground black pepper

hummus or baba ghanoush, to serve

1 Preheat the oven to 200°C (400°F/Gas 6). Lay the wraps on a work surface and brush all over on both sides with the olive oil.

2 Scatter them with the rosemary and Parmesan and season well with pepper. Place on a baking tray.

3 Bake them at the top of the oven for 5–7 minutes until golden brown, puffed up and crispy. Watch them carefully for the last minute, as they burn quickly.

4 Remove them from the oven, then transfer to a wire rack to cool. When they are cool, break them into jagged, irregular pieces and serve with hummus or baba ghanoush.

NUTRITION PER SERVING	
Energy	295kcals/1242kJ
Carbohydrate	39g
of which sugar	1g
Fat	10.5g
of which saturates	4g
Salt	0.8g
Fibre	2.2g

Multi-seed crackers

Use whichever seeds you like – but reserve larger seeds for decorating so that the crackers do not split.

Low carb

Low saturated fat

Low salt

MAKES 45–50
PREP 20 MINS
COOK 12–15 MINS

150g (5½oz) wholemeal flour

75g (2½oz) plain flour, plus extra for dusting

50g (1¾oz) butter, in pieces, softened

½ tsp fine salt

2 tbsp sesame seeds

2 tbsp linseeds

2 tbsp pumpkin seeds, plus extra for decorating

2 tbsp sunflower seeds, plus extra for decorating

1 tbsp clear honey

1 egg white

1 Preheat the oven to 200°C (400°F/Gas 6). In a large bowl with your fingertips, or in a food processor using the pulse-blend setting, blend the flours, butter, and salt until the mixture resembles fine crumbs. Mix in all the seeds.

2 Dissolve the honey in 100ml (3½fl oz) of warm water. Make a well in the flour and mix in the water to form a soft dough.

3 Turn the dough onto a floured surface and knead it briefly. Roll out as thinly as possible – aim for 1–2mm (¹⁄₂₄–¹⁄₁₂in) thick.

4 Cut the dough into 4 x 6cm (1½ x 2½in) crackers. Leave on the work surface.

5 Whisk the egg white with ½ tablespoon of water and brush the crackers. Scatter the additional pumpkin and sunflower seeds over, and gently press in.

6 Transfer to two baking sheets using a fish slice, and bake for 12–15 minutes, turning carefully halfway, or until both sides are crisp and golden brown. Leave to cool on their trays. Store in an airtight container for up to 2 weeks.

NUTRITION PER SERVING

Energy	38kcals/157kJ
Carbohydrate	3g
of which sugar	0.4g
Fat	2g
of which saturates	0.8g
Salt	trace
Fibre	0.7g

Veggie burgers

These delicious burgers are a great alternative to meat, and contain protein and lots of vitamins and iron.

Low carb

Dairy free

Low salt

MAKES 8
PREP 15 MINS,
PLUS CHILLING
COOK 12–15 MINS

2 tbsp olive oil

1 onion, finely chopped

½ celery stick, finely chopped

1 small carrot, grated

½ small courgette, grated, excess moisture squeezed out

1 garlic clove, crushed

400g can mixed beans, drained and rinsed

50g (1¾oz) fresh breadcrumbs

1 tsp dried mixed herbs

2 tbsp sunflower oil

FOR A GLUTEN-FREE OPTION
use gluten-free breadcrumbs

1 Heat the oil in a heavy-based saucepan. Cook the onion, celery, carrot, and courgette for 5 minutes over a medium heat until softened. Add the garlic and cook for a further minute. Cool.

2 Put the beans in a bowl and mash with a potato masher to a texture you desire. Add the vegetables, breadcrumbs, and herbs, and mix.

3 Use damp hands to form eight 6cm (2½in) patties, pressing them lightly between your palms. Cover and chill for 30 minutes.

4 Heat the oil in a frying pan and cook the burgers for 3–4 minutes on each side, turning carefully, until browned and crispy. Serve warm with ketchup.

try this....
Edamame bean burgers

In step 2, replace the canned beans with 250g (9oz) **edamame beans**. Place the beans in a pan of boiling water for 5 minutes, drain well, and then mash or purée. Add the vegetables, breadcrumbs, and some fresh **mint** to replace the mixed herbs, and mix well. Continue with steps 3–4 as above. Serve with **sweet chilli dipping sauce** (see p320).

NUTRITION PER SERVING	
Energy	112kcals/468kJ
Carbohydrate	12g
of which sugar	2.5g
Fat	6g
of which saturates	0.8g
Salt	0.5g
Fibre	3.4g

Salt and pepper squid

Squid is an economical source of low-fat protein. It is also high in selenium (an antioxidant), copper (vital for forming red blood cells), and B vitamins.

Low saturated fat

Dairy free

SERVES 4
PREP 10 MINS
COOK 6–8 MINS

1 tbsp sea salt flakes

1 tbsp black peppercorns

4 tbsp plain flour

4 tbsp cornflour

¼–½ tsp chilli flakes (optional)

4 squid tubes, cleaned, about 300g (10oz) in total

300ml (10fl oz) vegetable oil, for deep-frying

lemon wedges, to serve

1 Using a mortar and pestle, crush the sea salt and peppercorns until fine. Place the flours in a bowl and stir in the sea salt, pepper, and the chilli flakes (if using).

2 Make a slit down one edge of each squid pouch and open it out flat. Using a sharp knife, score a diamond pattern on the inside of each pouch. Cut each into eight pieces. Dust the pieces in the seasoned flour.

3 Heat the vegetable oil to 180°C (350°F) in a medium, heavy-based pan. To check the temperature of the oil without a thermometer, carefully lower a cube of bread into the oil. The oil is hot enough when a piece of bread, dropped in, sizzles and starts to turn golden brown after 1 minute.

4 Cook the squid, in four batches, for 1½–2 minutes, or until golden brown, returning the oil to 180°C (350°F) between batches. Transfer to a plate lined with kitchen paper to drain, then place into a warm oven to keep warm. Repeat, working quickly, to cook all the squid. Serve piping hot, with lemon wedges.

NUTRITION PER SERVING	
Energy	264kcals/1108kJ
Carbohydrate	24.5g
of which sugar	0.5g
Fat	12.5g
of which saturates	2g
Salt	3.9g
Fibre	0.5g

Prawn and guacamole tortilla stacks

These tasty Mexican-style canapés are simple to make. Assemble the stacks just before serving to keep them fresh.

Low carb

Low saturated fat

Dairy free

Low salt

MAKES 50
PREP 15 MINS,
PLUS MARINATING
COOK 10–15 MINS,
PLUS COOLING

5 wheat or corn tortillas

1 litre (1¾ pints) sunflower oil

2 ripe avocados, stoned and skinned

juice of 1 lime

Tabasco sauce

4 tbsp coriander, finely chopped, plus extra as a garnish

4 spring onions, trimmed and finely chopped

sea salt and freshly ground black pepper

50 large cooked, peeled cold water prawns

FOR A GLUTEN FREE OPTION
use gluten-free tortillas

1 Cut at least 100 discs out of the tortillas with a 3 cm (1¼in) pastry cutter. Heat the oil in a medium-sized saucepan. Drop the tortillas into the oil, a handful at a time, and deep-fry until golden. Do not overcrowd the pan, or the tortillas will not crisp up properly. Remove them with a slotted spoon, drain on kitchen paper, put aside, and allow to cool.

2 In a bowl, mash the avocados with half the lime juice, a dash of Tabasco, 3 tablespoons of the chopped coriander, the chopped onions, and sea salt and pepper to taste.

3 When there are about 30 minutes left before serving, marinate the prawns with the remaining lime juice and the remaining 1 tablespoon chopped coriander in a small bowl.

4 To serve, pipe a little guacamole onto a tortilla using a piping bag with small plain nozzle, top it with another tortilla, pipe more guacamole on top, and finish with a prawn and a little of the remaining coriander as a garnish.

try this....
Minted pea and prawn tortilla stacks

In step 2, replace the guacamole with **minted pea purée**. Cook 400g (14oz) frozen **peas** for 4–5 minutes, then drain and place in a blender with 2 tablespoons **mint sauce** and 150g (5½oz) **half-fat crème fraîche**. Purée until smooth.

NUTRITION PER SERVING	
Energy	47kcals/197kJ
Carbohydrate	4g
of which sugar	0.2g
Fat	2.5g
of which saturates	0.5g
Salt	0.2g
Fibre	0.5g

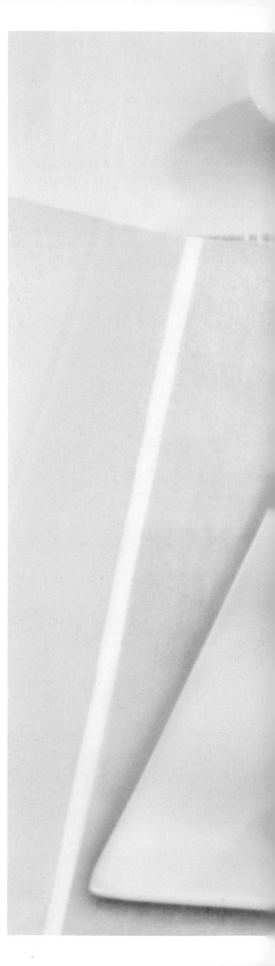

Lemongrass-marinated prawn skewers

Lemongrass gets its distinctive lemony fragrance from lemonal, which has antifungal and antimicrobial properties.

> Low carb
>
> Low saturated fat
>
> Dairy free

SERVES 4
PREP 15 MINS,
PLUS MARINATING
COOK 10 MINS

2 garlic cloves, roughly chopped

½ red chilli, deseeded and roughly chopped

2 lemongrass stalks, bottom (thickest) one-third only, peeled of hard layers, and roughly chopped

2.5cm (1in) fresh root ginger, finely chopped

1 tbsp chopped coriander roots or stalks

2 tbsp fish sauce

2 tsp soft light brown sugar

1 tbsp lime juice, plus lime wedges, to serve

40 raw, shelled and deveined king prawns

1 Prepare a barbecue for cooking. To make the marinade, simply put all the ingredients, except the prawns, in a blender or food processor and blitz to a fine paste.

2 Toss the king prawns in the marinade, cover, and leave in the fridge to marinate for 1 hour. Meanwhile, soak eight bamboo skewers in water, as this will help to stop them burning on the barbecue.

3 Thread five prawns onto each skewer, threading through the top and bottom of the prawn to make a curved "C"-shape. Grill the prawns on the barbecue for 2–3 minutes on each side, until pink and charred in places. Serve with a squeeze of lime.

NUTRITION PER SERVING	
Energy	128kcals/541kJ
Carbohydrate	3g
of which sugar	3g
Fat	1g
of which saturates	0.1g
Salt	2g
Fibre	0g

Crispy polenta fish fingers with easy tartare sauce

Home-made fish fingers are fun and healthy, and a light polenta coating gives them a lovely crunchy finish. Coley is sustainable, making it a good substitute for cod.

Dairy free

Low salt

SERVES 4
PREP 10 MINS,
PLUS CHILLING
COOK 5 MINS

400g (14oz) skinless firm-fleshed white fish fillets, such as coley

2 tbsp plain flour

1 egg, lightly beaten

100g (3½oz) fine polenta

salt and freshly ground black pepper

sunflower oil, for frying

FOR THE TARTARE SAUCE

2 cornichons, coarsely grated

6 heaped tbsp good-quality mayonnaise, preferably home-made mayonnaise

1 tbsp white wine vinegar

1 tbsp capers, very finely chopped

finely grated zest of ½ lemon

1 heaped tbsp finely chopped dill

1 Cut the fish into 2cm- (¾in-) thick strips. Pat it dry with kitchen paper. Lay the flour, egg, and polenta out in three shallow bowls. Season the flour well.

2 Coat the fish fingers by dusting them first with the flour, then dipping them in the egg, then rolling them in the polenta, until they are well covered. Put them on a plate, cover with cling film, and chill for 30 minutes. This helps the coating to stick.

3 Meanwhile, make the tartare sauce. First, put the grated cornichons onto a chopping board and chop again, finely, with a sharp knife. Mix the cornichons, mayonnaise, vinegar, capers, lemon zest, and dill, and season well. Cover and chill until needed.

4 Heat a large, deep-sided frying pan and add enough oil to cover the base. Fry the fish fingers for 2 minutes on each side, turning carefully, until golden and crisp all over. Rest them on a plate lined with kitchen paper while you cook the rest. Serve with home-made chunky oven fries or Cajun-spiced potato wedges and the tartare sauce.

NUTRITION PER SERVING	
Energy	478kcals/1988kJ
Carbohydrate	23g
of which sugar	0.5g
Fat	32g
of which saturates	4.5g
Salt	0.8g
Fibre	1g

Prawn kebabs

A popular way to enjoy the jumbo prawns caught off the coast of North Africa is to thread them onto skewers and grill them quickly over charcoal.

Low carb

Low saturated fat

Dairy free

Gluten free

SERVES 4
PREP 10 MINS,
PLUS MARINATING
COOK 6 MINS

16 large prawns

juice of 2 lemons, plus 1 lemon extra, cut into wedges, to serve

4 garlic cloves, crushed

1 tsp ground cumin

1 tsp pimentón (Spanish paprika)

sea salt

8–12 cherry tomatoes

1 green bell pepper, cut into bite-sized squares

oil, for greasing

1 Shell the prawns down to the tail, leaving a little bit of shell at the end. Remove the veins and discard. Mix together the lemon juice, garlic, cumin, paprika, and a little salt and rub over the prawns. Leave the prawns to marinate for 30 minutes.

2 Meanwhile, prepare the charcoal grill. Thread the prawns onto metal skewers, alternating with the tomatoes and green pepper pieces, until all the ingredients are used up.

3 Place the kebabs on an oiled rack over the glowing coals and cook for 2–3 minutes on each side, basting with any of the leftover marinade, until the prawns are tender and the tomatoes and peppers are lightly browned. Serve immediately with lemon wedges.

NUTRITION PER SERVING	
Energy	106kcals/444kJ
Carbohydrate	2.5g
of which sugar	2.5g
Fat	4g
of which saturates	0.6g
Salt	0.4g
Fibre	1.5g

Chinese minced prawn toasts

These fabulous snacks are always far better when home-made, and are a real children's favourite. The paste can be made ahead and put in the fridge.

Low saturated fat

Dairy free

SERVES 4
PREP 10 MINS
COOK 10 MINS

175g (6oz) raw king prawns, shelled, deveined, and roughly chopped

1 tsp cornflour

2 spring onions, finely chopped

½ tsp finely grated fresh root ginger

1 tsp soy sauce

1 tsp sesame oil

1 egg white

4 large slices of day-old white bread, crusts removed

sunflower oil, for deep-frying

30g (1oz) white sesame seeds

1 Put the prawns, cornflour, spring onions, ginger, soy sauce, sesame oil, and egg white into a food processor, and process to a fairly smooth paste.

2 Cut each piece of bread into quarters and spread with a little of the prawn paste, taking care to go right up to the edges and mounding it up slightly so that all the paste is used up.

3 Heat a 5cm (2in) depth of oil in a large, heavy-based frying pan or deep fryer. It is ready when a crust of spare bread, dropped in, sizzles and starts to turn golden brown. Spread the sesame seeds out on a plate. Press each piece of bread, prawn-side down, into the sesame seeds, so each is topped with a thin layer.

4 Fry the prawn toasts in small batches, sesame seed-side down, for 1–2 minutes, until becoming golden brown, then carefully turn them over and fry for a further minute. Drain the cooked toasts on a plate lined with kitchen paper while you fry the remaining pieces. Serve hot.

try this....
Chia and sesame prawn toasts with chilli sauce

Replace the white bread with **Granary** and half the sesame seeds with **chia seeds**. To make a sweet chilli dipping sauce, mix 6 tablespoons **sweet chilli sauce** with 2 tablespoons **rice wine vinegar**.

NUTRITION PER SERVING

Energy	287kcals/1200kJ
Carbohydrate	20g
of which sugar	1.5g
Fat	17g
of which saturates	2.5g
Salt	1g
Fibre	1.5g

Oysters with shallot and vinegar dressing

Take great care when shucking an oyster, as the knife can slip all too easily. For safety's sake, wrap your knife-free hand in a thick towel to protect it.

Low carb

Low saturated fat

Dairy free

Gluten free

SERVES 4–6
PREP 15 MINS

24 oysters in their shells

crushed ice

4 tbsp red wine vinegar

1 large or 2 small shallots, very finely chopped

1 To prepare the oysters, discard any that have opened or do not close tightly straight away, when tapped on the work surface. Use an oyster knife, and hold the oysters over a bowl as you open them. Carefully shuck the oysters one by one, catching any liquid in the bowl and transferring the opened oysters in their shells and their liquid to the fridge as you go.

2 Arrange the oysters on an oyster plate with ice, or pack four serving dishes with lots of crushed ice and place the oysters on top.

3 Mix the vinegar and shallots together and put into a small dish. Place in the centre of the oysters – or the middle of the table – and serve.

NUTRITION PER SERVING	
Energy	125–84kcals/ 530–353kJ
Carbohydrate	0.9–0.6g
of which sugar	0.9–0.6g
Fat	2.4–1.6g
of which saturates	0.4–0.2g
Salt	2.3–1.5g
Fibre	0.5–0.3g

Grapefruit scallop ceviche skewers

The scallops need at least three hours to marinate, which gives you plenty of time to get ahead.

Low carb

Low saturated fat

Gluten free

Low salt

MAKES 20
PREP 20 MINS,
PLUS MARINATING

40 queen scallops or 20 king scallops

grated zest and juice of 1 grapefruit

juice of 2 limes

4 tbsp olive oil

1 fresh red chilli, deseeded and finely chopped

½ red onion, finely chopped

½ tsp salt

1 tbsp finely chopped coriander

1 spring onion, finely sliced

1 If using king scallops, slice in half crossways.

2 Combine the scallops, zest and juice of grapefruit, juice of lime, oil, chilli, onion, and salt in a non-metallic bowl. Cover and refrigerate for 3 hours, stirring occasionally.

3 Remove scallops with a slotted spoon. Toss to coat with coriander and spring onion. Thread two queen scallops or two king scallop halves onto each of the 20 wooden skewers or toothpicks (7.5cm/3in). Serve chilled with herbed yogurt dip.

NUTRITION PER SERVING	
Energy	48kcals/200kJ
Carbohydrate	1g
of which sugar	1g
Fat	2.5g
of which saturates	0.4g
Salt	0.2g
Fibre	0.1g

Spinach and garlic pizza

This Valencian version of the Neapolitan pizza is given a juicy topping of greens finished with a Middle Eastern sprinkling of pine nuts, raisins, and olive oil.

| Low saturated fat |
| Dairy free |
| Low salt |
| High fibre |

SERVES 2
PREP 10 MINS, PLUS RISING AND PROVING
COOK 20 MINS

100g (3½oz) strong bread flour

salt

25g (scant 1oz) fresh yeast or 1 tsp dried yeast

1 tbsp olive oil, plus extra for greasing

FOR THE TOPPING
about 500g (1lb 2oz) spinach leaves, rinsed

1–2 garlic cloves, slivered

1 tbsp pine nuts, toasted

1 tbsp raisins or sultanas

olive oil, for drizzling

1 Sift the flour with a little salt into a warm bowl. Dissolve the yeast in 4 tablespoons warm water, sprinkle with a little flour, and leave for about 15 minutes to froth.

2 Make a well in the flour, then pour in the oil and the yeast mixture. Draw the flour into the liquid and knead the dough into a smooth ball. Place the dough in a bowl, cover with cling film or wipe with an oiled palm, and leave in a warm place for 1–2 hours, until doubled in size.

3 Preheat the oven to 220°C (425°F/Gas 7). Wash the spinach, drain all but a little water and cook it sprinkled with a little salt in a lidded pan. As soon as the leaves start to wilt, remove from the heat, squeeze dry, and chop roughly. Set aside.

4 Knead the dough well to distribute the air bubbles and cut in half, then pat or roll each piece into a round about 1cm (½in) thick. Transfer to a lightly oiled baking tray, top with the spinach, sprinkle with garlic, pine nuts, and raisins, drizzle with a little olive oil, and leave for 10 minutes to prove.

5 Bake for 15–20 minutes, until the crust is puffy and blistered at the edges.

NUTRITION PER SERVING

Energy	360kcals/1506kJ
Carbohydrate	47g
of which sugar	9g
Fat	13g
of which saturates	1.5g
Salt	0.9g
Fibre	9g

try this....
Spinach and ricotta pizza

At the end of step 3, roughly mix the spinach with 200g (7oz) **ricotta cheese** and 3 tablespoons **Parmesan cheese**. Continue with steps 4 and 5 as above.

Four fruits power bar

These bars are best eaten the day you make them, to get the maximum goodness from the freshly sprouted grains. Sour cherries give them a sharp flavour.

Low saturated fat

Dairy free

Low salt

MAKES 16
PREP 30 MINS, PLUS
SOAKING AND DRYING

150g (5½oz) wheat grains

150g (5½oz) dry apricots

50g (1¾oz) raisins

50g (1¾oz) blackcurrants

50g (1¾oz) sour cherries

50g (1¾oz) walnuts, soaked for 4 hours, dried and lightly pan-toasted

50g (1¾oz) sesame seeds, pan-toasted

1 To sprout the wheat grains, soak for 12 hours or overnight. Rinse the grains thoroughly and put in a large glass jar (grains expand to two to three times their initial volume). Cover the opening and neck of the jar with muslin cloth and attach it with string or a strong rubber band. Place at a 45° angle in a well-lit spot but not in direct sunlight. Rinse the grains each morning and evening by pouring water through the muslin and emptying it out.

2 The sprouts are ready when seedlings approximately 0.5–1cm (¼in) in length appear. Rinse the seedlings thoroughly in clean water, strain, and spread on a clean cloth to dry. The sprouted grains are ready to use when they are dry to the touch. Place the apricots and raisins in a blender and blend to a paste. Add half of the sprouted grains and blackcurrants and blend until crushed (but not blended to a purée).

3 Transfer to a mixing bowl and add the rest of the grains, berries, and the cherries. Mix well with a wooden spoon. Chop the walnuts into small chunks and add them to the mix. Sprinkle the sesame seeds on a flat surface. Roll out the mixture, or press it with clean hands, over the seeds into a rectangle 1cm (½in) thick. Use a sharp knife to cut the mixture into small rectangular bars. Place the bars on a rack and leave to dry out for a few hours.

NUTRITION PER SERVING

Energy	111kcals/464kJ
Carbohydrate	16g
of which sugar	8g
Fat	4g
of which saturates	0.6g
Salt	trace
Fibre	2g

Cranberry, orange, and chocolate quinoa bars

The perfect breakfast on the go or handy snack, these sweet, chewy, and wholesome bars feel like a treat, but pack a big nutritional punch and will keep you full all morning.

Dairy free

Gluten free

Low salt

MAKES 12
PREP 20 MINS,
PLUS COOLING
COOK 5 MINS

125g (4¼oz) almonds, roughly chopped

125g (4¼oz) quinoa flakes

40g (1¼oz) sunflower seeds

40g (1¼oz) chia seeds

100g (3½oz) dried cranberries

125g (4½oz) puffed rice cereal

50g (1¾oz) dark chocolate chips

grated zest of 2 large oranges

85ml (2¾fl oz) coconut oil

120ml (4fl oz) clear honey

30g (1oz) light brown sugar

1 Place the almonds, quinoa flakes, sunflower seeds, chia seeds, dried cranberries, puffed rice cereal, chocolate chips, and orange zest in a bowl. Mix well with a wooden spoon and set aside. Grease and line a 20 x 25cm (8 x 10in) baking tin with greaseproof paper.

2 Heat the oil, honey, and sugar in a saucepan over a medium heat. Cook, stirring occasionally, for about 5 minutes, or until the sugar has melted and the mixture is bubbling. Set aside to cool for about 2 minutes.

3 Pour the cooled honey mixture into the dry ingredients. Mix using a wooden spoon until well incorporated, making sure the chocolate chips have melted and are evenly combined. Spoon the mixture into the prepared baking tin. Press down firmly with the back of a wooden spoon to make a roughly even layer.

4 Place the baking tin in the fridge for at least 4 hours, to allow the mixture to cool and harden. Remove from the fridge, turn out onto a chopping board, and cut into bars. These can be stored in an airtight container in the fridge for up to 5 days.

NUTRITION PER SERVING

Energy	292kcals/1222kJ
Carbohydrate	34g
of which sugar	20g
Fat	15g
of which saturates	6g
Salt	0g
Fibre	3g

Matcha latte

There isn't a hint of bitterness in this blissfully creamy tea. The powdery matcha makes a bubbly froth when whipped and imparts a pale green tinge to this easy-to-make choco-rich latte.

Gluten free

SERVES 2
PREP 5 MINS
COOK 10 MINS

350ml (12fl oz) plain sweetened almond milk

15g (½oz) white chocolate

2 tsp matcha powder, plus extra to garnish

120ml (4fl oz) water heated to 80°C (175°F)

1 Heat the milk and chocolate in a saucepan on a medium heat, stirring constantly, until the mixture simmers and becomes creamy. Remove from the heat and set aside.

2 Whisk the matcha powder and hot water in a bowl to form a thin paste. Add the hot milk and chocolate mixture and whisk briskly until foamy. Pour into cups. Garnish with a pinch of matcha powder and serve hot.

NUTRITION PER SERVING	
Energy	82kcals/343kJ
Carbohydrate	9g
of which sugar	9g
Fat	4g
of which saturates	1.5g
Salt	0g
Fibre	0g

Coconut matcha

Naturally sweet and creamy, this smoothie is a great afternoon pick-me-up. The coconut cream brings healthy fatty acids to the mix, while the avocado provides a good dose of potassium and vitamins K and C.

Gluten free

SERVES 2
PREP 5 MINS
COOK 5 MINS

2 tbsp coconut flakes

½ avocado

1 tsp matcha powder

150ml (5fl oz) coconut-flavoured yogurt

300ml (10fl oz) chilled coconut water

1 Preheat the oven to 180°C (350°F/Gas 4). Place the coconut flakes on a baking tray and toast for 4½ minutes, or until golden brown.

2 Place the flakes in the blender along with the remaining ingredients and blend until creamy. Serve in chilled glasses with a straw.

NUTRITION PER SERVING	
Energy	307kcals/1284kJ
Carbohydrate	16g
of which sugar	15g
Fat	24g
of which saturates	15g
Salt	0.5g
Fibre	4.4g

Roasted chicory mocha

Cacao nibs are slightly bitter in their raw form, but full of antioxidants, while roasted chicory, long used as a coffee substitute, helps to remove toxins from the body and aids digestion. Their combined goodness makes for a potent drink.

Dairy free

Gluten free

SERVES 4
PREP 5 MINS
COOK 5–7 MINS

2 tbsp coarsely ground roasted chicory root

12 raw cacao nibs, crushed

900ml (1½ pints) boiling water

honey or sugar, to taste

1 Place the roasted chicory and cacao nibs (including husks) in a teapot.

2 Add the boiling water and leave to infuse for 4 minutes.

3 Strain the infusion into cups or mugs and sweeten with honey or sugar to taste. Serve at once.

NUTRITION PER SERVING

Energy	70kcals/293kJ
Carbohydrate	8g
of which sugar	6g
Fat	4.5g
of which saturates	2.5g
Salt	0g
Fibre	1g

Raspberry lemon verbena

The raspberries create a beautiful shade of coral, while the verbena is calming, soothing, and a natural tonic that aids digestion. The lemon flavour is tangy but not acidic.

Low carb
Low saturated fat
Dairy free
Gluten free
Low salt

SERVES 4
PREP 5 MIN
COOK 6–8 MINS

10 large raspberries, fresh or frozen, plus 4 extra, to garnish

3 tbsp dried lemon verbena leaves

900ml (1½ pints) boiling water

1 Place the raspberries in a teapot and muddle them using a muddler or pestle.

2 Add the lemon verbena leaves and pour in the boiling water. Infuse for 4 minutes. Strain into cups or mugs, and garnish each with a raspberry.

NUTRITION PER SERVING	
Energy	3kcals/13kJ
Carbohydrate	0.5g
of which sugar	0.5g
Fat	0g
of which saturates	0g
Salt	0g
Fibre	0.4g

Figs on the terrace

Aromatic sage has a powerful flavour that combines with sweet figs in this Italian summer tea.

Low saturated fat

Dairy free

Gluten free

Low salt

SERVES 2
PREP 10 MINS
COOK 10 MINS

2 fresh or dried figs, quartered

2 fresh sage leaves, or ¼ tsp dried whole sage leaves

100ml (3½ fl oz) boiling water, plus 400ml (14fl oz) water heated to 85°C (185°F)

2 tbsp Longevity White tea leaves (Shou Mei)

ice cubes

1 Divide the figs and sage between two tumblers. Muddle with a muddler or pestle, then add the boiling water. Leave to cool.

2 Place the tea leaves in a teapot, add the heated water, and infuse for 2 minutes. Then strain into the tumblers and stir to mix with the fig and sage. Leave to cool. Stir and add the ice cubes before serving.

NUTRITION PER SERVING	
Energy	24kcals/100kJ
Carbohydrate	4.5g
of which sugar	4.5g
Fat	0g
of which saturates	0g
Salt	0g
Fibre	1g

Kiwi and pear juice

Kiwis are nutrient-dense, offering good nutrition for few calories. Pears are also very low in calories, and a good source of minerals.

Low saturated fat

Dairy free

Gluten free

SERVES 1
PREP 5 MINS

2 kiwi fruit, peeled

1 large ripe Conference pear

¼ cucumber

large handful of baby spinach

1 Chop the fruits into large chunks. Feed all the ingredients into a juicer and blend until smooth.

2 Pour the juice into a glass, add an ice cube, and serve immediately.

NUTRITION PER SERVING	
Energy	154kcals/581kJ
Carbohydrate	29g
of which sugar	29g
Fat	0g
of which saturates	0g
Salt	0g
Fibre	5g

Blackberry lemonade

Blackberries have antioxidant, kidney-toning, and detoxifying properties while an infusion made from their leaves enhances the anti-inflammatory effects. Serve with ice, or as a warm drink for a sore throat.

Low saturated fat

Dairy free

Gluten free

Low salt

SERVES 2
PREP 10 MINS
COOK 13–15 MINS

4 tsp dried blackberry leaves, or 12 fresh leaves

300g (10oz) blackberries, rinsed

2 lemons, juiced, plus a few thin slices for decoration (optional)

3 tbsp maple syrup

1 To make an infusion with the leaves, boil 300ml (10fl oz) of water, pour over the leaves, and leave to infuse for 10 minutes. Strain the mixture, reserving the liquid to use in the lemonade. Discard the leaves.

2 Place the blackberries in a food processor or blender and blitz to a pulp. If you don't like the gritty texture of the seeds in your drink, strain the pulp through a colander and collect the smooth juice.

3 Pour the lemon juice, blackberry juice, and 250ml (9fl oz) of the blackberry leaf infusion into a jug, add the maple syrup, and stir well. Pour into large glasses, decorate each with a slice of lemon, and serve.

NUTRITION PER SERVING	
Energy	118kcals/494kJ
Carbohydrate	27g
of which sugar	25g
Fat	0g
of which saturates	0g
Salt	0g
Fibre	6g

Lemon balm and honey purée

This purée requires young leaves, so is best prepared in late spring. Add 1–2 teaspoons to boiling or chilled water.

| Low saturated fat |
| Dairy free |
| Gluten free |
| Low salt |

MAKES 125G (4½OZ)
PREP 5 MINS

20g (¾oz) fresh lemon balm leaves

100g (3½oz) runny honey

juice of ½ lemon

1 Place the leaves in a blender or food processor, add the honey and lemon juice, and blend until you get a smooth green purée.

2 Dilute with water and drink. The purée will last for a week or two, if kept refrigerated.

NUTRITION PER SERVING

Energy	12kcals/50kJ
Carbohydrate	3g
of which sugar	3g
Fat	0g
of which saturates	0g
Salt	0g
Fibre	0g

Health boost juice

This is a beneficial tonic, especially in the winter. Onion squash supplies anti-inflammatory and antioxidant properties, while ginger can improve digestion. Grapefruit helps ward off colds and celery helps detoxify the body.

Low saturated fat

Dairy free

Gluten free

SERVES 2
PREP 15 MINS

100g (3½oz) onion squash

1 small piece fresh ginger root, skin on

1 large grapefruit, peeled and pith removed

2 celery sticks and leaves, roughly chopped

1 Cut the squash in half, scoop out all the seeds, and discard or reserve them to roast later and use as an ingredient in other recipes, or as a topping for salads and soups. Leave the skin on the squash to benefit from its nutrients and chop the flesh if necessary, so it fits through the hopper of your juicer.

2 Juice all the ingredients and combine in a jug. Strain through a sieve to remove the grapefruit pips and serve immediately in long glasses.

NUTRITION PER SERVING	
Energy	53kcals/222kJ
Carbohydrate	11g
of which sugar	7g
Fat	0g
of which saturates	0g
Salt	0g
Fibre	4g

Chilled pea and avocado soup shot

Vibrant green and silky, this quick-to-make recipe celebrates the flavours of summer. Home-made stock is a good source of protein and niacin, a B vitamin that helps our nerves to function.

Low carb

Low saturated fat

MAKES 20
PREP 5 MINS
COOK 5 MINS

140g (5oz) frozen peas

2 ripe avocados halved, peeled, and stoned

4 spring onions, trimmed

4 tbsp lemon juice

10g (¼oz) fresh coriander

chilli powder to taste

600ml (1 pint) chicken stock, chilled

1 tbsp sour cream

salt and freshly ground black pepper

TO GARNISH

50g (1¾oz) sour cream

2 tbsp finely chopped coriander

1 Blanch the peas in boiling water for 2 minutes and drain.

2 Purée all the ingredients together in a food processor until smooth, and taste to check the seasoning.

3 Garnish with the sour cream and finely chopped coriander.

NUTRITION PER SERVING

Energy		43kcals/179kJ
Carbohydrate		1g
of which sugar		0.6g
Fat		4g
of which saturates		1g
Salt		0.2g
Fibre		1g

try this....
Edamame, kale, and avocado soup shots

Replace the peas with **edamame beans**, then add 2 large handfuls of **baby spinach**, and replace coriander with 1 tablespoon **fennel**.

Icy ginger yerba mate

Traditionally, South American yerba mate is served in a gourd cup, sipped through a bombilla straw, and passed from guest to guest. Here is an easy iced version with a little zing from ginger and honey.

Low saturated fat

Dairy free

Gluten free

SERVES 2
PREP 5 MINS
COOK 5–7 MINS,
PLUS CHILLING

2 tbsp yerba mate leaves

½ tsp grated ginger root

500ml (16fl oz) water heated to 90°C (195°F)

1 tsp honey

ice cubes

1 Place the leaves and ginger in a teapot. Add the hot water and steep for 5 minutes.

2 Strain into a glass jug. Add the honey and stir. Leave to cool, then chill in the fridge. Pour into two tumblers and add the ice cubes.

NUTRITION PER SERVING	
Energy	12kcals/50kJ
Carbohydrate	3g
of which sugar	3g
Fat	0g
of which saturates	0g
Salt	0g
Fibre	0g

Valentine's special

This is a feel-good drink: nutritious, healthy, and life-enhancing. It contains antioxidant-rich soft fruits and coconut water, which help rehydrate the body and reduce feelings of fatigue.

Low saturated fat

Dairy free

Gluten free

SERVES 2
PREP 5 MINS

½ punnet raspberries, washed

½ punnet blueberries, washed

a dash of rose syrup

¼ tsp cardamom seeds, crushed (no more than 10 pods)

2 tbsp pistachio nuts, shelled

250ml (9fl oz) coconut water, to top up

1 Put all the ingredients in a powerful food processor or blender and blitz to a smooth consistency. If serving immediately, pour into long glasses and serve. Otherwise the drink will last for up to 2 days if stored in a tightly sealed bottle and refrigerated.

NUTRITION PER SERVING	
Energy	146kcals/ 611kJ
Carbohydrate	12g
of which sugar	12g
Fat	7.5g
of which saturates	1g
Salt	0.3g
Fibre	2.5g

Strawberry and macadamia smoothie

This healthy twist on strawberries and cream uses a cream made from coconut pulp and macadamia nuts. The nuts are a rich source of monounsaturated fatty acids, which are reputed to lower cholesterol.

Gluten free

SERVES 4
PREP 5 MINS

50g (1¾oz) macadamia nuts

250g (9oz) fresh strawberries

300ml (10fl oz) 0% Greek yogurt

200ml (7fl oz) coconut water

1 Place all the ingredients in a blender or food processor and pulse to give a smooth, silky texture.

2 Pour into four glasses and serve.

NUTRITION PER SERVING	
Energy	171kcals/715kJ
Carbohydrate	9g
of which sugar	9g
Fat	10g
of which saturates	1.5g
Salt	0.2g
Fibre	3g

Banana and berry smoothie bowl

Pistachios are high in fat, which helps the body to absorb the vitamins provided by the fruit: A, E, and K.

SERVES 1
PREP 25 MINS

1 ripe banana, peeled, sliced, and frozen

25g (scant 1oz) frozen raspberries

2 heaped tbsp fat-free Greek yogurt

50–100ml (1½–3½fl oz) cow's, almond, or oat milk

FOR THE TOPPING

3 strawberries, sliced

5 blackberries, halved

10 blueberries

1 tbsp sugar-free muesli

4 shelled pistachio nuts, roughly chopped

FOR A GLUTEN-FREE OPTION
use gluten-free muesli

1 Remove the banana from the freezer and leave for about 20 minutes, or until the banana is just beginning to soften to the touch but the centre is still frozen. Transfer to a blender with the raspberries and yogurt, then purée until smooth, adding enough milk to get a thick, creamy consistency.

2 Transfer the mixture to a bowl and arrange the fruit and muesli on top.

NUTRITION PER SERVING	
Energy	278kcals/1145kJ
Carbohydrate	39g
of which sugar	28g
Fat	8g
of which saturates	2g
Salt	0.1g
Fibre	6g

DESSERTS

FRUITS

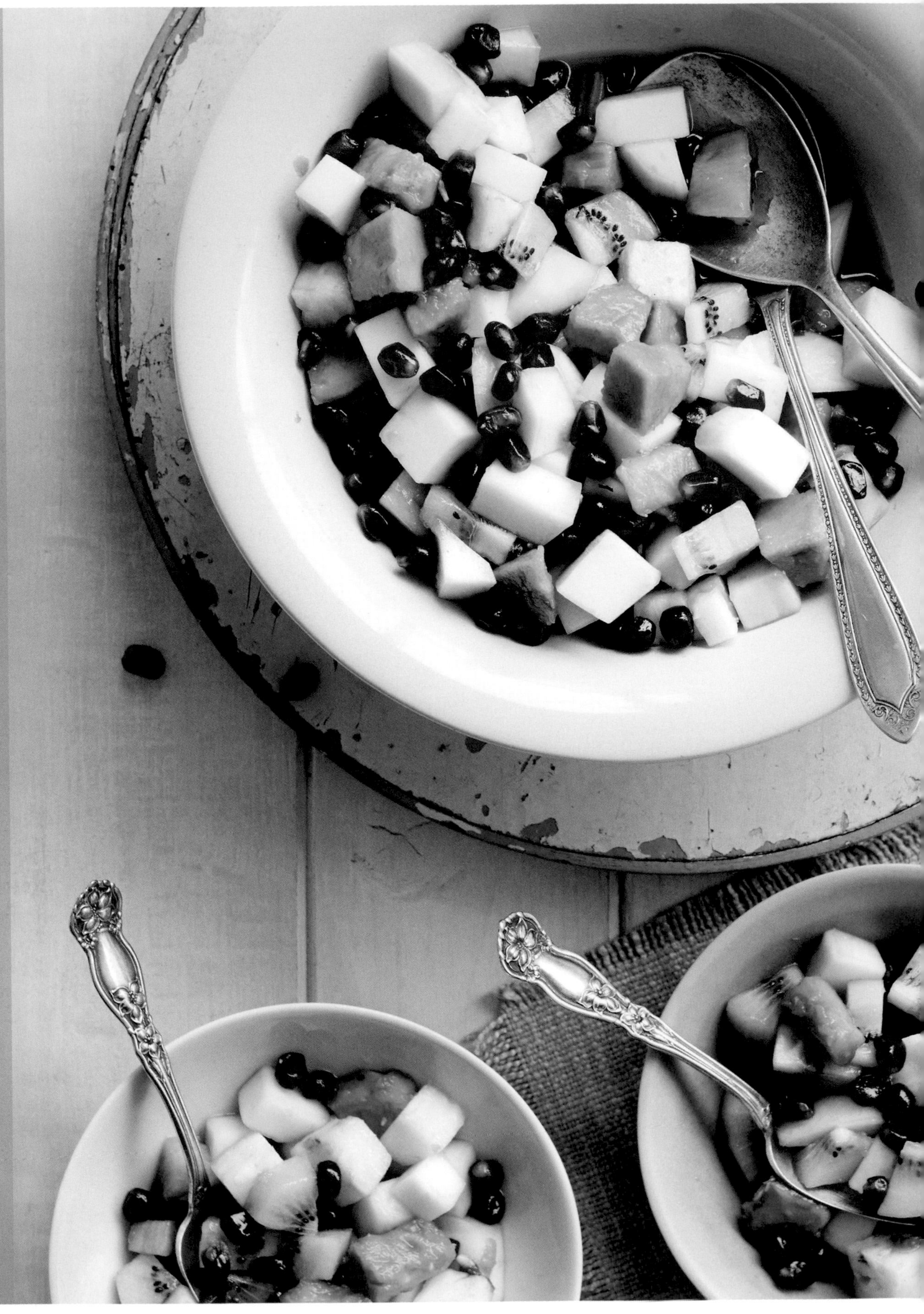

Fruit salad with minted sugar syrup

Cut the fruit into small pieces, so that this fruit salad offers a few flavours in a single spoonful. The minted sugar syrup helps to bring out the flavour of the ingredients.

Low saturated fat

Dairy free

Gluten free

Low salt

SERVES 4
PREP 15 MINS
COOK 5 MINS, PLUS
COOLING AND CHILLING

1 ripe mango, peeled and cut into 1cm (½in) cubes

2 ripe kiwis, peeled and cut into 1cm (½in) cubes

100g (3½oz) ripe papaya, peeled and cut into 1cm (½in) cubes

100g (3½oz) pineapple, cut into 1cm (½in) cubes

seeds from 1 ripe pomegranate

FOR THE SYRUP

50g (1¾oz) caster sugar

1 tbsp lemon juice

10 large mint leaves

1 For the syrup, place the ingredients in a small heavy-based saucepan. Pour over 50ml (1¾fl oz) cold water.

2 Bring to the boil, stirring frequently, until the sugar dissolves. Remove from the heat, pour into a heatproof bowl, and leave to cool. Then chill until needed.

3 Combine all the fruits in a large serving bowl, reserving one-quarter of the pomegranate seeds. Strain the syrup into a jug. Discard the mint leaves.

4 Pour the syrup over the fruit and toss well to coat. Scatter over the reserved pomegranate seeds and serve. It is best served within 4 hours of preparation.

NUTRITION PER SERVING

Energy	120kcals/502kJ
Carbohydrate	26g
of which sugar	26g
Fat	0g
of which saturates	0g
Salt	0g
Fibre	4g

Moroccan orange salad

Slices of fresh orange are made more exotic and flavoursome with rosewater, pomegranate seeds, and pistachio nuts.

Low saturated fat

Dairy free

Gluten free

Low salt

SERVES 4
PREP 15 MINS

4 oranges

1–2 tbsp runny honey

2 tbsp rosewater

good pinch of ground cinnamon

seeds from 1 pomegranate

small handful of chopped pistachios (optional)

handful of mint leaves, to decorate

1 Slice off the top and bottom from each orange and place on a chopping board. Carefully slice off the skin and pith, leaving as much flesh as possible, and following the sides of the orange so you keep the shape of the fruit. Slice the oranges horizontally into thin strips, discarding any pips as you come across them. Arrange the orange slices on a serving platter. Pour over any remaining juice.

2 Drizzle with the honey and rosewater, and sprinkle with the cinnamon. Scatter with the pomegranate seeds and pistachios, if using, then decorate with the mint leaves and serve.

NUTRITION PER SERVING	
Energy	111kcals/464kJ
Carbohydrate	17g
of which sugar	17g
Fat	3g
of which saturates	0.5g
Salt	0g
Fibre	2.4g

Sweet spiced freekeh with fresh figs

Inspired by the cuisine of the Middle East, the high-fibre freekeh in this dish is cooked with sweet spices and served with honey, pistachios, and figs.

Low saturated fat

Low salt

SERVES 4
PREP 5 MINS
COOK 25 MINS

100g (3½oz) cracked freekeh

1 star anise

4 cardamom pods

1 tsp ground cinnamon

½ tsp grated fresh root ginger

¼ tsp grated nutmeg

¼ tsp salt

8 fresh figs, stems removed

4 tbsp honey, plus extra to serve

40g (1½oz) pistachios, roughly chopped

2 tbsp chopped mint leaves

4 tbsp Greek yogurt, to serve

1 Place the freekeh, star anise, cardamom, cinnamon, ginger, and nutmeg in a large saucepan. Add the salt and cover with 500ml (16fl oz) of water. Place the pan over a medium heat and bring to the boil. Then reduce the heat to a simmer and cook for about 15 minutes, or until all the liquid has been absorbed.

2 Meanwhile, preheat the grill to its medium setting. Grease and line a baking tray with greaseproof paper. Cut a cross in the top of each fig, cutting almost to the bottom so they open up like a flower. Place on the baking sheet and drizzle with 2 tablespoons of honey. Place the tray under the grill and cook for 10 minutes, or until the figs are lightly grilled.

3 Remove and discard the star anise and cardamom pods. Add the remaining honey to the cooked freekeh and mix well. Divide the freekeh mixture between four plates. Top each plate with two grilled figs and a quarter of the pistachios. Garnish with mint and drizzle with honey, if you wish. Serve with Greek yogurt.

NUTRITION PER SERVING

Energy	253kcals/1065kJ
Carbohydrate	42g
of which sugar	23g
Fat	6g
of which saturates	1g
Salt	0g
Fibre	1g

Chocolate-dipped strawberries

Dip strawberries in rich, dark chocolate for a treat that may help lower the risk of heart disease and stroke, and also prevent memory loss.

SERVES 8
PREP 15 MINS
COOK 5 MINS

400g (14oz) strawberries, not too ripe

100g (3½oz) good-quality dark chocolate, more than 60 per cent cocoa solids, broken into pieces

1 Wash and dry the strawberries well. Try to leave the hulls in, as this makes the finished fruit easier to pick up.

2 Put the chocolate in a small heatproof bowl and place over a saucepan of simmering water, making sure the bowl does not touch the water. Stir frequently and remove it as soon as it melts.

3 Line a large sheet with greaseproof paper. Hold each strawberry by its leaves and dip the end in the chocolate, so half of the fruit is covered in chocolate. Allow any excess chocolate to drip off back into the bowl, then place the strawberries on the baking sheet, making sure they do not touch each other.

4 Put in a cool place to set. These should be served the same day, as the chocolate will soften if the strawberries are over-ripe, or if they are kept in the fridge for too long.

NUTRITION PER SERVING	
Energy	77kcals/324kJ
Carbohydrate	10g
of which sugar	10g
Fat	3.5g
of which saturates	2g
Salt	0g
Fibre	1g

Red fruit medley

This German dish, *Rote Grütze*, translates as "red grits". Its red berries are anti-inflammatory.

| Low saturated fat |
| Dairy free |
| Gluten free |
| Low salt |

SERVES 4
PREP 10 MINS
COOK 5 MINS

250g (9oz) cherries, pitted

175g (6oz) raspberries

150g (5½oz) redcurrants

115g (4oz) blackberries

115g (4oz) strawberries, quartered if large

stevia, to taste

2 tbsp cornflour

1 Place the fruits in a saucepan with 150ml (5fl oz) of water and slowly bring to the boil.

2 Combine the stevia and cornflour with 2 tablespoons cold water to form a paste, then stir into the fruit. Cook gently, stirring, until the mixture thickens.

3 Allow to cool, then spoon the mixture into individual dishes.

NUTRITION PER SERVING	
Energy	122kcals/510kJ
Carbohydrate	24g
of which sugar	13g
Fat	0g
of which saturates	0g
Salt	0g
Fibre	5g

Warm fruit compote

This dish is ideal for autumn and winter, when supplies of fresh fruit are limited. Serve with yogurt on the side and runny honey drizzled over, if you like.

Low carb

Low saturated fat

Gluten free

Low salt

MAKES 10
PREP 10 MINS
COOK 10 MINS

30g (1oz) butter

6 dried prunes, chopped

6 dried apricots, chopped

2 large apples, peeled, cored, and chopped

1 firm pear, peeled, cored, and chopped

1 cinnamon stick

2 tsp sugar

2 tsp lemon juice

yogurt and honey, to serve

1 Melt the butter in a heavy saucepan over a medium heat. Add the fruit and cinnamon stick. Cook gently, stirring often, until the fruit has completely softened.

2 Stir in the sugar and heat for a further couple of minutes, or until the sugar has dissolved.

3 Remove the pan from the heat, sprinkle with lemon juice, and serve warm with a spoonful of yogurt and a drizzle of honey.

NUTRITION PER SERVING

Energy	68kcals/288kJ
Carbohydrate	9g
of which sugar	9g
Fat	3g
of which saturates	2g
Salt	trace
Fibre	2g

Grilled peaches with ice cream and granola

Grilled peaches are one of summer's tastiest treats. Paired here with a healthy amaranth and millet granola, they are easy to prepare and can also be stored overnight for a filling wholegrain breakfast.

High fibre

SERVES 4
PREP 10 MINS
COOK 20 MINS

4 peaches, pitted and halved

2 tbsp grapeseed oil

4 scoops of vanilla ice cream

FOR THE GRANOLA

100g (3½oz) rolled oats

50g (1¾oz) uncooked amaranth

50g (1¾oz) uncooked millet

75g (2½oz) almonds, chopped

40g (1½oz) pumpkin seeds

1 tbsp virgin coconut oil

2 tbsp maple syrup (grade B)

½ tsp vanilla extract

¼ tsp ground cinnamon

¼ tsp sea salt

FOR A GLUTEN-FREE OPTION
use gluten-free oats

1 Preheat the oven to 180°C (350°F/Gas 4). For the granola, place all the ingredients in a large bowl and toss to combine. Spread the mixture evenly in a baking tray and place in the oven. Bake the granola for 10–15 minutes or until the oats and nuts are lightly browned. Remove from the heat and leave to cool.

2 Meanwhile, set the grill at its medium setting. Brush the peach skins with the oil and place under the grill for 2–3 minutes, on each side, until tender. Remove from the heat. Place the grilled peaches in serving dishes, then top with a scoop of vanilla ice cream and the granola. Serve immediately.

NUTRITION PER SERVING	
Energy	630kcals/2636kJ
Carbohydrate	60g
of which sugar	26g
Fat	35g
of which saturates	10g
Salt	0.4g
Fibre	6g

Pineapple flambé

Rings of fresh pineapple flambéd in rum or brandy make a smart restaurant-style dessert. Pineapple contains bromelain, which has anti-inflammatory properties.

Low saturated fat

Gluten free

Low salt

SERVES 4
PREP 10 MINS
COOK 10 MINS

1 pineapple

4 tbsp dark rum or brandy

2 tbsp fresh lime juice

25g (scant 1oz) salted butter

50g (1¾oz) light soft brown
 sugar

quark or Greek yogurt,
 to serve

ground cinnamon, for dusting

1 Peel and thinly slice the pineapple. Cut out the tough core using a small round cutter or the tip of a sharp knife.

2 Put the pineapple slices and any pineapple juice into a large frying pan with the rum and lime juice and heat. Light the alcohol by carefully tilting the pan into the gas flame, or by using a match, and allow the flames to die down.

3 Dot the pineapple with butter and sprinkle with sugar. Shake the pan while heating gently, until the butter melts, the sugar dissolves, and the mixture thickens to a glaze. Serve with quark or Greek yogurt and a dusting of ground cinnamon.

NUTRITION PER SERVING	
Energy	185kcals/774kJ
Carbohydrate	24g
of which sugar	24g
Fat	5g
of which saturates	3g
Salt	0g
Fibre	2g

CHILLED AND FROZEN

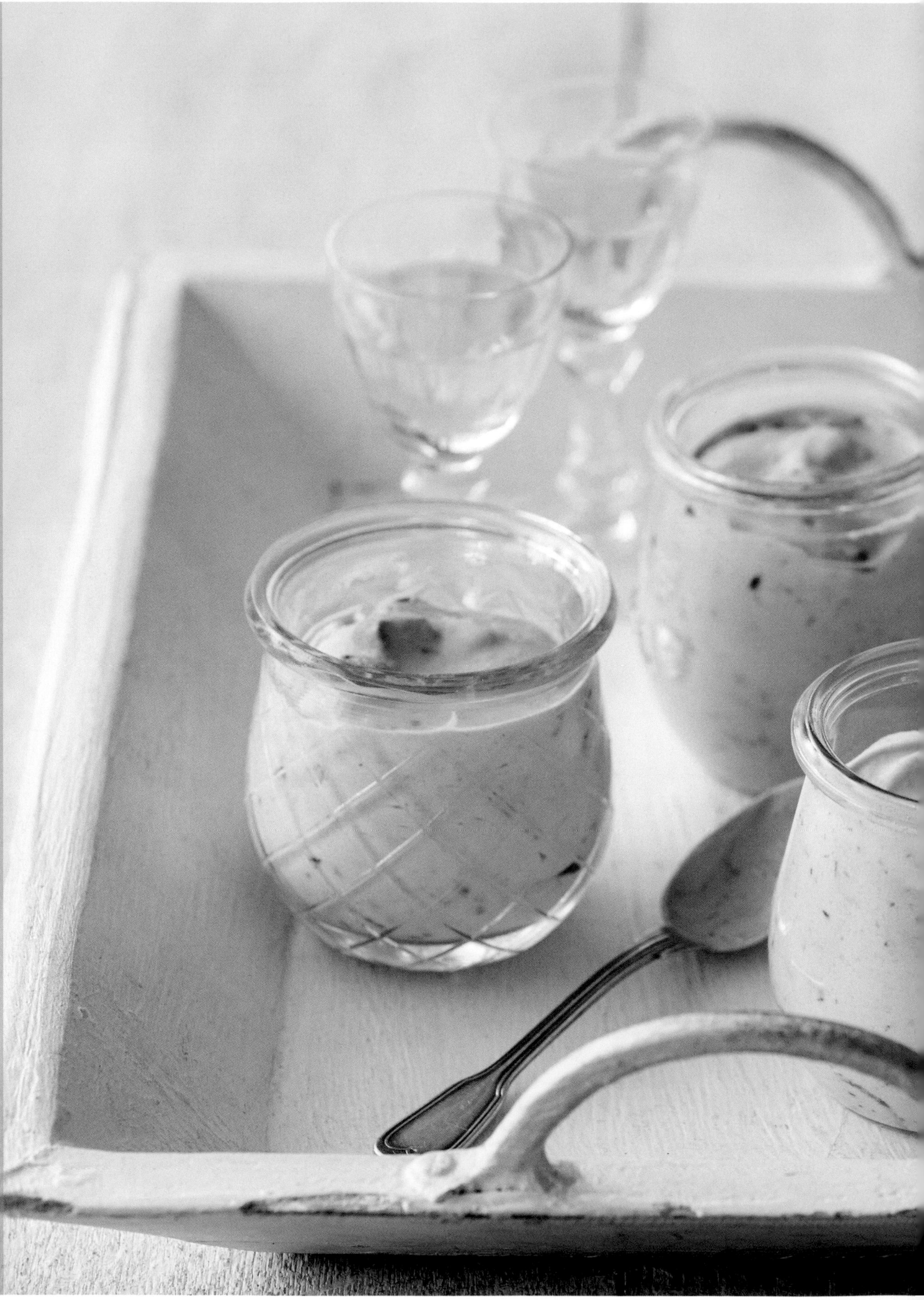

Summer fruit fool

Traditionally, fruit fools contained only stewed fruit and custard. Modern fools feature fresh fruit purée to create a brighter flavour and fluffier texture – they have become a classic in their own right.

Low saturated fat

Gluten free

Low salt

MAKES 4
PREP 10 MINS,
PLUS CHILLING

400g (14oz) mixed hulled strawberries, raspberries, and blueberries

30g (1oz) caster sugar, plus 1 tbsp extra

200g (7oz) quark

150g (5½oz) full-fat Greek yogurt

½ tsp vanilla extract

1 Slice the strawberries so that they are a similar size as the other fruit. Combine all the fruit with 1 tablespoon of sugar in a large bowl. Then pulse two-thirds of the mixture in a food processor to form a purée.

2 Beat the quark in a bowl until smooth. Add the yogurt, vanilla extract, and remaining sugar. Fold the mixture gently, so that you lose as little air as possible.

3 Gently fold the fruit purée into the quark mixture until no streaks remain.

4 Fold the reserved fruit into the mixture. Divide the mixture between four 100ml (3½fl oz) glass jars or glasses, cover, and chill for 2 hours, before serving. You can cover and store them in the fridge for up to 1 day.

try this....
Apricot and passion fruit fool

Drain 2 cans of **apricots in natural juice**, then purée the flesh. Mix 200g (7oz) quark with 150g (5½oz) full-fat Greek yogurt and then stir in the apricot purée. Add **honey** or a **calorie-free sweetener**, like **stevia**, to taste. Spoon into jars or glasses, top each one with seeds from 1 **passion fruit**, then serve.

NUTRITION PER SERVING

Energy	151kcals/632kJ
Carbohydrate	16g
of which sugar	16g
Fat	4g
of which saturates	2.5g
Salt	0.1g
Fibre	3.5g

Vanilla pudding with raspberries

This simple pudding is no more than a chilled vanilla custard. Serve it with raspberries, which are rich in antioxidants, for a sweet-sharp flavour contrast.

Gluten free

Low salt

SERVES 4
PREP 10 MINS
COOK 10 MINS,
PLUS CHILLING

100g (3½oz) caster sugar

3 tbsp cornflour

3 large egg yolks

½ tsp salt

500ml (16fl oz) semi-skimmed milk

15g (½oz) unsalted butter

3 tsp vanilla extract

30–40 raspberries, to serve

1 Place the sugar, cornflour, egg yolks, and salt in a large bowl. Pour in half the milk and whisk until well combined and smooth.

2 Heat the remaining milk in a saucepan over a medium-low heat, until steaming. Pour half the hot milk into the yolk mixture, in a steady stream, whisking constantly to combine. Then pour the yolk and milk mixture back into the pan and mix well to combine.

3 Increase the heat to medium and bring to the boil, stirring constantly. Reduce the heat to a simmer and cook for a further 1 minute, stirring, until the mixture has thickened. Remove and strain through a fine sieve into a large bowl.

4 Whisk in the butter and vanilla extract until evenly combined. Cover with cling film, making sure it touches the top of the pudding. Chill for at least 3–4 hours. Serve it with raspberries. You can store the pudding in an airtight container in the fridge for 2–3 days.

NUTRITION PER SERVING

Energy	288kcals/1205kJ
Carbohydrate	43g
of which sugar	33g
Fat	9.5g
of which saturates	4.5g
Salt	0.8g
Fibre	2g

Eton mess

Using yogurt gives this crowd-pleasing dessert a healthy twist. It is also particularly quick if you use ready-made meringue.

Gluten free

SERVES 6
PREP 10 MINS,
PLUS CHILLING

200ml (7fl oz) whipping cream

300ml (10fl oz) 2% fat Greek yogurt

1 tsp vanilla extract

150g (5½oz) ready-made meringues

300g (10oz) strawberries, chopped quite small

150g (5½oz) raspberries

1 Whisk the cream until it is very stiff, then carefully fold in the yogurt and extract.

2 Place the meringues in a freezer bag and bash with a rolling pin to break into uneven pebble-sized pieces. It's nice to have a mixture of large pieces and smaller crumbs, for the best texture.

3 Fold together the cream mixture, the meringues, and the fruit. Cover and chill for at least 1 hour before serving.

NUTRITION PER SERVING	
Energy	288kcals/1205kJ
Carbohydrate	29g
of which sugar	29g
Fat	15g
of which saturates	9g
Salt	0.1g
Fibre	2.7g

Strawberry mousse

This speedy dessert is bound to be a hit with the kids. Strawberries are high in fibre, which helps to regulate blood sugar, and their bright red colour is caused by anthocyanidin, a powerful antioxidant.

SERVES 4
PREP 20 MINS,
PLUS CHILLING

450g (1lb) ripe strawberries

170g can evaporated milk, well chilled

30g (1oz) caster sugar

200g (7oz) Greek yogurt, plus extra to serve

1 Slice a strawberry and set aside for decoration. Divide half the strawberries between four dessert glasses and place the remaining strawberries into a food processor and blend to a purée. Push through a sieve to remove the seeds. If you do not have a food processor, mash with a fork before pushing through a sieve.

2 Using an electric whisk, whisk the milk in a large bowl until doubled in volume, which will take 6–8 minutes. Whisk in the sugar and stir in the strawberry purée and Greek yogurt until well combined. Spoon the whisked mixture into the glasses and chill for 15–20 minutes.

3 Serve decorated with a little extra yogurt and the reserved strawberry slices.

NUTRITION PER SERVING	
Energy	211kcals/ 883kJ
Carbohydrate	22g
of which sugar	22g
Fat	10g
of which saturates	6g
Salt	0.3g
Fibre	4g

Apricots with amaretti biscuits and mascarpone

Apricots are delicate and should be handled with care. They are rich in vitamin A and carotenes, both essential for good vision.

Low salt

High fibre

SERVES 4
PREP 15 MINS

8 amaretti biscuits

200g tub reduced-fat mascarpone

16 ripe apricots, halved and stoned

handful of blanched almonds, halved

1 Lightly crush the amaretti biscuits with a rolling pin, then divide among four individual glass dishes. Lightly whip the mascarpone with a wooden spoon until thickened.

2 Layer the apricots and mascarpone on top of the amaretti biscuits, finishing with a layer of mascarpone. Sprinkle with the almonds and serve.

try this....
Apricots with ginger and quark

For a lower-fat version, replace the mascarpone with **vanilla quark**, and replace the amaretti biscuits with 8 **ginger nuts**.

NUTRITION PER SERVING	
Energy	436kcals/1824kJ
Carbohydrate	36g
of which sugar	35g
Fat	24g
of which saturates	8g
Salt	0.1g
Fibre	7g

Mango, orange, and passion fruit fool

This creamy, golden fruit fool, which is rich in vitamin C and fibre, can be whizzed up in minutes. The passion fruit offers potassium.

Gluten free

Low salt

SERVES 4
PREP 10 MINS,
PLUS CHILLING

3 large, ripe mangoes, stoned and flesh roughly chopped

zest of 1 large orange

4 tbsp orange juice

400g (14oz) Greek yogurt

sugar-free sweetener, to taste

4 passion fruit, seeds extracted

1 Place the mango and orange zest and juice in a food processor or blender. Process until smooth. Stir in the Greek yogurt and add sweetener to taste.

2 Divide the mixture among four glasses or bowls, and chill for at least 30 minutes.

3 Spoon the seeds from the passion fruit on top of the fool and serve.

NUTRITION PER SERVING	
Energy	229kcals/962kJ
Carbohydrate	28g
of which sugar	26g
Fat	10g
of which saturates	7g
Salt	0.2g
Fibre	4.5g

Traffic-light jellies

Fresh, sugar-free fruit juices make a healthier jelly. These take most of the day to set, but only minutes to make.

Low saturated fat

Dairy free

Gluten free

Low salt

MAKES 10
PREP 15 MINS,
PLUS SETTING
COOK 5 MINS

1 packet gelatine leaves
   (12 x 1.75g leaves)

3 x 500ml cartons fresh fruit
   juice, such as pineapple,
   cranberry, kiwi, and apple
   (try to get different colours)

1 Put three leaves of gelatine in a shallow bowl and cover them with cold water. Allow them to soften for 3–5 minutes until pliable.

2 Heat one fruit juice gently over a low heat in a small saucepan. When the gelatine is soft, remove it from the water and squeeze out the excess. Take the pan off the heat. Add the gelatine, whisking to dissolve. Cool, then divide equally between 10 small 150ml (5fl oz) plastic glasses. Chill to set.

3 Repeat the process with the second jelly, making sure you choose a contrasting colour to the first. Make sure the second fruit juice mixture is cold before pouring it carefully on top of the set jelly.

4 Repeat the process with the final fruit juice and return to the fridge to set before serving.

NUTRITION PER SERVING	
Energy	61kcals/260kJ
Carbohydrate	12g
of which sugar	12g
Fat	0g
of which saturates	0g
Salt	trace
Fibre	0.2g

Elderflower jelly with grapes

Elderflower gives a delicate fragrant flavour to these pretty jellies and a memory of summer.

SERVES 4
PREP 15 MINS,
PLUS SETTING
COOK 5 MINS

75ml (2½fl oz) elderflower cordial

4 gelatine leaves

4 tbsp whipped cream, to serve

8 seedless green grapes, to serve

1 Measure 600ml (1 pint) cold water in a jug and stir in the cordial. Place the gelatine leaves in a small bowl, and add 4 tablespoons of the elderflower mixture. Leave to soak for 10 minutes, or until the gelatine is very soft. Place the bowl over a pan of barely simmering water, and stir until the gelatine has completely dissolved.

2 Add the gelatine to the elderflower mixture, and stir well. Pour into four glasses, then chill on a tray in a refrigerator for at least 2–3 hours, or until set. Serve the jelly in the glasses, topped with whipped cream and a few grapes.

NUTRITION PER SERVING	
Energy	132kcals/552kJ
Carbohydrate	14g
of which sugar	14g
Fat	6g
of which saturates	4g
Salt	0g
Fibre	0.2g

Quick banana ice cream

This is the quickest and easiest "ice cream" you will ever make! Bananas contain tryptophan and vitamin B_6, which may help boost your mood.

Low saturated fat

Dairy free

Gluten free

Low salt

SERVES 4
PREP 5 MINS,
PLUS FREEZING

4 ripe bananas
1 tsp vanilla extract

1 Simply peel the bananas, chop them into 2cm (¾in) chunks, and place them in a freezer container. Seal, and put in the freezer until frozen.

2 When the bananas are frozen solid, process them in a food processor with the vanilla extract, until you have a smooth, thick ice cream. You may need to scrape down the sides a couple of times during the process.

3 Either eat the softened banana ice cream immediately, or freeze for a few minutes for it to firm up once more before serving.

try this....
Quick banana
and peanut
ice cream
....
In step 2, add 100g (3½oz)
crunchy peanut butter and
continue as above.

NUTRITION PER SERVING

Energy	86kcals/360kJ
Carbohydrate	19g
of which sugar	17g
Fat	0g
of which saturates	0g
Salt	0g
Fibre	1.4g

Banana and cranberry ice cream

Ice cream without cream – ideal for those allergic to cow's milk. Ripe bananas can help lower blood pressure, while cranberries have antibacterial properties.

| Low saturated fat |
| Dairy free |
| Gluten free |
| Low salt |

SERVES 4
PREP 10 MINS,
PLUS FREEZING
COOK 10 MINS

4 ripe bananas, sliced

200g (7oz) cranberries

1 tbsp caster sugar

1 tsp vanilla extract

50g (1¾oz) pistachio nuts, shelled and chopped

1 Put the bananas and cranberries in the freezer and remove when semi-frozen. If they are completely frozen, allow to thaw slightly for about an hour. Place them in a blender or food processor and blitz until the fruits are coarsely combined and still have some texture. Divide between four freezerproof serving bowls (enamel bowls are freezer-safe) and place in the freezer for 3 hours. Alternatively, freeze the ice cream in a clean plastic container.

2 Meanwhile, place the sugar in a small saucepan over a low heat and add just enough water to wet the sugar. When the sugar has dissolved completely, add the vanilla extract and mix in the pistachios, then remove from the heat and allow to cool.

3 Remove the bowls, or container, from the freezer, allow to sit at room temperature for a short while, then use an ice-cream scoop to divide the ice cream between four serving bowls. Drizzle the sugar solution and nuts over the top of each portion and serve.

NUTRITION PER SERVING

Energy	212kcals/898kJ
Carbohydrate	34g
of which sugar	28g
Fat	6g
of which saturates	0.8g
Salt	trace
Fibre	3.5g

Mango sorbet

Freezing any food will diminish its flavour, so be sure the fruit is at its peak of ripeness. The citrus juices in this recipe heighten the taste and balance the mango's sweetness.

| Low saturated fat |
| Dairy free |
| Gluten free |
| Low salt |
| High fibre |

SERVES 6
PREP 25–30 MINS,
PLUS FREEZING
COOK 2–3 MINS

100g (3½oz) caster sugar, plus more if needed

3 mangoes, total weight 1.25–1.35kg (2¾–3lb)

juice of 1 lemon

juice of 1 orange

lime zest, to serve

NUTRITION PER SERVING

Energy	202kcals/845kJ
Carbohydrate	44g
of which sugar	44g
Fat	0g
of which saturates	0g
Salt	0g
Fibre	7g

1 Combine the sugar and 120ml (4fl oz) water in a small saucepan. Heat until the sugar has dissolved, then boil the syrup for 2–3 minutes, until it is clear. Set aside to cool.

2 Peel the mangoes. Cut each mango lengthwise into two pieces, slightly off-centre just to miss the stone. Cut the flesh away from the other side of the stone. Cut away the remaining flesh. Cut all the mango into cubes. Purée it in batches, in a food processor, until smooth.

3 With the blade turning, pour in the cooled syrup and citrus juices. Taste, adding more sugar if it is tart, remembering the flavours will be dulled by freezing.

4 Pour the sorbet mixture into an ice-cream maker and freeze until firm, following the manufacturer's directions. Meanwhile, chill a bowl in the freezer.

5 Transfer the sorbet to the chilled bowl. Cover it and freeze for at least 4 hours to allow the flavour to mellow. If necessary, transfer the sorbet to the refrigerator to soften slightly. Scoop the sorbet into chilled glasses and serve immediately, sprinkled with lime zest.

Espresso granita

This coffee-flavoured granita is simple to prepare. Make sure the texture is crystallized, like shaved ice.

Low saturated fat

Dairy free

Gluten free

Low salt

SERVES 4
PREP 5 MINS, PLUS
COOLING AND FREEZING
COOK 5 MINS

100g (3½oz) caster sugar

½ tsp pure vanilla extract

300ml (10fl oz) very strong espresso coffee, chilled

1 Set the freezer to its coldest setting and place four freezerproof serving bowls or glasses in the freezer. In a small saucepan, dissolve the sugar in 300ml (10fl oz) cold water over a medium heat. Increase the heat and bring to the boil, then boil for 5 minutes to make a light syrup.

2 Pour the syrup into a shallow, freezerproof dish. Stir in the vanilla extract and coffee, then set aside to cool completely.

3 Transfer to the freezer. Use a fork to break up the frozen chunks every 30 minutes or so. Continue to do this for 4 hours, or until the mixture has the texture of shaved ice, then leave the granita in the freezer until ready to serve.

NUTRITION PER SERVING	
Energy	101kcals/423kJ
Carbohydrate	25g
of which sugar	25g
Fat	0g
of which saturates	0g
Salt	0g
Fibre	0g

Pink grapefruit and rose water sherbet

A sherbet is a cross between an ice cream and a sorbet. It is simple to prepare, and does not require a specialist ice-cream maker.

Low saturated fat

Gluten free

Low salt

SERVES 6
PREP 15 MINS, PLUS
CHILLING AND FREEZING

250g (9oz) caster sugar, plus extra for sprinkling

grated zest of 1 large pink grapefruit

450ml (15fl oz) pink grapefruit juice

1 tbsp rose water

350ml (12fl oz) whole milk

1 large egg white

12–16 large edible rose petals, washed and dried

1 Place the caster sugar, grapefruit zest and juice, and rose water in a blender. Pulse for 2 minutes, until it is well combined and the sugar has dissolved.

2 Transfer the mixture to a bowl and chill for 1 hour. Then transfer to a blender, add the milk, and pulse until well combined. Pour the liquid into a 1.5 litre (2¾ pint) shallow freezer-proof container.

3 Transfer to the freezer, scraping the frozen edges into the centre of the container with a fork every 45 minutes, breaking up any larger ice crystals with the back of the fork. Repeat this process for 3 hours, or until the mixture is well frozen, but not solid, then freeze until needed.

4 Whisk the egg white in a bowl and use to brush the rose petals. Sprinkle the petals evenly with caster sugar, shake off any excess, and leave to dry. Serve the sherbet decorated with the rose petals. You can store the sherbet in the container in the freezer for up to 1 month.

NUTRITION PER SERVING	
Energy	233kcals/975kJ
Carbohydrate	50g
of which sugar	50g
Fat	2.5g
of which saturates	1.5g
Salt	0.1g
Fibre	0g

Yogurt, honey, and pistachio semifreddo

This modern take on semifreddo has a firm texture, as eggs are omitted from the recipe – this also means that it keeps for much longer in the freezer.

Low salt

Gluten free

SERVES 8
PREP 20 MINS,
PLUS FREEZING

400g (14oz) full-fat Greek yogurt

6 tbsp runny honey, plus extra to serve (optional)

grated zest of 1 large orange

200ml (7fl oz) Elmlea double light cream

60g (2oz) unsalted and skinned pistachios, finely chopped

1 Line a 450g (1lb) loaf tin with cling film. Whisk the yogurt, honey, and orange zest in a large bowl until smooth and well combined. In a separate bowl, whisk the cream to form soft peaks and carefully fold into the yogurt mixture. Then fold in three-quarters of the pistachios.

2 Pour the mixture into the prepared tin, cover with cling film, and freeze for at least 6 hours. Then remove from the freezer, take off the cling film, and invert the tin over a large serving plate. Shake the tin lightly, if needed, to release the semifreddo.

3 Peel off the cling film. Sprinkle with the reserved pistachios and a drizzle of honey, if desired, and serve immediately. You can store the semifreddo, covered in the freezer, for up to 3 months.

NUTRITION PER SERVING

Energy	205kcals/858kJ
Carbohydrate	14g
of which sugar	13g
Fat	15g
of which saturates	9g
Salt	0g
Fibre	0g

try this....
Mixed dried fruit and rum semifreddo

Soak 300g (10oz) **mixed dried fruits** in 4 tablespoons **rum**. Mix the dried fruits with the yogurt, and omit the honey and orange zest. Continue with the recipe as directed above.

BAKES

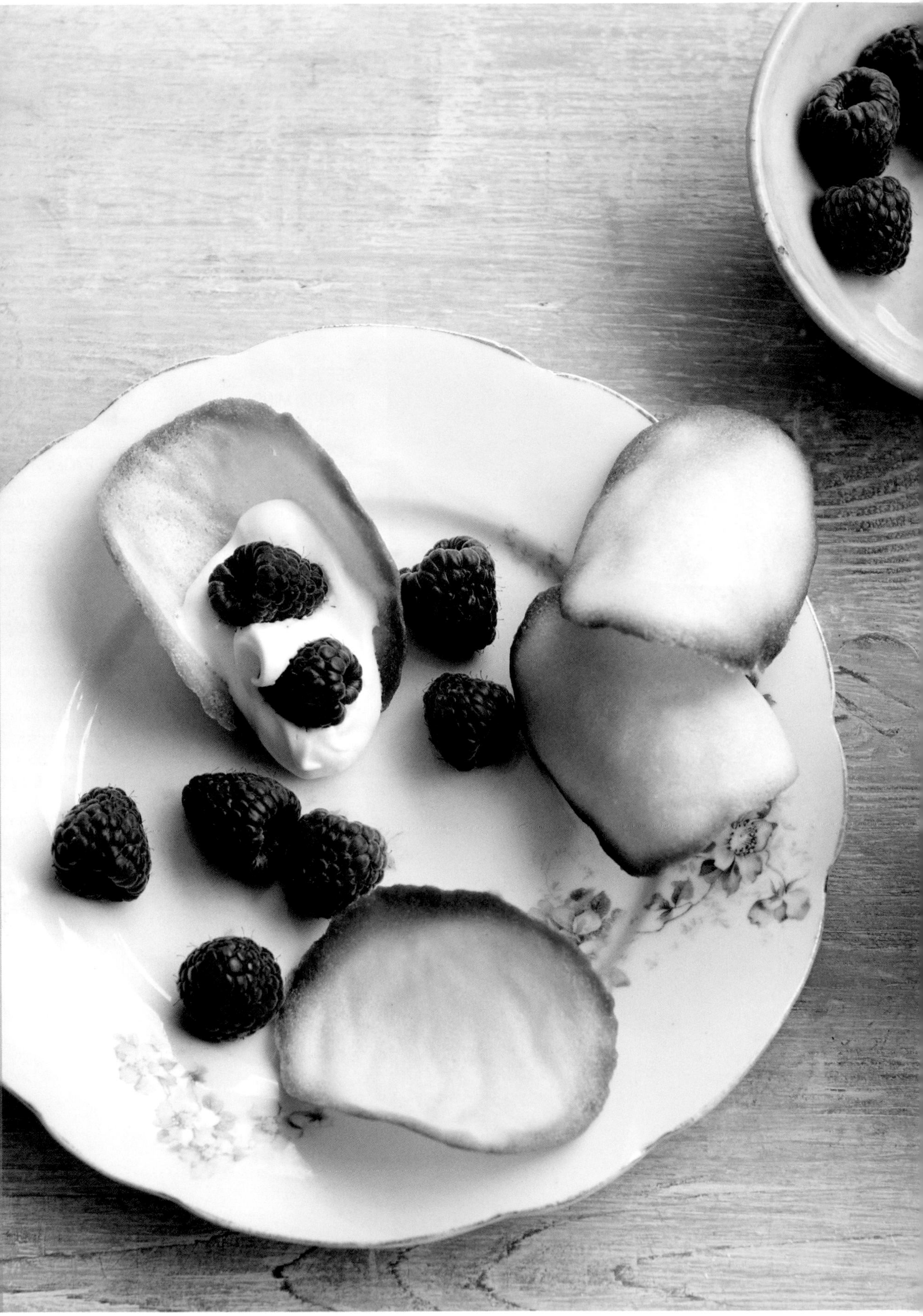

Simple tuiles

Tuiles are easy to make, but the art lies in timing the bake and shaping them properly. Serve with yogurt and fruit, or use to decorate desserts such as mousses and sorbets.

MAKES 16
PREP 15 MINS
COOK 6–7 MINS,
PLUS COOLING

50g (1¾oz) unsalted butter, softened

50g (1¾oz) icing sugar, sifted

1 egg, beaten

50g (1¾oz) plain flour, sifted

vegetable oil, for greasing

Greek yogurt, to serve (optional)

raspberries, to serve (optional)

1 Preheat the oven to 200°C (400°F/Gas 6). Place the butter and sugar in a large bowl and whisk together until light and fluffy. Add the egg and whisk well to combine. Then fold in the flour.

2 Draw four 8cm (3¼in) wide circles on four sheets of baking parchment, turn them over, and place on baking sheets. Spoon the batter into the traced circles, using the back of a wet spoon to smooth it out to a thin layer. Bake on the top shelf of the oven for 5–7 minutes, until the edges are golden brown.

3 Remove from the oven, and use a palette knife to lift and drape the tuiles over a greased rolling pin. You have only seconds to shape them before they harden. Bake for a further minute to soften them, if needed.

4 Once cooled, gently transfer the tuiles to a wire rack to cool and dry completely. Serve them with Greek yogurt and raspberries, if desired. You can store the tuiles in an airtight container for up to 5 days.

NUTRITION PER SERVING

Energy	52kcals/218kJ
Carbohydrate	6g
of which sugar	3g
Fat	3g
of which saturates	2g
Salt	0g
Fibre	0g

try this....
Tuile cups with mango and pomegranate

To make tuile cups, draw 4 x 12cm (1½ x 5in) circles in step 2. Then, in step 3, shape the tuile over an orange. Allow the tuile to cool, and then fill with mixture of diced **mango** and **pomegranate seeds**. Serve with a scoop of **frozen yogurt**. Makes 10.

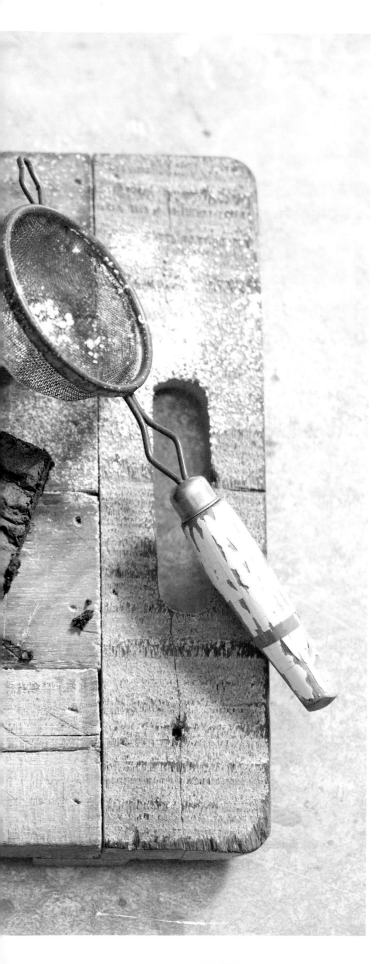

Chocolate brownies

There is no point pretending that brownies are a nutritional powerhouse. They're not. But using fruit helps to reduce the amount of refined sugar. And let's face it, we all want a treat from time to time.

| Low saturated fat |
| Dairy free |
| Low salt |

MAKES 9
PREP 10–15 MINS
COOK 25–30 MINS

220g can of prunes in syrup, drained and pitted

125g (4½oz) plain chocolate

2 egg whites

75g (2½oz) plain flour, sieved

200g (7oz) caster sugar

pinch of salt

½ tsp vanilla essence

50g (1¾oz) pecan nuts, chopped

icing sugar, for dusting

1 Preheat the oven to 200°C (400°F/Gas 6). Grease and line the base of an 18cm (7in) square shallow cake tin with non-stick baking parchment.

2 Place the prunes in a food processor and blend to make a smooth purée. Transfer to a large mixing bowl.

3 Break the chocolate into a heatproof bowl and place over a saucepan of simmering water. Stir occasionally until melted. Remove from the heat and allow to cool slightly.

4 Beat the egg whites until stiff, then beat the melted chocolate, flour, caster sugar, salt, and vanilla essence into the prune purée and mix well. Stir in the nuts. Fold in the egg whites.

5 Transfer the mixture into the prepared tin and bake for about 25–30 minutes, or until firm to the touch. Leave in the tin to cool for 5 minutes, then transfer to a wire rack to cool completely.

6 Cut into nine squares and dust with icing sugar.

NUTRITION PER SERVING	
Energy	176kcals/715kJ
Carbohydrate	20g
of which sugar	14g
Fat	8g
of which saturates	2.5g
Salt	0.2g
Fibre	2g

Vanilla tapioca pudding

Tapioca is a high-carbohydrate food that can be bland. This pudding is anything but bland – it is rich and creamy with a good textural contrast from the tapioca pearls.

Low saturated fat

Gluten free

Low salt

SERVES 6–8
PREP 10 MINS,
PLUS SOAKING
COOK 20 MINS

750ml (1¼ pints) semi-skimmed milk

70g (2¼oz) small pearl tapioca

2 large egg yolks

¼ tsp salt

50g (1¾oz) dark brown sugar

50g (1¾oz) caster sugar

1 vanilla pod

30 blackberries, to serve

single cream, to serve

1 Pour 200ml (7fl oz) milk into a heavy-based saucepan. Add the tapioca pearls and stir to mix. Leave the mixture to soak for about 45 minutes.

2 Stir in the remaining milk. Add the egg yolks, salt, and both lots of sugar, and whisk well to combine. Split the vanilla pod with a sharp knife, add to the pan, and stir well to mix.

3 Bring the mixture to the boil over a medium heat, stirring constantly. Reduce the heat to a simmer and cook for 15 minutes, stirring occasionally, until the tapioca pearls are soft and the pudding has thickened slightly.

4 Remove from the heat and discard the vanilla pod. Serve warm with blackberries and a swirl of cream; serve it chilled for a thicker texture. You can store it in an airtight container in the fridge for 2–3 days.

NUTRITION PER SERVING

Energy	190kcals/795kJ
Carbohydrate	33g
of which sugar	23g
Fat	4g
of which saturates	2g
Salt	0.3g
Fibre	0.4g

Index

Entries in **bold** indicate ingredients
or types of dish.

Prawn and asparagus
stir-fry with polenta

Quinoa and
fennel salad

Pea, mint, and avocado soup with quinoa

Moroccan orange salad

Swordfish in
salmoriglio

Polenta with tomato, mozzarella, pesto, and Parma ham

Taramasalata

**Banana and berry
smoothie bowl**

Acknowledgments

DK would like to thank the following:
Recipe testing: Jane Lawrie. **Proofreading:** Claire Cross,
Cincy Jose, Seetha Natesh. **Design assistance:** Juhi Sheth.
Indexing: Vanessa Bird. **Cover illustration:** Amy Holliday.

All photography © Dorling Kindersley

 Penguin Random House

DK UK
Project Editor   Caroline Curtis
Senior Art Editor   Sara Robin
Senior Jacket Creative   Nicola Powling
Pre-Production Producer   Rebecca Fallowfield
Senior Producer   Stephanie McConnell
Managing Editor   Stephanie Farrow
Managing Art Editor   Christine Keilty

DK INDIA
Project Editor   Arani Sinha
Senior Art Editor   Ira Sharma
Editors   Sugandh Juneja, Shreya Sengupta
Art Editor   Bhavika Mathur
Assistant Art Editor   Anjali Stella Gari
Deputy Managing Editor   Bushra Ahmed
Managing Art Editor   Navidita Thapa
Pre-Production Manager   Sunil Sharma
DTP Designers   Satish Gaur, Anurag Trivedi,
   Manish Upreti

First published in Great Britain in 2016 by
Dorling Kindersley Limited,
80 Strand, London WC2R 0RL

A CIP catalogue record for this book is available
from the British Library.
ISBN 978-0-2412-3710-6

Colour reproduction by Alta Image
Printed and bound in Slovakia

All images © Dorling Kindersley Limited
For further information see: www.dkimages.com

A WORLD OF IDEAS:
SEE ALL THERE IS TO KNOW
www.dk.com